The User Interface
Concepts & Design

The User Interface
Concepts & Design

Lon Barfield

Centre for Mathematics and Computer Science, Amsterdam

ADDISON-WESLEY PUBLISHING COMPANY

WOKINGHAM, ENGLAND • READING, MASSACHUSETTS • MENLO PARK, CALIFORNIA • NEW YORK
DON MILLS, ONTARIO • AMSTERDAM • BONN • SYDNEY • SINGAPORE
TOKYO • MADRID • SAN JUAN • MILAN • PARIS • MEXICO CITY • SEOUL • TAIPEI

© 1993 Addison-Wesley Publishers Ltd.
© 1993 Addison-Wesley Publishing Company Inc.

The programs in this book have been included for their instructional value. They have been tested with care but are not guaranteed for any particular purpose. The publisher does not offer any warranties or representations nor does it accept any liabilities with respect to the programs.

Many of the designations used by manufacturers and sellers to distinguish their products are claimed as trademarks. Addison-Wesley has made every attempt to supply trademark information about manufacturers and their products mentioned in this book. A list of the trademark designations and their owners appears below.

Cover designed by Designers & Partners, Oxford
and printed by The Ethedo Press, High Wycombe, Bucks.
Camera-ready copy prepared by the author.
Printed and bound in Great Britain by William Clowes, Beccles, Suffolk.

First printed 1993

ISBN 0–201–54441–5

British Library Cataloguing in Publication Data
A catalogue record for this book is available from the British Library.

Library of Congress Cataloging in Publication Data is available

Trademark Notice
PostScript™ is a trademark of Adobe Systems, Inc. Hypercard™, Macintosh™ are trademarks of Apple Computer, Inc. Coca-Cola™ is a trademark of Coca-Cola Corporation. FrameMaker™ is a trademark of Frame Technology. X Window System™ is a trademark of Massachusetts Institute of Technology. MS-DOS™ is a trademark of Microsoft Corporation. NeXT™ is a trademark of NeXT Corporation. Olympus™, XA2™ are trademarks of Olympus Optical Ltd. Oracle™ is a trademark of Oracle Corporation. Sun™, OpenWindows™ are trademarks of Sun Microsystems, Inc. UNIX™ is a trademark of UNIX System Laboratories, Inc.

To my nan.

Dwn Howells

1908 – 1990

Preface

This book

This book is about user interface design: designing those parts of a system that the user comes into contact with so that they are easy to understand, easy to get to grips with and easy and efficient to work with. A system, in this context, can be anything that is designed to be used, from a swing door all the way up to the most sophisticated computer graphics system. Similarly the user, the person using the system, can be anybody from an ordinary member of the public opening that door without thinking about it, to an expert in a specialized area requiring complex computer tools to get a job done.

The chapters that follow will introduce some of the concepts in user interface design in general and extend the ideas to the field of user interface design for computer systems. It is not a 'recipe book' with chunks of computer programs that you can copy out and use in your own programs. Instead, it will help you think about the user interface for yourself and formulate your own designs and solutions.

At present there is a lot of staking out of territory going on between computer scientists, mathematicians, psychologists and industrial designers regarding computer–user interface design. Everybody wants to treat it as a cosy little offshoot subject of their own discipline. Eventually, a deadlock will be reached since the subject cannot be confined to just one area and (as the dust settles) the other disciplines will realize that computer–user

interface design has arrived, having quickly risen to become a discipline in its own right, with its own collection of literature and its own courses at universities. This book is not about the psychology of computer–user interface design, or the computer science of it, or the human factors of screen layouts and keyboard layouts. It is about computer–user interface design from a computer–user interface designer's point of view.

The target audience

The people I have expressly designed this book for are those who are just beginning to get involved in computer–user interface design, either through academic study or as practitioners of the subject.

Academically, computer–user interface design is becoming more and more important. It is changing rapidly from being a third-year computer science option to a mainstream first- or second-year subject. Coupled with this growth in importance is the realization that the subject is not just confined to the computer sciences. It is a true multidisciplinary study which embraces many different subjects. As a result it is starting to find its way into psychology and industrial design courses, and some institutions, realizing that it is fast becoming a discipline in its own right, are now running complete, four-year courses devoted to the subject. This book is for those students just starting a course in computer–user interface design in whatever context, or for more mature students and researchers who want a new viewpoint on the subject.

In industry too, computer–user interface design is becoming a key issue as competition increases and the purchasers of systems become more discerning when looking for a new product. Practitioners of computer–user interface design in industry should also benefit from this book. There are no easy solutions to designing user interfaces, but I hope to provide them with some of the building blocks from which they can construct effective methods and new interfaces.

Prior knowledge

No in-depth knowledge of any one field is required, but readers should have a background of a fairly logical nature and some familiarity with the key areas, such as experience with using computers. It doesn't matter whether you have used them for word processing, drawing plans, spreadsheets or accounting. You just need to have seen how they go about things and to have had a go

at using menus, windows and icons. (One way to get a grounding in this is to get a friend to show you an Apple Macintosh and spend an hour or two experimenting with it.) Readers should also have done some general design and problem-solving work. This could be in any field: designing and writing computer programs, designing a scientific experiment to test a theory, designing the layout of a kitchen – anything that gives you a taste of what it feels like to work through a design problem.

The terms used

As any new branch of a science evolves, it develops its own terminology, creating new terms and borrowing some from other disciplines. The subject matter of this book has its own collection of terms. The interface between the user of a system and the system itself used to be referred to as the Man–Machine Interface, (MMI). This term is still in use today in some circles, but most people have stopped using it on the grounds that it is old fashioned and somewhat sexist; it conjures up images of rows of men using huge noisy machines! A more modern term is HCI meaning Human–Computer Interaction or the Human–Computer Interface. However, this can be too specific in that it refers only to the interface between users and computers.

The terms I have chosen to use are 'the user interface', meaning the interface between a user and a system in general, and 'the computer–user interface', meaning the specific interface between a computer system and the user of that computer system. I feel that the term 'computer–user interface' more accurately sums up the nature and background of the discipline, and that 'user interface' is less of a mouthful than 'human–computer interface'.

I have decided to use female personal pronouns throughout the book. I find the exclusive use of male pronouns more and more difficult to tolerate in text books, and although it is possible to avoid personal pronouns when writing this sometimes leads to artificial-sounding text.

This policy also has the effect of making you realize how strong some of your inbuilt assumptions are about the gender of people referred to in text books. The strength of assumptions in general and the questioning of them are both important factors when it comes to the design of user interfaces.

Producing this book

Initially, this book was typeset using the computer typesetting language Latex and the diagrams were drawn using the graphic commands from the PostScript language. This sounds good, but it is an indication of the current state of computer–user interface design that the suite of diagram drawing programs available to me had deficiencies so severe that I eventually decided to work out the layout of the diagrams on millimetre graph paper and then translate them directly to PostScript commands by hand. Further complications arose with the simple task of including these diagrams in the text, the whole exercise being a good illustration of how computers and bad user interfaces can make it easy to do complicated things, but complicated to do easy things.

Eventually I switched to the interactive document preparation system FrameMaker which eased some of the problems, but the graphics facilities still could not provide me with the range and versatility I needed, so the figures remained 'hand-crafted' in the PostScript language.

From a hardware point of view the final stages of production, text layout and so on, were carried out on a Sun Sparcstation, a Silicon Graphics Indigo and a Compugraphic phototypesetter at the Dutch Centre for Mathematics and Computer Science (CWI). Much of the initial text work and diagram design was done at home and at various cafés using the highly portable Rotring Renaissance system.

Finally, I should mention that the early stages of the book design, the correlation of ideas, the chapter groupings and their ordering, were all carried out using lots of pieces of card spread out on the floor. Why is it, when I have access to the information-handling capabilities of a powerful computer, that I organize this information using bits of card and a floor? Am I just stuck in my ways or is it through the lack of a well-designed, easy to use system to help with the task?

Acknowledgements

To begin with I want to express my gratitude to those who provided the environment in which this book was written: the CWI in Amsterdam, my co-workers here, the 'gezelligheid' of the AA and CST departments and in particular my two colleagues in the Views project, Steven Pemberton and Eddy Boeve. As well as the CWI, I am also grateful to those involved in the other research environment I worked in, namely, SERC at the University of Utrecht. Then there are those who assisted with the book itself,

reviewing, commenting and proofreading. My thanks to Lynda Hardman, Steven and Eddy (again), Lambert Meertens, Gerrit van der Veer, Dick Rijken and Jamie Barr. Thanks also go to Nicky Jaeger and Simon Plumtree of Addison-Wesley for good feedback and guidance in the writing stages and Alan Grove for helping hold it all together in the production stages. Finally a special thank you to my lover and friend Wendelynne Heelis for her part in this book and in everything else.

Contents

Chapter 1

Introduction

1.1 Hello

Hello. Working out the opening sentences of a textbook is a very tricky task. You have to think about how the reader will react to what you are writing. You have to write in such a way that the reader will find it interesting but also in a way that gets across the information that you are putting into the book. This way of thinking about the reader, of writing the book with the reader in mind, is what user interface design is all about – designing those parts of something that the user comes into contact with, and bearing the user in mind as you do so. So, as I design the layout, the order of the contents, the wording and the diagrams of this book I am actually designing the user interface (albeit a simple one) to the material and ideas that are contained in it.

User interface design plays an important part in many disciplines, from the simple presentation of information in a book like this to the layout of controls in an aeroplane. Now that computers are starting to be used in so many areas of our everyday life, people are realizing that user interface design for computer systems plays a vital part in the system's efficiency. Both the designers of computer systems and the users are starting to accept that just being able to do a task on a computer is not the only important factor. The question 'can this goal be achieved with a computer?' is starting to be replaced by the question 'how easily can I, the user, achieve this goal using the computer?'.

1.2 What is the user interface?

The user interface of a system concerns itself with the system, the user of that system and the way in which they interact. It is composed of those parts of a system that are designed to be apparent to and manipulable by the user and those models and impressions that are built up in the mind of the user in response to interacting with these features. Thus the user interface incorporates elements that are part of the system, elements that are part of the user and methods of communicating information from one to the other. (See Figure 1.1.)

It follows from this model that there is a division between the elements of the system that are part of the user interface and those that are concerned with the internal workings of the system. This division between the internal functionality and the user interface is sometimes difficult to appreciate. It seems to be most apparent in technologies that are both mature (in that they have been redesigned many times) and complex. Their maturity means that the designers have had the time to make a strong division between the elements of the system that are to be hidden from the user and the elements that the user needs to be aware of and control. Their complexity means that the elements of the user interface are usually embodied by pieces of equipment of some sort, thus making the user interface a more concrete, tangible thing. A good example of such a technological area is car design. The car is a system and the driver is the user of that system. Most of the system is hidden away under the bonnet, but the driver can interact with and monitor the system by means of a suite of controls on the dashboard. There is thus a correspondence to Figure 1.1 with 'driver, dashboard, engine' corresponding to 'user, user interface, system'.

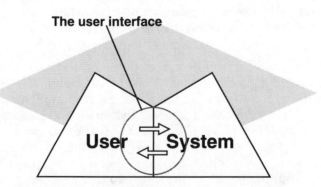

Figure 1.1 Visualizing the user interface.

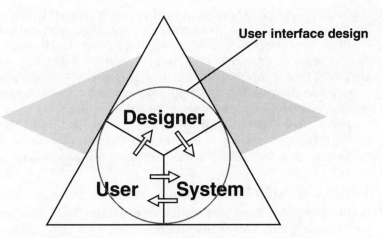

Figure 1.2   The user interface and the designer.

Computer systems too have a correspondence with Figure 1.1, but although the area is complex it is not yet mature enough for the sharp division between the user interface and the rest of the system to have been made. Also, the technical complexity of computer software is not as 'concrete' as in other technologies. The user interface of an interactive computer system, unlike the car dashboard, is not a collection of hardware devices. Some of it *is* embodied in hardware, like the keyboard and the mouse, but the great majority is embodied in less physical things: images, symbols and objects floating around on the screen and models within the computer's memory.

If we extend the scope of the area under discussion to include the design of the interface then we must bring in the other player in the field, the designer of the system (although with many systems there will be more than one designer). There are certain elements of user interface design which are part of the designer. There is a transfer of information from the designer to the system; the system itself is an embodiment of the designer's ideas, and there may be some transfer of information from the users to the designer, either through direct contact or through studies of the user group. The situation then is better illustrated by Figure 1.2.

1.3 The importance of the user interface

Right! I have pinned the concept of the user interface down a bit, but just isolating and identifying something is not justification enough to pursue it academically with books, papers and research. Is the discipline *really* that important? Why should people bother about making the layout of items on a computer screen 'look nice', or put lots of thought into the arrangement of buttons on a machine, or spend ages designing clever icons? Isn't it all a bit 'namby-pamby' to put all that work into making something 'comfortable' and 'user friendly'; a bit like spending ages building a comfy armchair into a tractor? The answer is that it isn't 'namby-pamby'; gradually people are coming round to the realization that computer–user interface design is much more than just nice screens and icons and it is a vital area. The notion of comfort alone is a lot more complex than it appears at first and the issues of safety and efficiency play an important part as well.

1.3.1 Comfort

Comfort is more than just sitting in a comfy chair. The comfort of the person using the system comes in many forms, each of which can be affected by how well the user interface is designed. The most well-known form of comfort is *physical* comfort: being relaxed, sitting in a good position, not over-straining or over-exerting muscles. Physical discomfort can have negative effects such as impairing concentration, and high degrees of discomfort can actually be damaging. With computer–user interface design physical comfort plays a part in the ergonomics of the keyboard, the mouse and the screen. It also plays an important part in the graphics used on the screen, in particular how readable the text is or bad contrasts between colours.

There are other types of comfort. Imagine sitting in a dentist's waiting room; the chairs are comfy, there are magazines to read and people to talk to, but is it relaxing? No! This is *psychological* or *mental* discomfort; it has to do with not feeling relaxed about non-immediate things. It is a very human quality and stems from our ability to worry about the future or worry about the past. Place a cat on a comfy chair and it will curl up and relax. Place a cat on a comfy chair before taking it to the vet and it will still just curl up and relax. This type of comfort plays a much greater role in computer–user interface design. It is about feeling relaxed when changing things within a computer program because you know you can change them back if things go wrong. It is about deleting old computer files from the computer's memory knowing that if you delete the wrong one you can always bring it back somehow, and it is about not worrying when experimenting with new computer-based tools because you know that they are designed so that even a novice can't have any nasty accidents with them.

Finally I shall probe the depths of woolliness to mention *spiritual* comfort. Sometimes, when you use a tool or a computer program that has been well designed it gives you a good feeling.

The more you know about how difficult it is to design good user interfaces the stronger that feeling is. It is the feeling that someone, somewhere has thought about *you*, the user, and shown some care for you. There's someone trying to do what is right, someone thinking about you and fighting for you. As I said, it is a good feeling.

1.3.2 Safety

How many domestic arguments have you heard because someone didn't set up the video recorder properly and ended up recording a quiz show instead of an opera? That's a user interface problem. So what's the big deal? Why expend all this effort for user interface design just so people don't make mistakes when recording their favourite television programmes? The point is that it is a general problem; the errors in design that caused the person operating the video recorder to select the wrong channel are similar to those that caused the pilot of a plane with a defective engine to select the wrong engine to be shut down leading to the crash of a passenger plane near the M1 motorway at Kegworth in Great Britain in January 1989.

As we start to depend more and more upon technology to help us with certain aspects of our life, we start to place more and more responsibility on the people controlling that technology. Mistakes made by these people can be costly: they may be in control of huge masses of steel travelling at high speeds or delicate processes involving dangerous reactions. Preventing mistakes from happening depends on many factors, one of the most important of which is how well the user interface to the system is designed.

The eventual verdict on the aeroplane crash I mentioned above was 'pilot error'. The fault did not lie with the system, but did it really lie with the pilot? Granted, some of the responsibility must lie with him – he is there on the spot flying the thing – but when a fully trained pilot trying to take the correct action in a stressful situation is able to do completely the *wrong* thing and believe that he is doing the *right* thing, then the designers of that system must accept a degree of responsibility for the errors. Maybe the jury in cases like this should be able to return the verdict of 'designer error'.

1.3.3 Efficiency

Everybody knows that if you do a job using well-designed and appropriate tools you do it faster, better, and with less mistakes. In short, you do it more efficiently. For more complex tasks involving the use of complex tools, efficiency depends on a well-designed user interface to the tool as well as good design in its functionality.

There are some links between efficiency and comfort. If you are using a tool to do a task and you know that it is taking hours instead of minutes because its user interface is badly designed, then you will probably resent working in such an inefficient way and the result will be psychological discomfort.

1.4 The book's structure

This book takes an approach to computer–user interface design that at first may seem rather novel. It discusses it from a designer's point of view. But how does computer–user interface design relate to other areas of design, and how does the book cover the relevant areas?

Design can be seen as resembling a tree. The trunk of this tree is 'basic design' – the appreciation, techniques and ideas that are relevant in all areas of design. As one progresses up this trunk different, and more specialized, areas of design branch off from the main body. Most of these branches need some extra input of knowledge concerned with their specialized field. Many branches will branch again and again as that particular field of design splits into ever more specialized areas. Each new branch may require new knowledge concerned with its specialization. Take a look at Figure 1.3. One of the areas of design that branches off from the trunk of basic design is automobile design. This needs a large input of specialist knowledge concerned with the design of cars in general: material properties, automobile stability, engine properties, wind resistance theories and driver ergonomics. Automobile design itself then splits up into more specialised areas, one of which is racing car design. Again this requires a new input of knowledge over and above the knowledge for designing cars in general.

Now let us examine computer–user interface design in a similar way. (See Figure 1.4.) Here user interface design branches off from basic design and requires specialist knowledge such as psychology, graphic design, typesetting and human physiology. Further along this branch we find, among other specializations, *computer*–user interface design. This requires extra information about computer science and a host of other disciplines.

This book works its way up this tree structure. It starts with basic design, then moves onto user interface design and finally on to computer–user interface design. Along the way it takes a brief

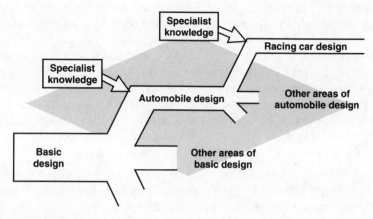

Figure 1.3   Basic design and automobile design.

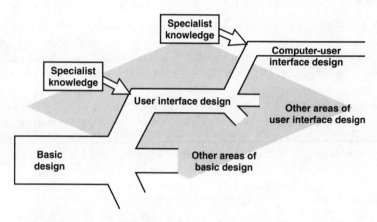

Figure 1.4   Basic design and user interface design.

look at a few other offshoots and at some of the specialist knowledge and key concepts needed for both user interface design and computer–user interface design.

1.4.1 Chapter overview

The first three chapters set the scene for the material in the book. Chapter 1 is a general introduction, Chapter 2 outlines some of the important factors in the design process, in particular, design for use, and Chapter 3 looks more rigorously at interactive systems and how to describe them.

The next six chapters then discuss some of the key areas and concepts in user interfaces. Chapter 4 describes abstraction and presentation, two useful concepts for designing systems that involve the communication of information to users. Chapter 5 takes these ideas a step further and takes a deeper look at graphics and the presentation of dynamic systems. Chapter 6 investigates mental models and user models of interactive systems. Chapter 7 looks at the feedback given to the user by interactive systems and how this relates to errors. Chapter 8 then analyses the controls that make up part of the user interface. Chapter 9 gives a few guidelines for approaching user interface design and then takes us through some examples of design, drawing on the material already covered.

Chapter 10 introduces computers into the picture. It gives a brief overview of computing, explaining what you do and do not need to know about the subject in order to be involved in computer–user interface design. It explains the main differences that computers bring to the field of user interface design and outlines a framework for analysing the computer–user interface.

Next the computer–user interface is considered using the framework mentioned above, and some of the key concepts covered earlier are re-examined. Chapter 11 takes a look at task analysis and goals. Chapter 12 examines the nature and design of the underlying computer models that systems are based on and how these models can be presented to the user. The fundamental styles of interaction between the user and the computer are covered in Chapter 13, while Chapter 14 deals with the design of user models of systems. Chapter 15 covers the controls and devices that are presented on screen by the computer and Chapter 16 looks at the graphics used in computer user interfaces and at how animation helps communicate information.

Finally, in Chapter 17 some examples of computer–user interface design are worked through and Chapter 18 takes a look at the state of user interfaces in industry and raises some questions about the underlying goals of user interface design. At the end of the book there is also an appendix containing a collection of guidelines for the exercises in the book and a bibliography.

1.4.2 Chapter structure

At the end of each chapter I have included a summary of what was covered. I have also appended exercises connected with the material covered in the chapter. These exercises are included for *exercise*, as the name implies, and not for evaluation. They are designed to 'stretch the muscles' of the reader's understanding, analysis and design capabilities. Between the chapters are short sketches to refresh the reader. They take a humorous look at real-world analogies of bad user interface design but they nevertheless have an educational side to them.

I have avoided putting references directly in the text, partly because this book is not intended as an overview of the state of the art in the area and partly because I feel it interrupts the smooth flow of a text. Relevant material is listed in the annotated bibliography at the end of the book

1.5 The information diagram

One of the many important things that an academic book should provide for the reader, besides new ideas, is a framework within which to place the ideas. Above I have outlined a framework for the general coverage of the book. I shall now outline another which appears in many of the chapters and brings together some of the concepts covered in this book. It is a style of diagram that describes relationships between information and different ways of representing or storing that information.

Let me start from the basics. Look at Figure 1.5. On the left is me, and the 'thought bubble' over my head contains my ideas about this book: the subject, how it will be structured and how it will be written. On the right *is* the book. It is an embodiment of the ideas in my 'thought bubble': not an exact one, however, as the book is structured in a linear way and my ideas are not, and not all my ideas are documented in the book. In writing the book there is a filtering and a translation of the concepts and the information from one form to another – from ideas in my head to the printed

Figure 1.5   My ideas and the book.

Figure 1.6   Converting the ideas into the book.

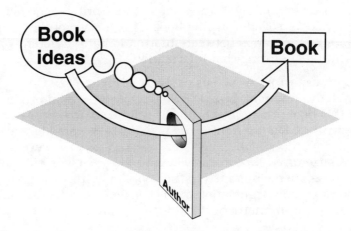

Figure 1.7   Stylized form of writing the book.

page. This translation has to be carried out by some agent, in this case it is me: see Figure 1.6. This diagram can be stylized and generalized to yield Figure 1.7. The author is replaced by a block with a hole in it, signifying that the translation process is carried out by him. Furthermore, to show that the concepts and ideas exist in the mind of the author they are shown as a thought bubble originating from him.

This whole process is reversed when someone reads the book and builds up their own ideas and concepts about the things I am trying to put across. (See Figure 1.8.) These simple translations can be strung together in chains to represent more complex processes and they will occur from time to time in the book.

Figure 1.8   Somebody reading the book.

1.6 The knife with no handle

I shall finish the introduction with an analogy that shows how unacceptable the current state of computer–user interface design would be if it occurred in other, more familiar, areas of design for use. Consider buying a computer-aided design system (CAD system). You go along to a big exhibition to look at what sort of things are available. You visit a stand displaying the latest in computer-aided design systems, a salesperson gives you a rundown on how powerful the system is and shows you glossy pictures of graphics done with the system. 'It can do *this* and *this*,' she says. You want to be able to do that and that. So you buy the thing... and a month later you are *still* struggling with the user interface, trying to make the system do what you want it to.

Imagine if the situation were the same with the purchase of a kitchen knife... you are at the exhibition talking to the salesperson. 'Just listen to this! It's got a nine-inch blade, Sheffield steel, tempered cutting edge, and here's some glossy pictures of finely cut up vegetables produced by it. It can do *this* and *this*.' You're convinced, you buy it, get it back home and open the box to discover that it hasn't got a handle! The salesperson wasn't lying, it *has* got all the features she listed, and you *can* use it to chop and slice vegetables so that they look just as good as those in the glossy pictures she showed you. The problem is that it's awkward, it's complicated, it's time consuming, and it involves learning completely new ways of chopping vegetables dictated by the silly design of the knife.

Finally, if it's anything like the computer industry, the knife company will make a further profit by offering you an expensive two-week long training course on how to get the hang of using your new knife!... Read on.

Chapter 2

Design

2.1 Introduction

In Great Britain and America in the late 1980s many new (and not so new) products were referred to with the word 'designer' as a prefix. Everything was 'designer' this and 'designer' that. There were designer jeans, designer furniture and even designer glasses and designer drugs! It seemed as if people had only just started to bring design into the manufacture of all these things. The truth is that things like this have always been designed, they can't *not* be designed. Even the most basic artefacts have had some thought put into their creation. Every bit of furniture is really 'designer furniture', every pair of glasses are 'designer glasses'. Some things have had a lot of thought put into them, and it shows. Sadly, other things have had very little thought put into them, and that shows as well. But the important point is: it has all been designed.

Design is a very human activity. Many animals build things: birds build nests, beavers build dams and bees build complicated honeycombs, but only humans *design* things. The key issue is the thought that goes into the process, planning it, mapping it out, evaluating it. Animals seem to build things by instinct. A beaver doesn't question the way in which it is building the dam, it just gets on with the job. Humans, on the other hand, build by design. When humans design something they put thought into it. They consider how to go about making it and what it will be like once it is finished. For simple things all this thinking can be done as you go along, trying things out 'on the fly', finishing one stage before thinking about the next. For more complex things, designing 'on the fly' can be very wasteful of time and resources and so the design process is usually carried out well before the construction stage.

Additionally, as I mentioned above, almost every modern human artefact *is* designed. The list of things is endless: telephone systems, cups, rucksacks, gardens, buildings, clothes, computers, doors. The thing being designed does not even have to be a tangible object; systems of ideas or rules are also designed. Consider an electoral system, the rules of law, dance steps, computer languages, economic policies, methods of communication like semaphore, Morse Code. All of these have been designed, even though none of them are *concrete* objects.

The analysis of design overlaps with computer systems in two main ways. Firstly, interactive computer systems need to be designed and designed well. Some understanding of the design process is a useful supplement to such design work. The other overlap is in implementing computer systems to support the design process – computer-aided design. Whether it be designing a building, a circuit board or a book, in order to support design you need to analyse it and work out the best ways of giving the support. There will be more about this in later chapters when computers are introduced.

2.1.1 Language and boomerangs

Any attempt to pin design down will lead to some grey areas. It is obvious that some things are designed and others are not, but in between there are a few things that may or may not be, depending on how you think about design. Human languages for example; are they designed or do they just evolve without any thought going into their creation? Some new, specialized words are chosen to describe new concepts and, as such, they could be said to be 'designed', but the main body of the language to which these words are added has evolved over centuries. Is it just random evolution, or a huge process of 'consensus design' with many individual decisions being made about which words to carry on using and which to discard?

And what about the boomerang? Modern boomerangs are designed using aerodynamics and so on, but the original aborigine boomerang came about as a result of evolutionary design in a similar way to language, coming into shape over many years as a result of trial and error practised by many people.

For the purposes of this book I shall look at the design process in two stages: firstly general design and then design for use. General design is about designing things to fit in with other inanimate objects. Design for use is about designing things to fit in with people. It is a specialization of general design with extra considerations and complications brought about by the inclusion of people into the process.

2.2 General design

First of all then let us examine design that does not take people into account, that is, designing things such as the internal components and workings of machines, railway bridges, pure engineering in general, systems of rules or languages for non-human use such as communication between computers: in fact, anything that people don't come into contact with under normal conditions. I say 'under normal conditions' because most things in this category will have *some* contact with people (I refer to them as 'service users'); the machine component must be fitted or repaired by a mechanic, the computer signals must occasionally be monitored by a computer technician, but in normal use they are hidden from most people. They are designed purely to do a job and fit in with those things around them.

Later on, in Section 2.3 [p 18], I shall explain how difficult it is to incorporate people as one of the factors in a design problem and how difficult it is to analyse the things that they do, but to start off with I shall consider the process of design without this extra complication.

2.2.1 The ideal configuration

One way of looking at design is as a complex juggling exercise involving many interrelated factors. The factors are those aspects of the design that the designer thinks are important. For example, when designing a cup the designer may abstract the following factors that she considers to be important: the cup's capacity, its weight, how comfortable it is to hold, what the rim of the cup feels like when placed to the lips, how well it retains heat, how easy a shape it is to clean and how stable it is when placed on a surface. Associated with most of these factors are ideal values. Some of them are just the maximum or minimum possible, but some have a more precise optimum value (like the capacity). Others are dictated by the environment that the object is being designed for. If it has to fit in some way with other objects, then the parameters that affect this ability to fit in have to be of a certain value or

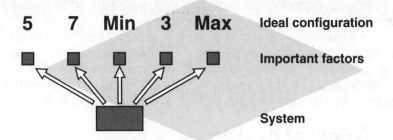

Figure 2.1   Important factors and the ideal configuration.

within a certain range of values. Consider designing a hatch to fit a hole; the dimensions of the hatch will be governed by those of the hole.

This collection of ideal values for each of the important factors is the ideal configuration. (See Figure 2.1.) However, when dealing with the real world it is difficult to achieve the ideal configuration.

2.2.2 The optimum configuration

Complexities arise because of the interdependence of many of the factors; changing one factor will affect others. Imagine I am designing a camera and I identify the important factors as being size, weight, performance, ease of use, robustness and cost. If there were no interdependencies in the factors my design would be simple: match-box sized, weight of a few grams, performance of a Hasselblad, robust as a tank and a cost of only a few pence. In reality there are many interdependences. If I increase the robustness then I will probably increase the weight unless I use special lightweight materials, but then the cost goes up. I can increase the performance by including lots of clever options but that may decrease the usability and increase the cost. So, the designer has to juggle these factors and interdependences and try to achieve an optimal configuration of them; a configuration where the value of each factor is as close as possible to its ideal value. This optimum configuration will have a correlation with the ideal configuration depending on how close all the optimum values are to the corresponding ideal values. If they are all close it will be high and vice versa. (see Figure 2.2.)

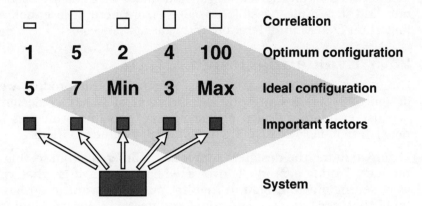

Figure 2.2   The optimum configuration and the correlation.

2.2.3 Relative importance

There is another complication to the process though. Achieving the ideal values for some factors may be more important than for others. The designer gives each factor a value of relative importance: 'Optimizing *this* factor is more important that optimizing *that* one.' The juggling of factors and values must then again be aimed at the goal of an optimal configuration but now this is the closest configuration to the ideal configuration taking into account the relative importance of the different factors. The proximity of each optimal value to its ideal value is weighted according to that factor's importance, and the most important factors are as close to their optimal values as possible while the less important factors are allowed to be further away.

2.2.4 Value systems

One key part of the design process outlined above is the building up of a value system for the problem: identifying the factors that are important and attaching values of relative importance to them.

In many areas of design these factors are easy to understand, quantify and manipulate. They are usually physical or economic factors such as weight, strength, cost of production and size. If the designer is designing something purely for herself then the attachment of values is not a problem; the designer will carry that out automatically. Whenever you make decisions based upon factors you attach values to them without thinking. However, the identification of all the relevant factors must be explicitly carried out, and it is quite possible to make errors here by overlooking important factors until later on in the design process.

2.2.5 Evaluating design

Evaluating a product – asking the question 'Is this product well designed?' – is tied in with the question of 'What is design?' because evaluating design depends upon the same principles as *doing* design: isolating factors and attaching values to them.

Evaluating the design of a product is different from testing a product. Testing a product involves checking that it is what you were setting out to design in the first place. If I want to design a table that can support one ton I can test my end product by putting a one ton weight on it and seeing what happens. If it collapses then it is *not* a solution to the design problem; if it holds, it *is*. However, two different designers could come up with two different designs for such a table, both of which *are* design solutions (they can both support one ton) but each is different. The question then is 'Which is the better designed of the two?'.

A design problem is characterised by a group of factors that are specified. With our table example the maximum weight is specified. All the factors that are not specified in this way are free to be manipulated by the designer in the process of achieving a solution. In doing so the designer will attach her own values to these factors and come up with her own personal design solution.

In evaluating the design the person doing the evaluation will judge the non-specified factors according to her own value system. The more similar this is to the value system of the original designer, the better the evaluator will believe the design to be. In some cases the evaluator's own value system will actually be modified as she evaluates the design. The designer may place emphasis on some factor that she believes to be important but that the evaluator has not considered until the moment she sees the design; then she thinks, 'Oh wow! That's clever, why didn't I think of that?' What she actually means by this is, 'Of course! it never occurred to me how important that feature was. Now I realize how important it is, and as this design places emphasis on it, it is a good design.'

2.3 Design for use

The search for a solution to a design problem becomes much more complex when people are involved as one of the factors. People are essentially complex; they are a product of nature. Artificial things are dreamed up in the head first and then produced, thus it is easy to reverse this process: to analyse an artificial thing and understand it. People, on the other hand, have come about naturally through evolution and, despite the application of many centuries of science, they are still not fully understood.

The human factors that play a part in the design process when designing for use can be split into two broad groups. The first are those factors of the body – the physical factors – and the second, those of the mind – the mental factors. When designing a door handle, for example, the physical human factors in the design mean designing the handle so that it is easy to reach, and easy and safe to operate. The mental human factors in the design mean designing it so that when someone is confronted with it they will realize that it *is* a door handle and they will understand what they must do to operate it.

Physical factors include such things as the size of different parts of the body, the strength a person can exert, how far someone can reach from a sitting position and what the best sitting position is. These factors are relatively easy to evaluate. Things can be simply measured or timed, people can be asked to perform physical actions repeatedly while being observed or videoed, and simple tests can be repeated over large numbers of people to yield average values. Physical factors have been playing a part in design for use for thousands of years.

Mental factors, on the other hand, are a relatively new consideration and have emerged because of the increasing complexity of modern interactive devices and systems. Mental factors include those aspects of the design that relate to what is going on in the mind of the user. Some of these factors are 'low level' and can be fairly easily measured by experiment in much the same way as physical factors are. In this category are things like attention span, memory span and memory capacity. However, most of the really interesting mental factors are 'high level' and woolly. These include questions like: 'How do people understand things?, 'How does a person think creatively?', 'Where do bright ideas come from?' and of course 'How do people design things?'

2.3.1 Value systems in design for use

The introduction of human factors and, in particular, mental factors makes the whole question of design a lot more complex. The designer is not designing according to her own wishes, she is designing for someone else – the user. This causes problems when it comes to value systems: problems that affect the initial specification of the value system for the design problem and problems that affect the subsequent evaluation of solutions to the design problem. The marshalling of factors and the attachment of values to them described in Section 2.2.4 [p 17] are prone to a degree of indirection when something is designed for use. The most important value system is no longer that of the designer, instead it is that of the end user of the system. The designer must carry out the design process in such a way that she follows the value system of the user. When weighing up changes in factors in the design problem she must ask herself, 'How important is this *for the user*?' This adoption of another value system raises the question of how the designer can find out what that value system is. One way is for the designer to play the part of the user herself and attempt to carry out the task that the user will be carrying out. She then becomes a user of the system and the value system she builds up as a result should be similar to that of other users.

The above is fine if it is a simple design-for-use problem like a pen or a tape recorder, but the process gets difficult if the problem is more complex. If it is something like the control panel for a railway signalling system then the designer will have to learn all about train scheduling before she can even start to become a user. In cases like this the designer must work with the users, talking to them and discussing aspects of the design problem in order to build up an idea of the user's value system. This type of interviewing ('picking the brains' of the user) is sometimes referred to as 'knowledge elicitation'. One disadvantage with this however is that the user may not have a very clear idea of how she actually goes about certain tasks, and any idea that she does have is bound to suffer some confusion when it is analysed and explained verbally to someone else. Indeed it is possible that the user could give an incorrect idea of what she is doing. In practice, as with design, the situation is not rigorous. No single method is used to build up the value system and there is lots of intermixing of methods depending upon the context of the design problem.

One classic example of misunderstanding or under-representing the user's value system was the mass of high-rise housing that was designed and built in the 1960s and 1970s. The designers of these tower blocks used a value system which was very different from that of the users (the inhabitants of the new buildings). The designers placed importance on things such as making use of the new materials and winning awards for their designs. When it came to what the users wanted, the designers emphasized the more machine-like factors of human living – the need to be warm, dry, and have good sanitation and services. They then, quite rightly, attached importance to these factors. However, they also overlooked many of the more spiritual and immeasurable factors of living, things like territory, control of surroundings, community, privacy and contact with neighbours. As a result their designs satisfied the factors that they perceived to be important but at the same time denied needs that many of the residents belatedly realized were just as important.

2.3.2 Evaluating design for use

Just as the introduction of people affects the design process so too does it affect the evaluation of design. Once again there is a difference between confirming that a design is indeed a design solution and judging how good a solution it is. The simple confirmation that a design is a design solution is more difficult since people are all different sizes and the question of whether a switch is accessible or not, for example, can depend upon who is reaching for it. The simulation of a design's behaviour is also made difficult when people are involved. When designing non-interactive things, simulation can take the form of constructing scaled-down models for testing or exposing prototypes to time-compressed testing: for example, running a vacuum cleaner continuously for days on end to determine if the design of the internal components can stand up to it. Some simulation is possible in designing for use; consider the building of architectural models for new buildings to see how they look. In general, however, the types of factors that you can evaluate from such simulations are very limited. Any testing has to be carried out with full-scale mock-ups and under normal time conditions.

2.4 Existing areas of design for use

Above I discussed design for use in a somewhat abstract manner. In more practical terms there are already a number of disciplines in existence concerned with design for use, in particular industrial design, architecture and town planning.

2.4.1 Industrial design

Industrial design is a discipline which has already been involved with the design of user interfaces for some time. The goal of industrial design is to design artefacts for human use so that they are pleasing to the user both to use and to look at. The discipline spans a wide range of complexity, going from simple household objects like cutlery through to complex systems like submarine control boards.

As well as the range of complexity, industrial design also covers a wide range with respect to those aspects of the user that the artefact is designed to fit in with. At the lowest end there is the design of objects to fit in purely with the physical dimensions of the user: helmets that fit the head, controls where everything is reachable and chairs that fit the human form. Further up on the same scale is the design of devices governed by the more physiological aspects of the user's bodily capabilities: designing display screens that are less harmful to the eyes and alarms that alert users without shocking them or interfering with their ability to respond. At the more psychological end of its scope industrial design involves designing devices, and especially the device's behaviour, to fit in with the mental side of humans: for example, their expectations, their previous experience and how they assess and integrate new information. This encompasses the design of products like complex control panels and information systems.

Many large office equipment companies that began by manufacturing typewriters, photocopiers and other office hardware are now expanding into computer markets with both hardware and software. The result of this is that their already established industrial design teams are having to push against the upper boundaries of industrial design, pushing the more psychological side of it outwards to embrace the design of user interfaces to these new, complex technologies.

Industrial design (and its related disciplines of ergonomics and human factors) has a history which is already several decades old, although some people might argue that humans have been designing for use for thousands of years (although this depends on your exact definition of design; see the boomerang discussion earlier in this chapter). Throughout its development industrial design has generated a large body of material applicable to user interface design, some of which can be generalized to apply to user interface design for computer systems.

2.4.2 Architecture and town planning

Many specializations of design for use concern themselves with the design of a product that is used to do one specific task. The user makes use of it for that one task and stops when that task is finished. In some cases that task may be a large part of a full-time job and its design then plays a very important part in the life of the person doing the job, but in the majority of cases the task is a minor one and shortfalls in the design of the product do not have a major effect upon the user. Seen in this light the responsibility of architecture to the public (the 'users' of a building) is very large indeed, since it is concerned with the design of an environment that people must live or work in for a large proportion of their life.

As well as this large effect on people's lives, architecture operates on a much longer timescale than other design disciplines. If I pick up a pen or sit in a chair I can quickly tell if it is well designed or not. Pens are designed for writing and chairs for sitting. But architecture designs things for living and working in. I can't try a building out by living in it or working in it just for a few minutes; both these concerns must be tested over a much longer duration of time. The realization that there are problems with the design of an office or a house may take a long time to emerge. Indeed, very often people fail to make the connection between their problems and the design of their environment.

The consequences of bad design are an important factor in architecture. If I find that my pen or my chair is unsuitable I can replace them without too much difficulty. But what if I start to think that my house or office is badly designed? Moving house is not a trivial task and neither is changing jobs. The problems associated with architecture become more accentuated when one moves up in scale to the level of town planning. The timescale is even longer; single buildings come and go within the framework of the overall town layout and the number of people affected is in the tens of thousands rather than in the hundreds.

Because of the large responsibilities architecture and town planning have to the public they are usually more advanced than other areas of design when it comes to taking account of the user and more answerable to the body of people who will be using their designs. As such they can give rise to solutions that can be generalized to other areas of design for use, including user interface design. One such solution that has emerged in recent years is 'community architecture': designing buildings and street layouts in consultation with the people who are going to live there. This embodies the ideas of involving the user right from the start of the design process and of having the prospective user evaluate the design at various points in its development

2.5 Summary

In this chapter I started off by trying to define exactly what design was. A model was outlined of the design process in general and I then talked about the importance of value systems within this process. From there I went on to discuss how this all related to the evaluation of design: that is, establishing whether something was well designed or not. This analysis was then made more specific by the consideration of 'design for use' – design problems where something was being designed for people to use. Again I looked at the importance of value systems and design evaluation. The chapter finished with a look at more established areas of design for use.

2.6 Exercises

2.6.1 Triggering cameras on kites

Almost as soon as the camera was invented people began attaching them to kites to try and take aerial photographs. The problems of triggering and aiming the camera when it is up in the air are approachable in many ways; a simple solution is to hang the camera from the kite in such a way that it always points directly down and then to trigger it by means of a clockwork timer which is set (while the camera is still on the ground) for several minutes' delay.

This whole area is a good example of a general design problem. Design a more advanced triggering and aiming system and try to document the process and the development of ideas maybe by tape recording the discussions or making notes.

2.6.2 Value systems

Draw up a list of the important factors to be considered when designing a camera and attach values to each of them on a scale of one to ten. Do it in a group and compare results. Think about the interdependences between the factors, (look back to Section 2.2.2 [p 16]). Have another go with something else: a tape deck, a car, a pen.

2.6.3 Design classics

Many existing designs are arrived at by gradual evolution; redesigning them involves just making small improvements to the existing design. Some designs that are regarded as being classic designs are achieved by designers doing away with current ideas and preconceptions about the thing being designed and starting from first principles. Have a go at designing a common household article from first principles, a folding chair or a desk lamp for example. Try and come up with a novel solution.

2.6.4 Things that get on your nerves

I have a big metal bikelock. It is fiddly to unlock it. I cannot do it with my gloves on. When the weather is really cold my hands end up getting frozen through contact with the cold metal even before I start my journey. Sometimes this gets on my nerves. Is there something at work or at home that gets on your nerves every time you use it? Why does it get on your nerves? Is it badly designed? If so have a go at redesigning it so that it doesn't get on your nerves.

2.7 Error messages: a sketch

Remember the analogy I drew at the end of the introduction, comparing a system that had a bad user interface to a knife without a handle? It was effective because it illustrated how unacceptable the current state of affairs with computer user interfaces would be if it were applied to areas of everyday life. Drawing analogies like this can be quite amusing, but it can also be a useful tool for thinking about user interfaces. What sorts of behaviour are acceptable to the users? Are there forms of interaction from real life that can be used as good metaphors in an interactive system?

Here is the first of the sketches that I am including. The two characters demonstrate what would happen if humans displayed some of the idiosyncracies of current computer–user interfaces. Hemelsworth is a rich, landed gentleman living in Broadoaks Manor. Barker, his butler to be, is way ahead of his time and, in his efforts to serve his master to the utmost, he will be continually attending the most up-to-date butlering courses.

Very often you come across systems that give you error messages. Something has gone wrong in the interaction between you and the computer and the computer tries to tell you what it is. Usually, however, the messages are very obscure and sometimes you must look up the error message in a manual which then explains what the computer system is really trying to say. Why the computer couldn't tell you in the first place I just don't know. What would it be like if people behaved like this?

Hemelsworth is waiting for his new butler to arrive. There is a knock at door. Hemelsworth opens it.

Hemelsworth: Hello.

Barker: Good morning. I'm your new butler, sir.

Hemelsworth: Oh, jolly good, I was rather wondering when you would arrive. What's your name?

Barker: Error code 3, sir.

Hemelsworth: That's an interesting name, 'Error code 3', what shall I call you for short?

Barker: Error code 145, sir.

Hemelsworth: But that's longer than 'Error code 3'. Wait a minute, 'Barker' was the name, wasn't it?

Barker: Yes sir.

Hemelsworth: Well come in Barker, come in. Would you like to join me for a cup of tea first?

Barker: Error code 19, sir.

Hemelsworth: What is all this 'error code' business?

Barker: They're error messages sir. Here. [*He presents Hemelsworth with a book*] You look up the error message in here and it tells you what you did wrong.

Hemelsworth: I'm not doing anything wrong am I? And why do I have to look it up in a book? Why can't you just tell me straight out?

Barker: Error code 65, sir.

Hemelsworth: Error code 65? Alright let's give this a try then... [*He leafs through the book*] Hmmm... 'Error code 65; too many questions at once'. Yes, well. Come in, let's have a cup of tea. I think I'm going to need one.

Chapter 3

Interactive systems

3.1 Systems

Any interactive computer program constitutes an interactive system; thus the ideas in this chapter are applicable and, although state-based notations may at first seem insufficient when dealing with the complexity of a computer system, they are useful when considering subparts of an interactive system as a whole: for example, the pressing and releasing of mouse buttons when interacting with a pop-up menu. Also, analysing interactive systems and presenting their behaviour graphically are both vital ideas when it comes to offering computer support for the design of such systems. Eventually people will design and implement computer–user interfaces not by writing long programs but by using a computer-aided design system (CAD system) to interact with some form of graphic notation for user interfaces which will then be translated into the real interface by the system.

So, let us start with systems. Although most people have a pretty good idea of what is meant by a system, it is one of those words that is difficult to pin down precisely. However, I shall have a go at explaining it.

Think of a commercial aircraft. One can talk about its electrical system, the internal lighting system, the flight control system, the navigation system, the fuel system and so on. Each of these systems is a collection of features that has something in common, or works together to achieve a common goal. For example, the navigation system includes all those features having something to do with navigating the aircraft. The fuel system refers to all the mechanics and structures that store the fuel on board and feed it to the engines. Some features can be part of two or more different systems; the radar in this aircraft is part of the navigation system and also part of the electrical system. Indeed, some systems can be completely contained within other systems; for example, the internal lighting system is contained within the electrical system.

There is a lot more to systems than is presented in this chapter, but the amount covered is sufficient for our discussion of interactive systems.

3.1.1 Static and dynamic systems

There are various ways of classifying and describing systems. One of the most important, as far as this book is concerned, is to distinguish between static and dynamic systems. The terms 'static' and 'dynamic' refer to how the system changes through time. A static system does not change, and a dynamic one does. As an example of a static system consider a cup. A cup, is a cup, is a cup. You can put it on a table and watch it for days but it won't do anything!

One could argue that a cup *does* change in time; it can be full of water, it can be upside down on the table, it can be full of coffee, and so on. However, in each of these cases the cup is a subsystem of a larger system, and it is its relationship to the larger system that is changing. A cup cannot be upside down on its own, it has to have something else there to be upside down in relation to. One could also argue that if you look at a cup in terms of its atoms it is a dynamic system, all those atoms are vibrating, it is *continually* changing. The purpose of this chapter is not to set out an unarguable collection of terms and assumptions for talking about systems, it is to put forward ideas that are useful to a designer of interactive systems. As such it should be remembered that in discussing various systems and making statements I shall be talking about things from the point of view of an ordinary person or user. So in this respect, a cup is a static system.

This book is about dynamic systems. A dynamic system is a system with one or more features that can have different states (for example a switch that can be off or on, or a door that can be open or closed). The state of the whole system is defined by the state of all of its features. The system moves from one state to another by changes in the states of its features. The transition from one state to another can happen in various ways. One way is just through the passing of time. Consider a kettle full of cold water sitting on a lit gas ring. After the passage of a certain amount of time its state has changed from being full of cold water and sitting on a lit gas ring, to being full of boiling water and sitting on a lit gas ring. Allow some more time to pass and eventually the water will boil away and it will be empty and sitting on a lit gas ring! Another way transitions can happen is by the system altering its own state. Think of a simple fan heater with a thermostat. The system keeps making the transition from 'fan on' to 'fan off' and back again as it attempts to keep its surroundings at an even temperature.

3.1.2 Interactive systems

As well as the classification of static and dynamic, dynamic systems themselves can be further broken down into two groups: interactive and non-interactive systems. The former are dynamic systems where some aspects of the way in which the system evolves through time can be influenced by a person using the system. The latter are systems that change their state without a user being able to influence these changes.

In Europe some escalators run all the time, even when no one is on them. Some escalators, on the other hand, are activated by the person treading on a pressure-sensitive switch as they approach them. They switch themselves off if no one has activated the pressure switch for a few minutes. Similarly, some traffic lights are non-interactive: they just give traffic the green light for certain periods of time. Other traffic lights *are* interactive: they have sensors that detect the presence of waiting cars and this influences the behaviour of the lights.

The two classifications described above are rather abstract. If the user has access to the electrical fuse box, or just a big enough hammer, many non-interactive systems can be redefined as interactive systems since they can be made to change their state by 'user actions'. Even without considering such extreme user actions it is possible to reclassify systems as interactive or non-interactive according to who the user is and how she is using it. Most systems need to be accessible to engineers and service personnel who are able to override the entire system and switch everything off. From their point of view any 'non-interactive' system is interactive. As I pointed out earlier, in this discussion on interactive dynamic systems, I shall be regarding the user in the simplest sense as just the normal end-user of the system.

3.2 Notating interactive systems

When dealing with the design of interactive systems there are occasions when it is useful to have a notation for expressing your ideas. Not only can you communicate your ideas to other people but the notation itself allows you to organize, analyse and manipulate the ideas in a more efficient way. With that in mind, let us put together a notation for describing interactive systems. Not an incredibly rigorous one, but enough to get the important ideas across.

The important things to be able to express are the separate states of the system and the transitions between them. I noted at the beginning of the chapter that a dynamic system is a system with one or more features that can have different states. Right, let's describe the complete system with a letter for each feature and a label in parentheses to describe what state it is in. Thus a light that can be on or off has two states: L(on) and L(off). The transitions can be shown on a diagram, by representing all the important states as circles and drawing arrows between them to represent the transitions. Mathematically speaking this is a 'connected graph', the circles are 'nodes' and the arrows are 'directed arcs'. But I shall just call it a state diagram.

3.2.1 Lights and switches

To illustrate this notation let us consider a simple example of a dynamic system: an ordinary household lamp with one switch. In the abstract we can consider this as a dynamic system with two elements – the lamp and the switch. Each of these can be in one of two states: feature L(lit), L(unlit) and S(on), S(off). Since I am considering the system at its simplest and most abstract I shall discount things like dead bulbs and bad wiring. The way the system is organized means that the lamp will only light when the switch is on. The states of L and S are linked. The system thus has only two states: S(on), L(lit) and S(off), L(unlit). Its behaviour is illustrated as a state diagram in Figure 3.1.

The two transitions are also shown. The user can flick the switch on or off: U:S(on) and U:S(off). The prefix 'U:' indicates that the user is responsible for the transition, and the feature and state following the prefix indicate the result of the transition. The only observation we can make from this simple example is that the user actions form a reversible pair; the user can do something and then do the reverse to get back to where they were. This is quite a common arrangement in interactive systems.

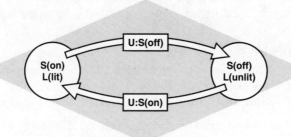

Figure 3.1   A simple lamp.

Next, a slightly more complex example: the same lamp, but with two switches, one on the lamp itself SL and the other on the wall socket SW. The lamp will now only be lit if they are both on: SL(on), SW(on), L(lit). The user can flick both the switches. The state diagram is shown in Figure 3.2.

In this figure the transitions drawn in grey form something called the 'common use loop'. This is the route through the transitions that is followed in normal operation (in the above example this means switching the light on and off by means of the switch on the lamp). A lot of simple interactive devices have this; the route is a loop and thus the normal operation can be repeated

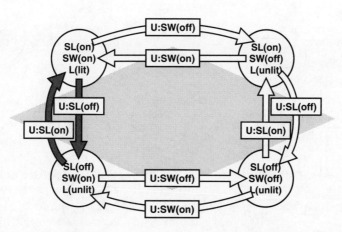

Figure 3.2   A lamp with two switches.

again and again. If the system is used intermittently one of the states on the common use loop will be the state where the system is waiting to be used again. This state is the 'neutral state'.

3.2.2 Kettles

Right, now let's move on to kettles. The old-fashioned electric kettles did not switch themselves off automatically. They just carried on boiling until the user intervened. (See Figure 3.3.)

The features are S, the switch, and W, the water in the kettle. W has three states: W(empty), W(full,cold) and W(full,hot). What new things have I introduced? To simplify things I have stopped showing the common use loop and I have replaced a reversible pair of user actions with a double-headed arrow. Another simplification is saying that the kettle has just three states. 'Full' includes many other states; in practice the kettle can be half full, quarter full or any amount full. As these states are all equivalent as far as boiling a kettle is concerned we group them together as one. I shall do a similar thing with the temperature of the water. The important state is when it is hot enough to use, to make a cup of tea for example. This is what I mean by 'hot'; all the other temperatures are grouped together as 'cold'. As well as user transitions we now have time transitions; if we leave the kettle alone for a while the water heats up or cools down. Time transitions are shown with a label T on them.

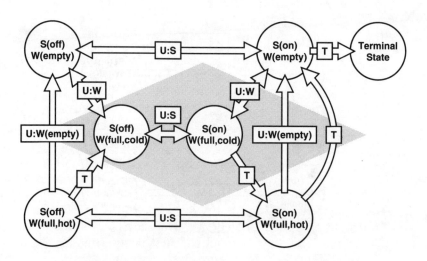

Figure 3.3 An old-fashioned electric kettle.

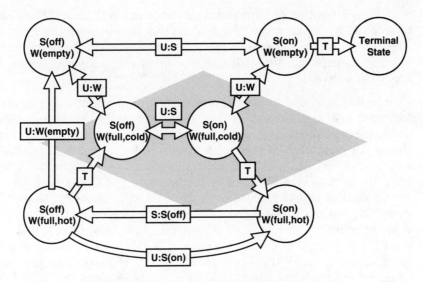

Figure 3.4 A modern electric kettle.

Out on its own on the right is a 'terminal state': if the kettle is left on while empty it overheats and the element burns out. Once the system reaches this state, that is it; there is no transition leading out of the state, the system is broken! Any state with a transition leading to the terminal state is a 'critical state'. In this case there is just one: S(on), W(empty). Avoiding the terminal state of this kettle is left up to the user. They must make sure it does not boil dry. If it somehow reaches the critical state they must make sure that the transition from the critical state is to a safe state by either filling it up with water or switching it off.

These days most electric kettles have a heat-sensitive switch inside them that switches the kettle off when it reaches a certain temperature. This transition is made by the system itself. (See Figure 3.4.)

The features are the same as above, except that 'hot' is now taken to mean hot enough to trigger the heat-sensitive switch. There is a new transition: when the S(on), W(full,hot) state is reached, the system automatically makes a transition by switching itself off. Previously there were three transitions from this state, two user transitions and one time transition. The system transition takes precedence over all these since it takes place as soon as the state is reached. There is no time for the user or time transitions to take place. System transitions are shown with the prefix 'S:'.

The critical state and terminal state are still accessible, but now only by user transitions entailing doing something silly, which can be easily avoided. Previously they could also be reached by time transitions: forgetting to do something sensible, which is less easy to avoid.

Both the above examples have a terminal state: it is possible to 'write off' the system by doing something wrong. The consequences of the terminal state in both cases are not too dire; the heating element of the kettle needs to be replaced or a whole new kettle bought. What if the consequences of the terminal state were more important? What if the system were, for example, a power station whose replacement would cost millions? It would be downright stupid if the safety of the system depended upon a user remembering to switch something off. In cases like this it is possible to design the system in such a way that terminal states (there may be more than one in a large system) are not present. Thus no matter what the user does, or forgets to do, such a state cannot be reached; the system is foolproof.

Terminal states may need to be removed because they are dangerous to the system. There are other states which are dangerous to the user or to other people; it would be a good idea if these dangerous states were also removed from the system's behaviour. Such a removal of a state can be achieved in two ways: by the linking of features or by constraining user actions... Bring on the microwave ovens!

3.2.3 Microwave ovens

Microwaves are a health hazard, thus care must be taken to ensure the safety of the user when designing the behaviour of a microwave oven. The user must not be able to expose herself to the microwaves. You could leave it up to the user (like I did with the first kettle we looked at) and print a warning in the instruction book, 'Ensure the oven is switched off when the door is opened' and hope that everybody remembers this and nobody makes a mistake. Or you could design the dangerous state out of the system.

Right, there is a door with two states: D(open), D(closed) and the switch, also with two states: S(on), S(off). There is also a timer control which can be used to switch the oven off after a certain period of time. These are the key controls at issue and I shall ignore the others. The state diagram of the system with no safeguards is shown in Figure 3.5.

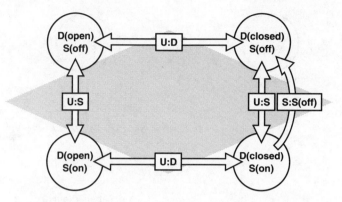

Figure 3.5 A microwave oven with no safeguards.

The use of the timer gives us an extra transition from D(closed), S(on) to D(closed), S(off). The dangerous state: D(open), S(on) is shown and there are two critical states leading to the dangerous state.

First let us seek a solution by constraining user actions. This means that in certain states (the critical states) the user is not allowed to make certain transitions (those leading to the dangerous state). For example, when the door is open and the oven is switched off the user is not allowed to switch the oven on. I can include the idea of constraints in our notation thus: (D(open), S(off) constrain U:S(on)). However, there are two critical states, so I also need to apply a constraint to the other one: (D(closed), S(on) constrain U:D(open)). These constraints give us the state diagram shown in Figure 3.6. The dangerous state has gone and thus there are no critical states.

The other approach is to link features; this means that certain user actions upon a feature will automatically affect other features. In the microwave oven I could say that opening the door automatically switches the oven off or, in our notation: (U:D(open) link S(off)). Once again, because there are two critical states, we must also say (U:S(on) link D(closed)). Thus the door closes automatically when the oven is switched on. This ensures that the dangerous state is not reachable from the other critical state. The resulting state diagram is shown in Figure 3.7.

Whereas the effect of constraints is to block off the transitions to the dangerous state, linking makes the transitions 'skip over' the dangerous state. In the abstract, linking is the better of the two solutions since constraining user actions can be confusing to the user – suddenly doors don't open or things can't

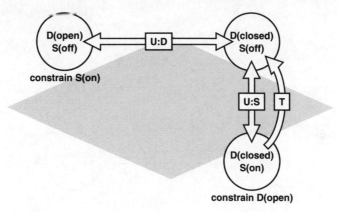

Figure 3.6 A microwave oven with constraints.

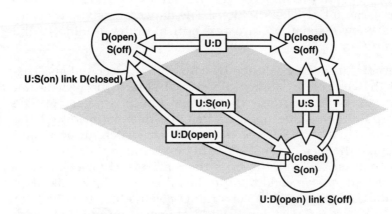

Figure 3.7 A microwave oven with linking.

be switched on. Also, if you compare Figure 3.6 and Figure 3.7, you see that with linking there are more transitions still available. The user can get directly from D(closed), S(on) to D(open), S(off) with just one transition whereas it takes two when constraints are used.

However, the linking of some features may be difficult to achieve, or it may lead to other problems in some systems: for example, the situation described above of automatically closing the microwave oven door when it gets switched on. Thus many systems use linking where possible and resort to constraints when linking is too difficult to achieve.

There are many other examples of similar arrangements of states occurring in anything involving a door with something dangerous behind it: spin driers, front-loading washing machines, torpedo tubes on board a submarine, the doors in a lift, air locks, photographic darkroom doors and the lids to food processors.

The notation outlined here has proved to be quite useful for describing the behaviour of simple devices. In the past couple of decades many different notations have been evolved, usually with peculiarities relevant to the type of system they are being used to describe. The more general such a notation is, the more complex and unwieldy it tends to be. If you are going to use a notation in a fairly non-rigorous way then the best approach is to have a browse through various different notations and put together your own, incorporating whatever features you think you might need.

3.3 Summary

In this chapter I discussed systems: what a system is and ways of classifying systems. I mentioned static and dynamic systems and then interactive and non-interactive systems. Interactive systems are what this book is all about and so I went on to develop a way of describing interactive systems with the help of state diagrams representing the different states of the system and the transitions between the states. Three types of transition were introduced:

◆ **Time transitions**
Caused by the passing of time.

◆ **System transitions**
Caused automatically by the system.

◆ **User transitions**
Caused by a user action.

Within the state diagrams certain key features were identified:

◆ **Common use loop**
The chain of states followed in normal use.

◆ **Neutral state**
The state in the common use loop where the system is waiting to be used.

◆ **Terminal state**
A state from which there are no outgoing transitions.

◆ **Dangerous state**
A state which may have dangerous consequences.

◆ **Critical state**
   A state with a transition leading to a terminal or dangerous state.

Methods of designing interactive systems so that terminal and dangerous states could be avoided were then discussed and illustrated with examples.

3.4 Exercises

3.4.1 Hot drinks machine

If you are reading this in an office or an educational establishment go along to the drinks machine, get a cup of coffee and draw a state diagram of the machine's operation. Start off with just a simple diagram showing the common use loop. What happens if the user is not 'well behaved'? Try making a selection before you put your money in, or not putting enough money in. Are there any options on the machine such as extra sugar? Can they be operated without putting any money in? Include them on the state diagram. Have another cup of coffee.

3.4.2 The common use loop and long queues

The design of the common use loop plays an important part in the design of systems that are used frequently. A good example is the cashpoint or automatic teller. You stick your plastic card in, key in your personal identification number, follow the instructions on the screen and end up with your card back and some money. Some cashpoints have quite time-consuming common use loops (including tasks like printing out a receipt of the withdrawal). This results in long queues building up at busy times.

   Draw the state diagram of the type of cashpoint you are familiar with, or design your own if you are not familiar with one. Redesign it to make the common use loop as short as possible, but still catering for people who may want special services (like a receipt or a check of their balance). Just for fun design one with a really long common use loop!

3.4.3 Protecting states

Ideally dangerous states and terminal states should be avoided in the design of a system. However, some devices have states which may have dangerous consequences but are nonetheless required and need to be accessible. Such dangerous states are not removed from the system but are protected by introducing extra states that need to be passed through before reaching the dangerous state. Consider a fire extinguisher or a gun; both have a trigger and a safety catch (something that has to be switched or unlocked before the trigger will work). The trigger has two states – T(pulled), T(not pulled) – and so does the safety catch – S(on), S(off). Draw the state diagrams and think of some other examples that have a similar arrangement of states.

3.4.4 Common use loops

In Figure 3.2 I showed the common use loop in grey. In the subsequent figures I left the common use loop out for simplicity. Have a look back at the figures and work out where the common use loop is for each of them.

3.4.5 State diagrams

Here is a list of simple interactive systems. Try drawing state diagrams for them:

◆ **A pelican crossing**
A pelican crossing is a pedestrian crossing with lights to stop the traffic, triggered by a button that the user presses when she wants to cross.

◆ **A simple alarm clock with a 'snooze' button**
A snooze button switches the alarm off for a few minutes (so that you can have a snooze) and then switches it back on again.

◆ **An airlock in a submarine**

◆ **A lock on a canal**
To get a boat from water at one level to water at another.

3.5 Losing files

You know the scenario – you are sitting in front of a word processor and are just putting the finishing touches to the document that you have been working on for the last day. You haven't done a save for a good half hour or so and suddenly you do something wrong and the system crashes (goes wrong and stops working). All your work over the last half hour is lost. Could it happen in real life?

In Broadoaks Manor, Hemelsworth has just finished dictating the final chapter of his book to Barker.

Hemelsworth: Well, that's the last bit done. Phew! Have you got it all down?

Barker: [*Holding up his note pad*] Yes sir.

Hemelsworth: Right, I'm going to start work on the diagrams. Could you bring me a cup tea please Barker?

Barker: [*Throwing the pad of dictated notes on to the fire*] Error code 42 sir.

Chapter 4

Abstraction and presentation

4.1 Introduction

Abstraction and presentation are two very powerful tools that occur in many different contexts. Much of user interface design is tied up with building abstract models and presenting them. This is important not just for information presentation but also at a deeper level when designing the underlying aspects and models that make up the interface. When dealing with information presentation, user models, feedback and computing the question continually arises, 'What are the key features and how can we best make the user aware of them?'

This chapter begins by explaining the concepts behind abstraction and presentation; it then goes on to consider more complex aspects, and finishes up by looking at the role played by abstraction and presentation in dynamic systems and interactive systems. In the opening sections, the concepts will be illustrated by considering a map. The map chosen is familiar to any visitor to London, and known by heart by many inhabitants of the city. It is the map of the London Underground System – the Tube. (Figure 4.1 shows a part of the black and white version of the map. In the colour version the Tube routes are drawn in different colours instead of different patterns.)

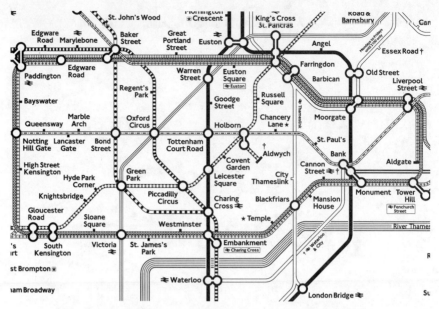

Figure 4.1   Part of the London Underground map.

4.2 Abstraction

First let us deal with the process of abstraction. Consider the Tube System. Let us try and describe it *completely*. We shall build up a list, a list of every conceivable fact or feature about the Tube System. As you might expect, the number of items of information we can come up with is huge. For starters:

◆   The Victoria Line links up four main British Rail stations.

◆   The Euston Tube station is sometimes crowded.

◆   The Hammersmith Tube station is above ground.

◆   The Circle Line goes round in one big loop.

◆   A lot of the Tube trains are silver.

◆   There is a new docklands branch to the system.

◆   Hampstead is the deepest station on the Tube.

Once we start along this road we can go farther and farther along it, coming up with vast amounts of Tube-related information such as:

◆   The spiral staircase at Tottenham Court Road smells slightly of fish and chips.

Figure 4.2   The real-world system.

◆ Baker Street station has very nice brickwork and lighting on the platforms.

◆ In 1988 two old Ovaltine posters were discovered during renovation work.

◆ One of the guards at Stockwell station hums a lot.

Furthermore, we are not limited to information about the state of the Tube as it is today. We could include how the Tube network evolved. When new lines were built. The dates on which the Queen travelled on the Victoria line and so on. Eventually we will have a collection of all the possible features of the Tube System: colours, smells, distances, employees, times, connections, everything! Together they form a complete description of the real world. Every aspect of it is documented in our list. This real-world system is represented as a big circle in Figure 4.2. A very simple figure, but one that will soon get more complex. This way of treating the real-world system is somewhat simplified. However, it is sufficient and it sidesteps some involved philosophical issues which are outside the scope of this book.

Imagine now that we have to assist people using the Tube System by providing them with information about it. We have amassed this vast body of features of the Tube System and from it we must abstract a collection of useful features to give assistance to the typical tube user.

4.2.1 The model of the user

The first question is, 'What do we mean by the average Tube user?' If we think about it for a while we can come up with a good idea of what they are like. They are using the Tube as a means of

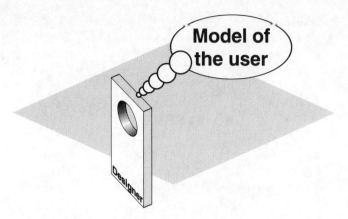

Figure 4.3   The designer and the model of the user.

transport. They want to get from A to B as directly as possible without getting lost or otherwise inconvenienced en route. They are not concerned with the history of the Tube, and comfort and station decor play only a minor role in their journey on the Tube. Gradually then, we (we will call ourselves 'the designer' from now on) build up in our mind a mental model of who our average Tube user is. There we are in Figure 4.3: the square is us (the designer), and the 'thought bubble' is our model of the typical Tube user.

4.2.2 The abstract model

Based on our model of the Tube user we now go through the collection of features of the Tube and select the useful ones. One good way of approaching the problem is to imagine what sort of questions a Tube user would ask. We would expect to hear things like:

> 'How do I get from Wimbledon station to Mornington Crescent with the least number of changes?'

> 'What is the nearest Tube station to Buckingham Palace?'

> 'If I arrive by British Rail at Liverpool Street station, will I find a Tube station there?'

We would probably not want to cater for rare questions like:

> 'When was the first time Prince Charles visited Charing Cross Tube station?'

So, from what we have decided so far about the user (no need of history, aesthetics and so on) we can immediately do away with the bulk of the information in the real-world system as we abstract features from it and build up our list of useful information, our abstract model. Eventually we can build up a list of features that are the most useful for the average Tube user. It could look something like this:

◆ The connections between stations.

◆ The relationship between the Tube network and the city.

◆ The names of the stations.

◆ The times of the trains from one station to another.

◆ The approximate duration of journeys between stations.

One important aim is to keep the abstract model as concise as possible, and to extract only the features which are most important to the user. There is a large body of features that can be ignored because, although they play a part in passenger comfort, they are not vital to the average user planning a journey. They include such things as the facilities at each station and the number of escalators from ground to platform level. Details about the train times and journey times are important, but as trains are frequent the times are not important in the planning of a journey. As such they can be presented separately on the appropriate platforms as supplementary information once a decision has been made about the route. The remaining features are then just concerned with position and connections. For each Tube station we need to have information about:

◆ Its position in relation to the rest of the city.

◆ Its name.

◆ Routes to take to reach each of the other Tube stations from it.

Such a collection of features as the one above, forms an abstract model of the Tube System. It is a model of a real-world system created by extracting only certain features from the whole description of that system. I can show what is going on by bringing Figure 4.2 and Figure 4.3 together, to produce Figure 4.4. Here we have the real-world system and the designer with a model of the user. The abstraction of features is represented by the arrow going from the real-world system to the abstract model, and, as this abstraction process is carried out by the designer, the arrow is shown passing through her. Also, like the model of the user, the abstract model exists as a mental model in the mind of the designer.

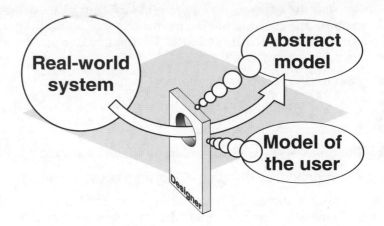

Figure 4.4   The creation of the abstract model.

4.3 Different abstract models

The selection of features that make up our abstract model was based on our model of a Tube user who was a passenger. What would the situation be if we were building up an abstract model for someone else? For a new member of staff or an electrician working there, for example, or for someone in a wheelchair who wanted to use the Tube System? In each case we would have a different model of the user and so end up with a different abstract model. The electrician would need to know where the cables and switches were located and what current they were carrying when in use. The person in the wheelchair would need to know which stations had lifts going to platform level and the least busy times to travel. Some features would be the same in the different models. Indeed some abstract models would contain *all* of the features present in one of the other models. For example, the abstract model for the member of staff would probably include all the features present in the model for the passenger as well as extra features, like access ways and stairs existing only for staff use. The extraction of different abstract models is shown in Figure 4.5.

Again, for each of these abstract models the designer has a corresponding mental model of the user in question. One abstract model could even be a history of the Tube System written for tourists, and it would therefore contain all those historical facts that we discarded earlier.

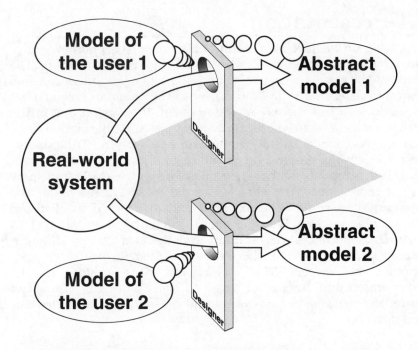

Figure 4.5 Extracting different abstract models.

There is an important general comment here about models of the user. As well as including aspects of the previous experience of the user and what her goal is in using the system, there are many occasions when the model of the user should include relevant aspects about the user's *environment* when using the system being designed: in particular, the personal environment and the general environment. The personal environment covers things directly related to the user which may affect their behaviour or capabilities: such things as having soapy (and thus slippery hands) in the bathroom, having full hands when going through a door or being busy with another task while doing the one in question. The general environmental considerations are more external to the user and more connected with the workplace: things like the noise level in the environment, the lighting, working space restrictions and so on. The importance of these factors should be weighted according to how likely they are to occur. Although these considerations do not play a major part in the Tube map, they are important in other situations.

4.4 Presentation

Well, what do we have as a result of the previous section? We have this talented designer, who has studied the Tube System and the needs of the people who use it, and she has come up with a fine abstract model that fulfils those needs. The question now is what do we do with this model? At the moment, it is just sitting in the designer's head somewhere. How do we get the information from that abstract model to the people who need it – the Tube users? We could sit our designer in an office and have passengers visit her one at a time to ask her their questions, or we could find some way of representing the abstract model in such a way that the representation could be duplicated and distributed to all those who need access to it. We shall refer to such a representation of an abstract model as a presentation and there are many different forms that it could take, the most convenient to use being text, graphics or speech. The concept of presentation can be incorporated into our earlier figure to give Figure 4.6. The act of converting the abstract model into its presentation is carried out by a designer.

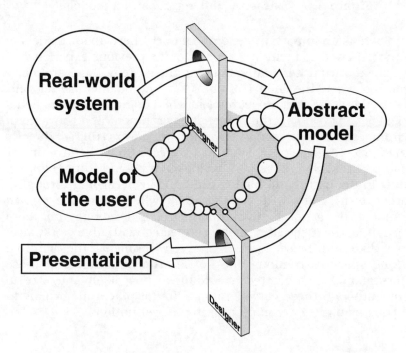

Figure 4.6   Abstraction and presentation.

The designer who builds up the abstract model here must also be the one to present it since you cannot transfer an abstract model directly from the mind of one designer to another.

4.4.1 Different types of presentation

Just as many different abstract models can be made from the real-world system, so too can many different presentations be made from an abstract model. The familiar Tube map, with each line picked out in a different colour, is just one way of setting the information down. The same information could also be presented as a black and white diagram with different textured patterns for the different lines, or it could even be just a written description of the lines and connections. As another example consider a clock. The real-world system is difficult to define exactly. It consists of all possible facts about what time it is *now*: the year, the month, the season, the date, the day of the week, the hour, the minute, the second, the tenth of a second, the hundredth of a second and so on. From this, we can extract a typical abstract model consisting of the hour and the minutes. This abstract model can then be presented in several different ways. Imagine that the time is twenty past seven. Figure 4.7 shows this time presented using different schemes. First, there is the familiar clock face with a long hand and a short hand, then it is expressed numerically, next it is written out in English, and finally in Japanese.

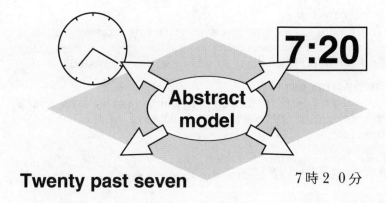

Figure 4.7   Different presentations of the time.

4.5 Classifying presentations

Presentations can be classified not only according to the medium they are realized in but also according to how that medium is used. The three most common media are:

- **Vocal**
  This covers the spoken word, either directly spoken by a person or 'second hand' from a recording of some sort.

- **Text**
  Text refers to any written language. The text can be in any physical form such as printed on paper or shown on a television screen.

- **Graphic**
  This covers all predominantly graphical two-dimensional presentations which may include text fragments, symbols, and pictures.

It is possible to make use of other media to present information. For example, the use of three-dimensional models plays a vital part in disciplines such as architecture. There is also the question of dynamic media which I shall deal with later. For now this discussion will concentrate upon the above three most commonly used media. The way that these different media are used can also be divided into three groups:

- **Simple use**
  The medium is used in as basic a way as possible without any embellishments.

- **Structured use**
  The medium has some sort of structure imposed upon it whereby the user can narrow her view of the presentation and select just the parts in which she is interested.

- **Interactive use**
  Here the medium is controlled by some form of device which interacts with the user and assists her in accessing the information.

There is some overlap between the last two categories since structured use must be interactive to some extent.

4.5.1 Vocal

When used in its simplest form, a vocal presentation of some body of information is usually a recording of a person reading through the information, while the user (the person accessing the information) has little or no control over it. A good example of this is the speaking clock: a telephone service where the subscriber dials a certain number and can listen to a recorded voice giving the current time at 10-second intervals. Inefficiencies with vocal presentations start creeping in when larger and more complex structures are presented. In such cases structured use of the medium is introduced into the presentation. Some mainline British Rail stations have train times to certain destinations recorded with a different telephone number for each destination. For example, if you are in London and you want to go to Manchester, you can dial a certain number and hear a voice reading through the train times from London to Manchester. This structuring of the presentation is becoming more possible with the introduction of digital telephone exchanges where the user can respond to questions or choices given in the recording by pushing the buttons on her 'phone during the call. The signals generated can access different parts of the recording, thus enabling the user to navigate her way through the information. For example, with the train times the user would dial one general train enquiry number and then respond to questions like:

'What is your destination? Leeds, push button 1. Manchester, push button 2.'

'What day are you planning on travelling? Monday, push button 1. Tuesday, push button 2.'

Earlier we considered presenting our abstract model of the Tube System vocally by sitting the designer of the abstract model in an office to answer passengers' questions. It is interesting to note that although this is inefficient in terms of human resources, it is still the method of obtaining information that most people prefer and trust. Despite train timetables and platform announcements, people will still ask a fellow passenger or a guard for confirmation of the destination of a train before boarding it. Interactive vocal systems still have a long way to go before they will command the same amount of user trust. The development of interactive vocal systems that can talk to and answer the user is still in its infancy. It involves two large and complex areas of computer science currently under research: speech recognition (identifying what words a person is saying) and the closely related field of knowledge engineering (understanding what the user means with those words).

4.5.2 Text

The use of vocal media, in their recorded form, relies heavily upon technology and involves many complexities. Text, however, has been around for thousands of years, and text-based techniques are thus more advanced. Let us return to the Tube System. If we were to design a textual presentation of our Tube model, the simplest way would be to write all the information down in very small print, in a big long list, and let the user sort it out. All the information would be there, and the Tube user could extract those parts relevant to her needs. However, imagine planning a Tube journey from Kew Gardens to Euston and being confronted with something like this in the foyer of the station:

'The best route from Holland Park to South Kensington is to take the Central Line, eastbound, and change at Notting Hill Gate to the Circle Line, southbound, which takes you to South Kensington. The best route from Temple to Leicester Square is to take the District Line, westbound, and change at Embankment to the Northern Line, northbound, which takes you to Leicester Square. The best route from St Paul's to...'

Presentation is not just a matter of making sure that all the information is there. The needs of the Tube user are just as important as completeness of information. Any Tube user faced with the above, would be delayed, confused, and probably annoyed as well! Structured use of text changes the presentation from one long stream that the user must wade through into an organized structure where the user can rapidly pinpoint the items of information that she needs without having to read through unnecessary information. In our Tube example the list could be organized alphabetically according to your station of departure, and within that according to your station of destination. So, a user going from Kew Gardens to Euston would look down the list to find the section concerned with Kew Gardens and, within that, the section with Euston as the destination:

'Destination: Euston

The best route from Kew Gardens to Euston, is to take the District Line, eastbound, and change at Victoria to the Victoria Line, northbound, which takes you to Euston.'

Interactive use of text relies on technological devices. Teletext systems, such as Ceefax and Oracle in the United Kingdom, present predominantly text-based information in a structured and interactive way. The user can navigate a route through the screens of information by selecting choices from the alternatives presented on the screen. More interactive use of text involves the use of computers to manage the system, and the subject is then referred to as 'hypertext'.

4.5.3 Graphics

If text has been around a long time, graphics has been around even longer – all the way back to cave paintings. Graphics is less abstract than text, easier to grasp and less dependent upon a fixed language. Simple use of graphics in a presentation of some body of information is difficult to define. There is no easy analogy to the single long recording of vocal media, or the one monolithic block of words in text-based presentation. Even the simplest of graphic presentations (diagrams) must have some thought and structure put into their creation, and 'simple graphics' spans a range from 'how-to-get-to-my-house' maps drawn on a scrap of paper to huge circuit diagrams or maps of areas of land. Within this range of presentations there is a huge variety of techniques for illustrating data graphically. You have only to watch the financial news on the television, the weather forecast or look at a map to realise the wide range of things that graphic communication includes.

Consider an abstract model consisting of the average monthly temperature recorded over one year. In Figure 4.8 this abstract model is presented in two ways: using text and using graphics. You can immediately see that the graphic presentation provides a far better overall view of an abstract model. The long-term trends and the shape are clear. The textual presentation does have some advantages however in that it is more helpful for precise information; you can see that the average temperature for May and October is the same, which is not immediately clear from the graphic presentation.

Structured use of graphics involves breaking a body of information down into areas that can be presented separately. This is quite a complex subject in its own right and it is dealt with in the next chapter. Interactive use of graphics uses technology, particularly computers. Such interactive use is usually video based (providing both still and moving pictures) and the subject then goes under the title of 'interactive video'.

The presentation of the Tube System is similar to the presentation of the graph above. The Tube user is interested in the 'overall picture'; they are not looking for one small item of information in amongst what is there. They want to know about the interrelationships between stations and lines and about the spatial relationships of elements to other elements. Thus graphics is the best presentation medium to describe those aspects of the

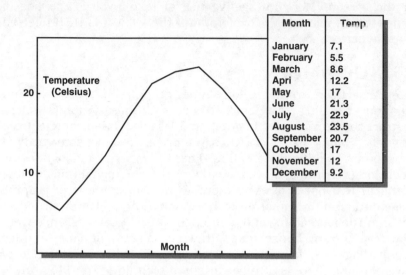

Month	Temp
January	7.1
February	5.5
March	8.6
Apri	12.2
May	17
June	21.3
July	22.9
August	23.5
September	20.7
October	17
November	12
December	9.2

Figure 4.8 Text and graphics presentations of information.

Tube System that we have been dealing with. The fact that graphics is the best medium in this case does not mean that graphics is best in general. Other presentation problems could require the use of other presentation media and choosing the medium to fit the problem depends not upon rules, but upon a good appreciation of the problem and its context.

Finally, presentations do not have to be realized in just one type of medium. Text and graphics are often mixed, and a lecture is a good example of a presentation that makes use of voice, text and graphics. There is a branch of computer science dealing with bodies of information that are presented using a mix of the three media; it is referred to as 'multimedia'.

4.6 Summary

This chapter concentrated on offering the user information about a real-world system. First I looked at how features can be extracted from a real-world system to form an abstract model of the system and how this abstraction can be based upon a certain model of the user of the information. I also showed how different abstract models of the same real-world system could be constructed for different groups of users.

I then moved on to the presentation of the abstract model. I considered different presentation media: vocal, text and graphics, and for each of these I looked at three different ways of using the media: simple use, structured use and interactive use.

4.7 Exercises

4.7.1 Hours and minutes

One of the examples we looked at was different ways of presenting the time. (See Figure 4.7.) What other possible ways are there? How about a linear clock face like that in Figure 4.9? The two digits at either end show the hours that the time is in between, and the small line indicates how much of the hour has elapsed. Something like this could be done using LCDs. Design a few alternative clock faces that show hours and minutes, and decide what advantages and disadvantages they have.

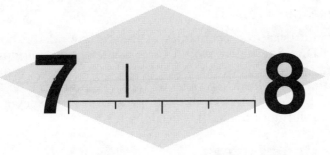

Figure 4.9   A different way of displaying the time.

4.7.2 Maps for cyclists

Maps are good examples of presentation and abstraction. If a map showed all the information about an area (grass type, soil composition, average temperature, age of roads, population numbers, picnic places) it would be unintelligible. Abstract models are built up according to who is going to use the map. General road maps have all sorts of information on them whereas tourist maps include extras like hotels and places with beautiful views. Imagine designing a small-scale map for touring cyclists. A lot of the information in the abstract model would be the same. What extra information would a cyclist be interested in? Bus shelters for when it rains? Bike shops for carrying out repairs? Steep hills? What other features are there and how might they be presented on the map?

4.7.3 The audio dashboard

At various times in automobile history designers have looked at the idea of an 'audio dashboard'. The motivation is that if drivers could have all the usual dashboard information supplied to them by means of sound, then they would not have to take their eyes off the road to look at the dashboard. This is a problem of presentation. The abstract model is the same but the presentation medium is different. The difficulty lies in communicating the information when it is needed and not over-using the medium. Consider oil pressure. You could have a recorded voice commenting on the oil pressure every ten seconds:

'Oil pressure normal,'

or

'Oil pressure high/low.'

This would drive the occupants of the car round the bend very quickly! One alternative would be to issue the warning message once only, but if the driver failed to hear it, or heard it and then forgot it, it could lead to problems. What would be the best way to manage warning signals like oil pressure? What about more complex information like the speedometer?

4.7.4 Book covers

Look through the books on computer science in a bookshop. Which ones have good covers that look interesting and tell you a bit about the subject covered by the book? Which have covers that are confusing and unrelated to the subject? Which covers are just downright boring? Choose some of the boring ones and design better covers for them.

4.8 Full file store

In the last sketch I talked about loss of information due to a system crash. Sometimes with a word processor such a loss of information can occur because the file store (the disk) is so full that there is not enough space left to save the file that you have been working on. There is not enough room and so you have to lose your work!

In Broadoaks Manor, Hemelsworth has just finished dictating the final chapter of the second version of his book to Barker.

Hemelsworth: Well, that's the last bit done again. Phew! Have you got it all down?

Barker: [*Holding up his note pad*] Yes sir.

Hemelsworth: Right, I'm going to start work on the diagrams. Barker, could you take this manuscript to the study and put it into the top drawer of my desk.

Barker: Certainly sir.

Barker leaves and returns a short time later.

Barker: Sorry sir, the top drawer was full so I burnt the manuscript.

Chapter 5

More about presentation

5.1 Introduction

The preceding chapter covered the presentation of information in quite a simple and abstract manner. Visual presentation of information is one of the key ways of getting information across to the user when dealing with the computer–user interface. All sorts of tricks and techniques have been used from the fields of typesetting and graphics and new ones have been invented just because of the abilities of the computer technology. The ability to present more complicated structures depends upon a better understanding of the issues involved and, because of the extra dimensions of time that computers bring to presentation, it is also useful to have a grasp of the concepts connected with the presentation of dynamic information.

5.2 Density of information

The crux of this book is that we are designing systems with the user in mind. We must therefore modify our design methods to accommodate any preferences and limitations that the user may have. In the field of presentation two important factors that must be balanced are the resolution of the information, and the physical size of its presentation. The human eye can only resolve so much detail per unit area. A street map shrunk down to the size of a postage stamp is very compact and portable, it contains all the information, but in terms of day-to-day usefulness it is hopeless. The information is too densely packed to be read by a person

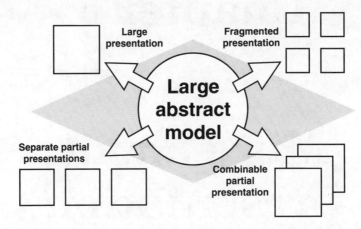

Figure 5.1   Four ways of coping with large presentation.

without using some sort of special equipment. Thus we can state that the presentation must not have too great a density of information. Contrary to this is the need to have the presentation of a physical size that makes its use both comfortable and efficient in the environment where it will most commonly be used. There are four ways of approaching this balancing act between resolution of information and size of presentation; they are described below and illustrated in Figure 5.1.

5.2.1 Large presentations

There are many areas where the solution is the obvious and simple one; just enlarge the presentation until all the information is resolvable. This is usually applicable to fields where small detail is important as well as the overall layout. This includes such things as cartographic maps (small details like telephone boxes are important along with layout information like the proximity of towns) and architectural elevations (small building details are important, and so too is the overall appearance of the building). The size of the presentation is deemed to be a factor secondary to the resolvability of the information and the overall layout. As a result such presentations can be large and cumbersome.

5.2.2 Fragmented presentations

In some cases the small local details are important, but decreasing the size of the presentation takes precedence over showing the overall layout. The result is typified by an 'A to Z' street map of a town (an 'A to Z' street map is one which is split up into sections and arranged in a book along with an index of street names). It is compact, it shows the local information, but is not ideally suited to showing the overall layout of the information.

Many such street maps also include a small-scale map of the whole area at the beginning: an overview. This is covered by a grid showing which areas of the town the pages refer to. I shall be looking at overviews further in Chapter 16.

5.2.3 Separate partial presentations

Another approach to reduce the information density is to break the information up and have several presentations.

This method is applicable to situations where the information can be separated into fairly unconnected blocks. The user is interested in the information in each block, and is less interested in how the information in one block relates to the information in other blocks.

A good example is a car manual. Instead of one huge diagram of the car showing absolutely everything, the information is divided up according to the separate subsystems within the car: braking system, electronics, steering. Each of these is presented separately. The presentations are usually very similar in structure (same size and shading) and they usually show the information overlying some common context such as a faint sketch of the body of the car.

One can see that this method would be inappropriate for abstract models where the relationship between the different parts is important: abstract models like that of the Tube System. If you had a separate small diagram for each line shown against the layout of the city it would be a nice compact little booklet, but finding connections and planning routes would be a nightmare.

5.2.4 Combinable partial presentations

Finally I shall look at a modification of the above method. There may be situations where the relationships between separate layers are important. The solution then is to give the user the ability to overlay separate presentations to see how they relate.

Overlays like this are used in town planning. A site map has different overlays showing things like land use, land ownership, communications, public facilities and so on. These may be combined to examine the relationships between them. A similar situation arises with architectural drawings showing the routes of different services within a building: heating, lighting, air conditioning and water.

5.2.5 Overviews and zooms

When I look at a map to find a particular detail I do not start at one corner and laboriously work my way across it reading every single street name. My first action is to look at the whole in order to get an overview of the area. Next I identify the part I am interested in, and only then do I narrow my perspective (zoom in) and start looking at the detail in that area. When I make that overview I am not looking at detail. I am interested only in a handful of large features that help me to put the rest in context. I look at the rivers, canals, the green splotches of parkland and at the main roads and railways. Usually maps are designed so that these key orientation features are more visible and more noticeable; they are in brighter, richer colours or drawn thicker and larger than other features.

5.3 Clarity and content

The clarity of a presentation, or part of it, is a measure of the ease with which a user can extract the information she needs. Information density is one factor affecting the clarity but there are other independent factors involved. The clarity of a particular feature of a presentation can be increased without affecting the content. A destination board mounted over a platform in the London Underground is shown in Figure 5.2. It indicates which

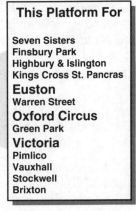

Figure 5.2   A destination board on the London Underground.

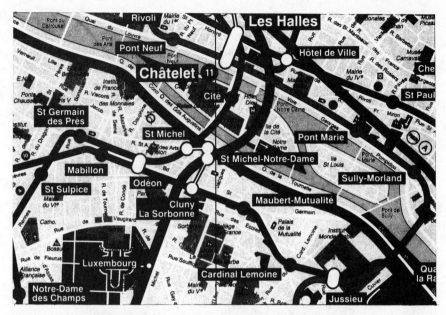

Figure 5.3   Part of the Paris Métro map.

stations are visited by trains calling at that platform. Some of the stations are more common destinations than others, thus many more people will be searching for these names on the list. These names can be presented in a bigger font to make them easier to locate, without sacrificing any other parts of the presentation.

However, there are situations where improving the clarity of one feature *will* affect the rest of the presentation. This leads to a balancing act similar to the one encountered above, improving the clarity of certain features at the expense of losing clarity in others. Indeed, some features may end up being removed altogether from the presentation (and the abstract model) in order to increase the clarity of some other feature. The measure of the importance of the features is derived from the designer's model of the user and how important the designer believes those features are to her. An illustration connected with the Tube System emerges when you compare the maps of the London Underground System (See Figure 4.1 [p 44]) and the Paris Underground System – The Métro (See Figure 5.3 which shows a part of the map in black and white. In the colour version the Métro routes are drawn in different colours). From the map of the Paris Métro we can see that the abstract model includes the exact positional information of the stations, and that this is included in the presentation by showing the network superimposed upon a street map of the city centre.

In the early days of the London Tube System the network was similarly superimposed upon a street map of the city. In the 1930s the map was redesigned: the clarity of the positional information of the stations and lines within the city was toned down until the map gave only a hint as to where the stations and lines were located, and the only features of the city that remained were some of the British Rail stations and the river Thames. However, this loss of positional information was balanced by an increase in the clarity of information about the layout and interconnectivity of the stations and lines. The layout was very clear and modular, with lines constrained to be vertical, horizontal or at 45-degree angles. The stations too were spaced out on the lines at regular intervals. The end result was a concise presentation, the style of which has been copied and applied to many other communications network maps throughout the world.

5.3.1 Active and passive organization

There are many ways in which information can be organized in order to make it a more efficient means of communication. Two broad categories are active organization and passive organization. Information can be said to be actively organized when the designer is trying to communicate information to the user (the person seeing the information) when that user is not actively searching for the information. The information is usually arranged with the aim of communicating the entire content to the user and examples can be found in advertising (billboards, letterheads, company logos, entertainment posters) and also in warning signs (warning symbols, road signs). For a discrete chunk of information like this you need to have a clear idea of precisely what it is that the user wants to know and, if there are several parts to the chunk, which of them are the most important. Take, for example, the advertising information for a textbook. The most important parts are the title, the author, the subject area and the price. Other less important parts might be the list of contents and reviewer's comments.

With passive organization the user is assumed to be the active agent, searching through the information to get to a particular part. Thus the information must be organized so that it helps the user navigate to the part she wants. The question then is how will they be trying to find the information they want? Usually they will have some item of information (a key) and will want to access more information related to this key. Sometimes the information may have to be organized so that the user can get to it using different keys. For example, in a dictionary of quotations the user may want to find a quotation by a particular person or a quotation on a particular subject. Problems arise when the two styles become mixed. This can happen when the amount of information to be communicated by an active organization of information becomes far too large. The users then begin treating it as a passive organization. A good example of this is the safety instructions handed out in aeroplanes. It is important information but, as there is little immediate need for it and there is a lot of it, nobody reads it thoroughly or even attempts to do so.

5.4 Icons

Abstraction and presentation also have a part to play when it comes to icon design. Think back to the last set of toilet doors that you saw. How did you know which one was the one you wanted? They probably had something marked on them to identify which was which. In Great Britain they are marked 'Ladies' and 'Gents', L and G, or they have small pictures on them of a man and a woman. Usually these are very simple stylized silhouettes of a trouser-clad man and a woman wearing a skirt.

The words 'Ladies' and 'Gents' on the doors are symbols. So too are the L and the G. Somewhere along the line you had to be told what they meant. The association between the pattern and the meaning was explicitly made, 'this pattern means this and that one means that'. The silhouettes of the man and the woman on the other hand are *icons*. They have an implicit association between pattern and meaning. The pattern resembles something with which the user is already familiar, and that something could already have several associated meanings for her. From the context of the icon the user is usually able to deduce its meaning.

Text has been around for a very short time as far as human evolution is concerned. Throughout most of their development humans have evolved while processing the world around them visually. Because of this we are far more adept at visual processing. Images can be recognized faster than text and single images can be selected from a group of images faster, and with greater accuracy, than a word from a group of words.

In many situations it may be difficult to find an icon that intuitively sums up the meaning that you want to convey so that a user coming across it for the first time will understand it. In such situations icons are sometimes still used in place of text because of the visual processing advantages described above, but the icons are used in a 'symbol-like' way; the icon is introduced to the user and its meaning is explained. Strictly speaking they are no longer icons but pictograms: simple pictures with an explicit associated meaning. A good example of this distinction can be found in road

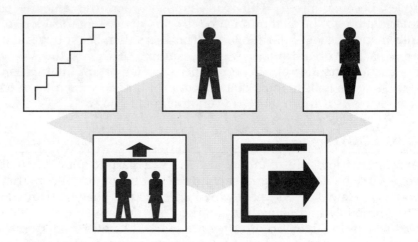

Figure 5.4   Abstracting essential features for icons.

signs. Some of the warning signs are quite obvious in their meaning; they show stylized pictures of men shovelling piles of materials or of falling rocks. Others are obscure and their meaning must be looked up in the driving regulations and learned.

I should mention here that we are once again dealing with people – the users. As a result the dividing line between real icons and 'symbol-like' icons is vague; it depends greatly upon the user's previous experience. Different users have different past experience; an icon that is intuitive and obvious to one user may have to be explained in detail to another.

Designing an icon involves the abstraction and clear presentation of the essential features of the concept you are dealing with. To draw an icon of a set of stairs for example you have to extract the key features of stairs in general and present just these. In a similar way the designers of the ladies and gents icons for toilet doors attempt to extract and present the essential visible features of (clothed!) men and women in a simple silhouette form, while people working on an icon depicting a lift have to be a little more inventive and find a graphic way of presenting the essential features of a lift. The best example of this sort of abstraction is the icon used in some stations to depict 'exit'. (See Figure 5.4.)

When designing icons for a new context it is sometimes possible to borrow them from other contexts since there is already a large body of icons in use in different areas of our life. One important consideration here is the overlap between the users of the new system being designed and the users of the system from which you are borrowing the icon. This overlap should be as great as possible to ensure that as many users as possible of the new system are familiar with the icon. One example of this is the use of the 'no entry' road sign on doors in office buildings and super-markets; here there is a good overlap since many of the people involved will also be road users.

The use of icons does not inherently imply good design. Many well-designed user interfaces do use icons, but they are indicative of good design only when they are a relevant solution to the problem. Their indiscriminate use does not result in a good interface and can often result in a bad one. A good example of this is the new photocopiers we have just had installed. In the old models the control panel was covered in icons. Some of the functions were easy to understand but others were more difficult. The worst was the darker/lighter copy control. It was not clear which of the two icons used implied 'darker' and which implied 'lighter'. You would often have to experiment in order to get some visible feedback.   The new copiers have clarified this situation by simply replacing these icons with the words 'darker' and 'lighter'.

5.5 Dynamic systems

The process of abstracting and presenting information about a system becomes more involved when we move on to consider dynamic systems. A dynamic system is one whose state changes with the passing of time. Some systems are obviously dynamic: for example, a clock. Other systems may seem static at first, but when considered over a long enough timespan they too are dynamic. The Tube System is a dynamic system; by that I am not referring just to the movement of the lifts and trains, but to the actual layout and interconnections. They are dynamic. New routes are added, stations are closed and so on. In the late 1980s a new line was added to the network – the East London Line. Because of this, the abstract model to be presented to the Tube user was changed to include the new line, and subsequently the presentation of this model (the Tube map) was altered. So the change in the real-world system 'filters through' to the abstract model and to the presentation. Changes in the Tube System layout take many months to carry out and the updating of the presentations (the Tube maps) can also take a long time without causing too much inconvenience to the user.

However, for dynamic systems with a much shorter timescale the abstract model and presentation must be updated at a proportionally faster rate. This is usually done automatically without involving human beings as part of the system. A good example (still following the theme of passenger transport) is the departure board in a station or airport. This is a list of the most imminent departures in order of departure time and it usually includes such information as the time of departure, the destination, and which platform the train will leave from. The list is displayed on some sort of electronically controlled board which can be rapidly altered. As the state of the real-world system changes, for example the first train on the list departs, the abstract model changes as well (since the abstract model does not include information about trains that have already gone) and subsequently the presentation (the departure board) follows the changes in the abstract model and the entry for that particular departure disappears from the board. (See Figure 5.5.)

5.6 Interactive systems

The next step after dynamic systems is to look at interactive systems; these are different from the interactive presentations encountered earlier. Interactive presentations are presentations of systems where the user can interact with the *presentation* to extract more information. With interactive systems the user interacts with, and changes, the *real-world system* thus causing changes in the abstract model and the presentation. See Figure 5.6, which I have simplified by combining the abstraction and presentation into one arrow.

Consider a set of lifts in an office. They have what could be called a 'departure board' on each floor informing the user which floor each lift is on. Each floor also has two buttons with which a

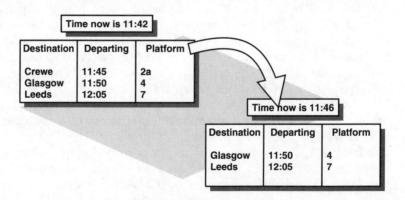

Figure 5.5   Changes in a departure board.

user can call for a lift: one to call for a lift to go up and the other to call for a lift to go down. These buttons light up when they are pressed and stay lit until the call for a lift is satisfied. The state of these two buttons indicates what lift calls are waiting to be satisfied. Once inside the lift the user can push buttons to request it to stop at different floors. All these buttons are in effect simple 'tools' with which the user can manipulate the state of the real-world system. The system is in one particular state and, by using the tools provided, the user can move it into another state.

Abstraction and presentation enable an abstract view of a system to be presented to the user. In the example of the lifts the user is unaware of all the electrical and mechanical activity taking place; she is only aware (via the 'departure board' and lit buttons) of the abstract model of the system, the whereabouts of the lifts and whether or not a lift has been called for the floor she is on. A similar situation is true of the 'tools' that the user can use to influence the state of the system.

The fact that there is a tool with which the user can change a particular aspect of the state of the real-world system, implies that that particular aspect is of importance to the user, and as such it is included in the abstract model. Thus each tool has a 'real effect'

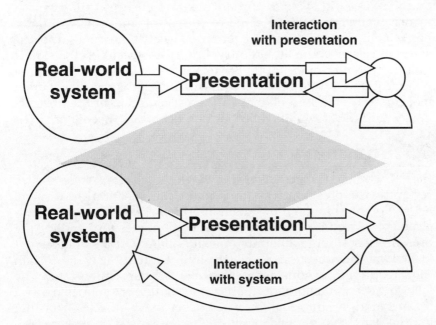

Figure 5.6 Interactive presentations and interactive systems.

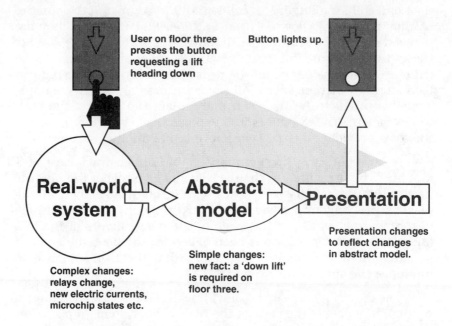

Figure 5.7   Changes in the state of a lift.

on the real-world system, and an 'abstract effect' on the abstract model. Signalling a lift to come to your floor and take you down has a complex real effect in terms of electric currents and the states of relays in the lift circuitry, but its abstract effect is simply that the abstract model of the system now includes the fact that a lift is required at that floor to go down. This change in the abstract model is reflected in a change in the presentation of the abstract model, and the 'down lift called' button lights up. (See Figure 5.7.)

5.7 Summary

Here I gathered together some of the important side issues regarding the presentation of information. I looked at the issue of density of information (how much information you can cram into a given space) and I considered different techniques for handling the presentation of large amounts of spatial data. On a similar note I looked at the question of clarity and content, leaving certain things out and emphasising features that are important. The following section on organization of information mentioned passive organization of information where the user searched for the information she wanted, and active organization where the information had to tell the user something she may not have been looking for.

After covering icons and icon design I moved on to abstraction and presentation in the context of dynamic systems and interactive systems.

5.8 Exercises

5.8.1 Five icons

Some of the most tricky icon problems are also the most common. Have a go at these five and see if you can come up with any solutions: two icons to be drawn alongside an electrical switch to indicate 'off' and 'on'; two icons to be drawn on opposite faces of a door, one to signify 'pull' and the other 'push'; finally, an icon to be printed on packing cases to indicate which side should be uppermost when stacking them 'this way up'.

5.8.2 Electrical wire colouring

In order to comply with European standards, the wires in a British domestic electric cable are coloured as follows:

◆ Live – brown.

◆ Neutral – blue.

◆ Earth – yellow and green stripes.

This is part of your user model when conducting electrical repairs. To most people these colours seem totally arbitrary and difficult to remember. Can you think of a better scheme of colours that makes use of mental models that people already have, thus making the colour scheme more obvious and easier to remember? Are there any special considerations you should give to your model of the user in this example?

5.8.3 Collecting icons

Earlier, I described the advantages that icons and pictograms have over text. A further advantage is that because they are graphic they are language independent; this is especially important in today's international environment (however, care should still be taken because icons can be *culture* dependent). If you look you will see icons all over the place. Keep your eyes open and maybe collect a list of icons you think are well designed and obvious and a list of those that you think are badly designed and ambiguous. Here are some good sources of examples:

◆ Road signs

- ◆ Photocopiers
- ◆ Hotel guides
- ◆ Stations, trains and airports
- ◆ Car dashboards
- ◆ Instructions and warnings on containers
- ◆ Other household/office devices (irons, washing machines, cameras, cassette decks)
- ◆ Catalogues of rub-down letters and symbols such as Letraset

5.8.4 Designing information structures

There are many sources of passively organized information available. For the following items of reference material specify what information the user is looking for and what bits of information they might be using as a key. How do they navigate through the structure to find the information they want?

- ◆ An atlas
- ◆ A recipe book
- ◆ A theatre programme
- ◆ A train timetable
- ◆ A book on user interface design
- ◆ A spelling dictionary
- ◆ A list of what's on at the movies this month

5.8.5 Built-in feedback

Instead of using icons to signify 'push' and 'pull' on a door, as in Exercise 5.8.1, is there some way of designing the door itself, or the handles, so that whether the user should push or pull is obvious without the need to decipher funny icons?

5.8.6 Planet guide

In a hotel guide you have a row of small icons underneath each entry forming a presentation of a concise abstract model of the hotel. They indicate whether or not it has a bar, a golf course, a sauna and serves cooked breakfasts.

Imagine a similar scheme describing planets for space travellers. What features would you need to extract about the planet for inclusion in the guide? Some obvious ones are: a breathable atmosphere, dangerous animal life and spaceport facilities. How would you present this information? What icons can you come up with?

5.8.7 More icons

Design some icons and test them out on someone else. Start with simple ones and then try and express more complex ideas. Give the person trying them out an idea of the context of the icon. Here is a list of ideas with contexts:

◆ Turn sound off (on a television remote control)

◆ Poisonous (a bottle)

◆ Fragile (a parcel)

◆ Do not bend (an envelope)

◆ Hot/cold (a heater control in a train)

◆ Open/close door (door control buttons)

◆ Lift overloaded (warning light in a lift)

◆ Sugar/powdered milk (sachets of powder in a cafe)

◆ Tea/coffee (a drinks machine)

◆ No change given (a drinks machine)

◆ Pause (a cassette player button)

◆ Redial last number (a telephone)

◆ Lost property (in a station)

◆ Silence (in a library)

◆ No food or drink (in a cinema)

◆ Contains additives, 'E numbers' (a food packet)

◆ Low in alcohol (a bottle)

◆ High in alcohol (a bottle)

◆ Delicious (a bottle)

◆ Call the police (button in a bank)

◆ Shake before opening (a bottle)

◆ Exciting film (a film advert)

- ◆ Romantic film (a film advert)
- ◆ Turn radio on (a spaceship control board)
- ◆ Open both airlock doors at the same time (a spaceship control board)
- ◆ Self destruct (a spaceship control board)

5.9 Same tasks, different commands

When dealing with a computer system you often find yourself in a variety of different computer environments: reading electronic mail with a mail-reading program, reading electronic news, working on a document with a word processor or simply moving files around with the operating system. Within each of these environments you have to learn the special commands to get things done. The strange thing is that there are lots of tasks that are the same in these different environments but each of them has its own special command. Consider deleting things. To delete an electronic mail message I use 'rmm', to delete a news item I must use 'ctrl-x', to delete a word it's 'esc-d' and if I want to delete a file it's 'rm' with UNIX and 'del' on a PC. There are examples of other common tasks as well as delete. Consider copy, paste, rename and new. They are all general tasks but each one has a different command according to its different context. Imagine if it were like that in real life...

> *Barker has just been on a special butler's training course where he has learned to obey special orders that must be given according to the object that the order is referring to. As we join them Hemelsworth is trying to instruct Barker to serve tea to him and Bertie (a patient friend of his).*

Hemelsworth: Damn! All these silly orders to remember. Umm... Elevate tray. Bring tray to table. Place tray... Now, the teapot, elevate teapot? No. What was it? Pick up teapot. Pour tea. Put down teapot.

Now what were the orders to do the same things with the milk jug? Raise milk jug. Dispense milk. Lower milk jug. Phew! It's hard work remembering all these different orders...

And now I'll get him to pour a cup for you, Bertie old chap. Pick up teapot. Pour tea. Lower teapot.

> *Barker picks up the teapot and pours the tea, but he does not replace the teapot.*

Barker: I'm terribly sorry sir, but I don't understand what you are saying.

Hemelsworth: What? I said, 'Lower teapot'.

Barker: I'm terribly sorry sir, but I don't understand what you are saying.

Hemelsworth: Oh I see! Wrong order. Umm... replace teapot.

Barker: I'm terribly sorry sir, but I don't understand what you are saying.

Hemelsworth: Oh drat! Wait a minute, I wrote it down here somewhere. Dashed sorry about this Bertie. Here we are, put down teapot.

Barker: Yes sir.

Hemelsworth: Phew! Now what were the orders for the cups? Maybe Barker is allowed to tell me. Barker! What are the orders to deal with the cups?

Barker: I'm terribly sorry sir, but I don't understand what you are saying.

Hemelsworth: Oh, drat and blast!

Chapter 6

User models

6.1 Introduction

Much of our interaction with the world around us, both natural and artificial, is done on the basis of user models. These user models govern our predictions and expectations of the effects of our interaction. When designing interactive systems these models are one of the most important factors affecting the interaction between the user and the system. Getting to grips with the concepts involved, and making the right decisions in designing the user model of the system, is vital.

Initially the concept of the user model is hard to grasp. It took me a long time after my initial encounter with the term to realize fully the complexity and generality of the idea. Since 'an interactive system' is such a general term, the concept of user models covers a wide range of areas from the use of basic devices through to arguments about philosophy and science.

In this chapter I shall begin by looking at user models in general using an assortment of examples. Then I shall concentrate on user models of artificial interactive systems.

6.1.1 Don't panic!

That upside-down text was intentional. Why was it intentional? Because it serves as a good way of introducing some of the concepts underlying this chapter. It is probably true that finding a block of upside-down text like that was unexpected in a book which, up until that point, had been well structured. So, what happened when you encountered it? You were confused, surprised, a little shocked maybe? And now in retrospect you may even find it amusing. Whatever you may have felt, the key factor is that it was *unexpected*. If the chapter had begun with a diagram, or a quote from someone famous, then you would not have been surprised because it would have fitted in with your expectations of the book. A block of upside-down text, however, was not something that you were expecting, and that is why it came as a shock.

From this opening illustration it would seem that whenever you pick up a book and start reading it you have a fairly definite model in your mind of what to expect and what not to expect from it. From your previous experience of reading books you have a general model of a book: the different ways in which it could be structured, where the index is, where to look for a summary of the book's contents, where to find the price and so on. Further to this, when you choose a specific book to read, the model of it in your mind becomes more complex. As well as the things that you expect from a book in general, there will be extra things that you expect from the particular book that you have chosen to read. If it is a book about maths or geometry you will expect lots of diagrams and mathematical symbols in it. If it is a book explaining some aspect of physics then the first chapters should be an introduction to the subject about to be covered, and if it is a whodunit then the detective will assemble all the characters in the drawing room and name the murderer on the very last page of the book.

So, as soon as you pick up the book, you have a model of what to expect from it in your mind. But it does not stop there. Even as you read the book your model of it will change. If the first page is in Polish then you would expect the rest of the book to be likewise in Polish. If, by the time you are halfway through, you have found it incredibly tedious, then you would expect it to continue in this manner and you would probably not finish reading it.

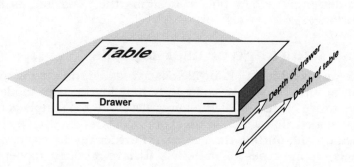

Figure 6.1 The short drawer.

6.1.2 The short drawer

As you have probably guessed by now, this user model you have of something is not just confined to books. It is a very general concept and can be applied to just about everything you can think of. Let us look at another example, a little more practical this time.

A relation of mine has a Victorian card table with a drawer in it. The table is about 70 centimetres deep but, because the table can extend and has a gate leg at the back, the drawer at the front is only about 30 centimetres deep. (See Figure 6.1.) Anybody new to this table who tries to open the drawer inevitably pulls it out way beyond its length and ends up holding the drawer by its handles while the contents spill all over the floor.

Just like the upside-down text in the book, the short length of the drawer is unexpected. When a 'user' sees the table they build up a user model of it, and this usually incorporates the notion that the drawer is as deep as the table. In their user model they imagine that they can pull the drawer out by more than 30 centimetres, but when they attempt to do so in reality they realize, too late, that the real table is different from their user model of it.

6.1.3 The importance of user models

When it comes to interactive systems, the model that a user has of the system (the user model) governs her interactions with it. Predictions and   expectations will be based upon the model; thus, in designing an interactive system, a lot of care and work should go into making the user model as clear and obvious as possible to the user. If the system's behaviour can be described by different user models then the question of choosing a good user model or even designing a new one to describe the behaviour is also of importance.

6.1.4 The range of user models

Since we spend most of our life observing and interacting with the world around us we are constantly building up user models of a whole range of things. At the lowest level are the simple common-sense models that we build up of our bodies as children by picking things up and putting things down. Further up the scale are user models of properties of materials (I have a rough model of the behaviour of wood and would not, for example, trust my weight to a long piece of two-centimetre square wood bridging a two-metre gap). We have user models of the physical size of things. Turning around when you are carrying a ladder can be tricky; you have to have a good user model of its size and how it will behave as you move with it. At the more complex end of the scale user models play a role in all sorts of areas, the philosophical questions surrounding our perception of the outside world and our attempt to understand it and make sense of it through science and religion (in effect 'user models for life').

6.1.5 Types of user model

User models of more simple interactive systems seem to be composed of two parts. Firstly there are the parts that are more physically oriented. These are connected with interaction with the physical aspects of the system: the properties like size, shape, weight and so on. Secondly there are the more conceptual parts of the user model; these can be reasoned about and verbalized. They are connected more with the behaviour, ideas and logic underlying the system. When interacting with a system some of the interaction will be based upon the physical user model and some will be based upon the conceptual user model.

Sport provides some good examples of the different levels of importance that the two sorts of model can have. Consider juggling. The user carries out actions according to her body's fast reaction to changes in the system; there is no time to pause and analyse what is happening or to reason about it conceptually. The whole thing depends upon a physical user model – the weight, behaviour and feel of the clubs being juggled. With snooker there is more of a conceptual part to the model. The players have time to examine the state of the system (the balls on the table) and to analyse and make predictions before deciding what sort of shot to make. A more physical user model then plays a part in the actual execution of the shot. Lastly, in a game of chess the interaction with the system is almost all based on a conceptual user model of the system covering things like the behaviour of the opponent and the possibilities opened up by certain moves.

6.1.6 Ingrained user models

As well as this difference between physically oriented and conceptually oriented models there is another difference. Some user models are really ingrained, you use certain things without thinking about the interaction. Other models are more unfamiliar and require definite thought and planning about the interaction. When building up user models, and especially when using them repeatedly, the user model becomes less of an unfamiliar model that needs thinking about and more of an ingrained one. There is, however, a time delay between information being part of a 'thinking user model' and becoming an integral part of an 'ingrained user model'. Here is a good illustration of this difference. A friend of mine set off to work one morning and discovered that her brakes were faulty. She knew that there was a garage a short distance ahead so she continued driving with extreme caution. Unfortunately she was not careful enough and eventually she gently rolled into the back of the car in front, giving it a dent and some scratches. Both drivers got out, looked at the damage and then, as there was a layby ahead, agreed to pull in there and sort out their insurance details. The dented car set off, pulled up in the layby and the driver got out in time to watch as my friend, forgetting all about her brakes, ran straight into the back of his car again, causing even more damage than the first time. She 'knew' that her brakes were faulty but she was driving the car using her habitual, ingrained user model wherein the brakes were fine.

The inclusion of facts that you know into this ingrained user model can come about in two ways. The first is through constant vigilance and reuse. Use the system a lot while all the time trying to be aware of the fact that the brakes are faulty (for example) and eventually you will need to concentrate less and less on the fact as it becomes a part of the ingrained user model. The other way is the imprinting of the fact by more direct means. This usually comes about by learning through experience. Making an error with nasty consequences can imprint the fact in the ingrained user model in a very direct way.

6.1.7 Muscle memory

When we consider the more physically oriented user models, especially those that are deeply ingrained, we come up against muscle memory. The user model is not conceptually stored in the 'thinking' part of the mind, but is somehow stored in those more basic parts concerned with physical things such as coordination and motor control. It feels as if the memory is actually in the fingers, in the muscles, hence the term 'muscle memory'. This is an important concept in the design of user interfaces. Let us have a look at a few examples of muscle memory when interacting with artificial systems.

I used to have a cashpoint card. To get my money out of the machine I had to key in my four-digit personal identification number (my PIN code). After several years I found that I remembered it more as a pattern of finger movements than as a number. This became clear to me one day when I thought too much about it! Instead of just letting my fingers key it in automatically I tried to remember what the four digits actually were; I couldn't, I kept getting it wrong.

Here's another example. Someone I know used to be a typist. Nowadays, when she needs to spell a word she is not able to remember it mentally but only through muscle memory. The result is that she will mime the finger movements on an imaginary typewriter keyboard and then analyse them, working backwards to arrive at the spelling!

Exploiting muscle memory in a system has several advantages. Once a sequence of movements is learned it can be reproduced easily and quickly and, because muscle memory is to some extent separate from mental memory, intermediate tasks based upon muscle memory are less disruptive to ongoing mental tasks.

One disadvantage of performing tasks dependent upon muscle memory is that it is that if you are under pressure it is difficult to relax sufficiently to allow it to work (as in the PIN code example above). Another disadvantage is that you can be prone to 'switching tracks' between similar muscle memories. I notice this sometimes when I type a word where the first few letters are the same as another word that I am familiar with. For example when typing the word 'thin', which is similar to the word 'this', my muscle memory will sometimes take over and before I know it I have typed 'this'.

Playing musical instruments is another area where muscle memory plays an important part, I have heard stories of concert pianist 'switching tracks' in a similar manner to my typing problem. They start performing a piece, reach a passage where it is very similar to another piece they know and before they realize it they are carrying on with that other piece. (Apparently the trick is to keep going until you get to another similar passage and then switch back to the original piece.)

It would seem valuable, therefore, to exploit muscle memory wherever possible when designing an interactive system. However, care should be taken to avoid similar muscle memory tracks, especially if the two operations with similar tracks result in very different outcomes.

Bearing the above in mind, let us take a look at some further examples of user models in the world around us.

6.1.8 The body

One of the most fundamental and accurate user models that we have is one that we are not usually aware of. This is simply because it is so well ingrained that we cannot imagine being without it, or remember what it was like not to have it. It is the user model that we have of our own body.

You cannot go back in time as we did with the car and ask, 'Do you remember what it was like to learn to use it?' Learning to use our body was something we did so early on in life that none of us can remember the struggle involved in picking up and manipulating a teaspoon when we first started feeding ourselves scrambled eggs. The only people who may get a reminder of these struggles in later life are stroke or accident victims undergoing rehabilitation.

There are several very basic examples of how accurate your user model of your body is. Since one of the most common actions that you perform is reaching out and picking something up, your user model for this action is particularly well developed. Try this. Sit up straight at a desk, the top of which has various things on it (books, papers, pens). You must keep your body still, and move just your arms. Look at some point on the desk (for example the corner of a particular book) and ask yourself if you can touch that point with your fingertips just by reaching out your arm (remember, moving *just* your arm). If you feel that you will not be able to reach it, where do you feel your fingertips will reach to when you stretch out your arm in that direction? After having gone through this process in your imagination, try it in reality. The accuracy of the prediction is usually surprising.

Here is another example: close your eyes and, with your elbows clear of your body but without your arms fully extended, try and bring the tips of your two index fingers together. Quite often you will find that they touch each other or come within about an inch of each other (I find it more accurate if I do it quickly). With your eyes closed there is hardly any information as to where your fingertips are. The operation is carried out purely upon the strength of your user model of your hands and arms.

6.1.9 Opening doors

This is something that you usually do without a moment's thought, but even here user models are playing their part. You bring your own user model of doors with you; your model of this particular door will be modified as you see it, read signs on it, and watch other people use it. Even as you open it you are interacting with it and maybe changing your model of it; if it is strongly sprung your model includes this and you push harder.

In Dutch trains the gangway doors in the carriages are sliding doors that automatically close after a few seconds. An English person like me, whose model of doors in trains is based on the British Rail version, will often try to close the door behind them and struggle for a few seconds before the door closes itself automatically.

6.1.10 Cars and lorries

Although the majority of our basic physical user models are built up in our childhood, there is one comprehensive and very common model that is built up later on in life, and that is the user model that drivers have of their vehicles.

Anybody who has learned to drive will remember how it felt when they took their first excursions in their parents car. The car was a huge block of metal, clumsy and heavy and seemingly possessed of a mind of its own. However, after a few years of experience the driver has built up a good model of the behaviour of the car, they can control it with great precision and can even carry out other tasks while driving: talking, listening to the radio or even buying stocks and shares over their car telephone.

By this time they also have a good model of the size of the car and how well it can fit in between gateposts or squeeze into small parking places. For the drivers of heavy goods vehicles the height of the vehicle is another important factor. Indeed this is actually included in the HGV (heavy goods vehicle) driving test in some countries. The driver signals from her cab for a bar to be lowered and raised until she thinks that she can just get her truck underneath it; when she is happy with the height she then drives her truck up to the bar to see how accurate her estimations were.

6.2 Model disagreements

Finding good illustrations of user models can be quite a difficult task since we are not normally aware of them. The best illustrations seem to occur when we have a definite disagreement between our user model of something and what that something actually is. The disagreement of model and reality is also an important area since it is a prime cause of errors in interactions. It is worth looking at examples to appreciate how errors and confusion can arise. The two opening examples (the upside-down text and the short drawer) were both examples of model disagreements. Here are some more.

6.2.1 Magic tricks

There is no feeling quite like that of watching the conclusion of a good magic trick. The magician finally opens the box (opens the curtains or whatever) and what we had expected to see is not there. There is a disagreement between our user model of the events taking place and what actually is taking place. What is more, the magician herself is promoting and supporting the audience's incorrect user model of what is happening. When she pretends to put a coin in a hat but palms it instead, she uses skilful body language and misdirection to support the user model that she really has put the coin in the hat.

When the hat is later shown to be empty the audience is faced with the paradox between their user model of the events they have just seen and their past user models of events in the real world. They saw the coin put in the hat and then they saw the empty hat, but previous experience tells them that things cannot just vanish. The only way to resolve this paradox is to reassess their user model of the real world (to believe that coins can vanish) or to assume that their user model of the events that they saw was wrong and in fact something totally different took place.

Strictly speaking, I should have used the term 'mental model' instead of 'user model' in the description above. This is because there is not really any interaction involved between the audience and the system (the trick itself). As an audience member I must sit and watch the proceedings in a passive manner; I cannot get up on stage during the performance and start poking around amongst the things on the magician's table.

6.2.2 Disagreements in physical size

If your user model of the physical size of some object is different from its true size then it must either be larger or smaller than the true size. If your user model is larger than the object's actual size, it will not often lead to problems. You will always allow enough space for your user model of the object and so there will be ample space for the actual object.

The problems arise when your user model is smaller than the object's true size. Classic examples usually occur in the driving of vehicles. The driver who drives into a multistorey car park has a good user model of her car – it will fit without any problems through the entrance she is approaching – but the actual size of the car is larger than her user model – she has two racing cycles strapped upright onto the roof rack.

6.2.3 Disagreements in the human body

As I have commented earlier, the user model of the human body is one of the most ingrained of user models. There are a few examples of disagreements, and because of the strength of the user model the effects are felt very strongly indeed. Your user model of your body *can* adapt to changes, for example my user model of my arm and my reach is longer than it was when I was a five-year old, but the user model can only adapt to a certain rate of change. If my arm became six inches shorter overnight, my user model would still be what it was before, and it would take some time for it to adapt to the new size. Thus examples of disagreements in the human body usually occur when the body or the brain is damaged in some way over a short timespan.

A missing tooth

Can you remember losing your milk teeth when you were young? Or have you more recently had a tooth pulled by the dentist? It is a very strange feeling. You have lost a tooth about the size of a bean and yet the gap left by it feels enormous and awkward and you find yourself continuously probing it with your tongue. There is only a small discrepancy between your user model (which still includes the missing tooth) and your actual body (which does not) but because your user model of your body is so ingrained even small disagreements lead to strong feelings of unease.

Ghost limbs

A somewhat strange illustration concerns the amputation of limbs. As well as the shock and physical problems experienced by amputees there are also psychological problems associated with the user model. Remember what was said above about my user model taking time to adapt if my arm suddenly became six inches shorter? Well this is what actually happens when a person has a limb amputated. Physically the limb is not there, but as far as the person's user model is concerned it *is* still there. This leads to very strange effects. If a leg is amputated the amputee may feel that the leg is still there, a sort of 'ghost limb'. As with the tooth example it takes time for the user model to realign itself with the new state of the body.

Anomalous body experiences

There are some disagreements caused not by physical changes in the body, but by changes in the user model itself. A common one is the feeling of having huge swollen hands when you are delirious. Other more serious disagreements can occur as a result of damage to certain areas of the brain (the parietal lobe). Some of these disagreements can be very severe with patients 'disowning' limbs; the limb is there, but it is not part of their user model and they cannot move it or even understand what it is doing there.

6.2.4 Disagreements in perception

Another interesting example of model disagreement crops up when we start to consider how our previous experience affects our perception of certain things. Part of our user model comes directly from our observation or interaction with the system in question, but another part comes from our previous knowledge of other systems we have seen or experienced that are similar to this one.

Sometimes the influence of past experience can overwhelm the contribution from direct observation and interaction. This leads to inaccurate user models and subsequent confusion or mistakes. Many good examples in this area can be found in optical illusions. With certain examples the reason that they work is that when you try and interpret one you bring all your previous visual processing experiences to bear on it, and your user model of what you are seeing is influenced by this. A familiar one is the Müller–Lyer illusion, shown in Figure 6.2. The question is, 'Which of the two lines between the arrow heads is longer?' It appears to be B, but if you measure them you find that they are both the same length.

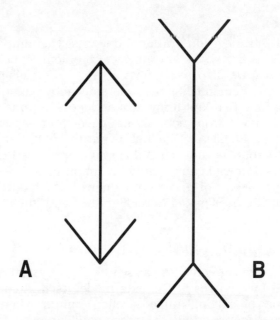

Figure 6.2   The Müller–Lyer illusion.

One explanation for this is that because of our previous experience of the effects of perspective on regular box-like structures, line A resembles the outside edge of a box or building and line B resembles the inside edge. (See Figure 6.3.) These perspective clues try to 'tell us' that B is further away than A. This affects our interpretation of the picture. The two lines appear

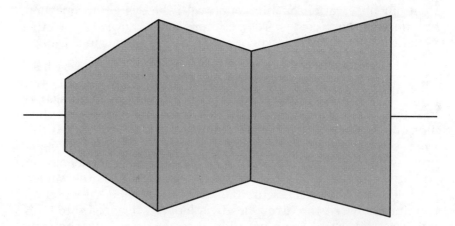

Figure 6.3   The effect of perspective on edges.

equal to the eye, but the brain, working on the perspective information, thinks, 'The two lines appear equal, B is further away than A, thus B must be longer than A.'

Apparently, a person who has spent their whole life away from artificial structures, for example someone living out in the bush, will perceive the two lines as being equal. They are unused to seeing regular box-like structures and therefore their perception of the optical illusion is not affected by past experience.

6.3 User models of artificial systems

Let us concentrate now on user models of artificial interactive systems, systems that have been designed. A user model is a part of the mental model you have of an interactive system. It is not the whole mental model, just the aspects of it that are concerned with the behaviour of the system and your interaction with it.

At home I have an automatic electric kettle. I have had it a long time and so my mental model of it is very detailed. It includes factors such as the fact that it is still shiny, it is made by Russell Hobbs, the inside of it needs descaling, most of it is made of stainless steel and so on. The part of this mental model that constitutes the user model includes all the factors to do with its use and behaviour: whether it is plugged in or not, whether it is switched on, whether it has got water in it, what the minimum amount of water is that it will boil, the special way of putting the lid on it, what it does if it boils dry and so on. We have these user models of all sorts of devices that we use: digital watches, cashpoint machines, drink vending machines and cars. Some are trivial like the user model of a simple light with a switch, while others are more complex like photocopiers, video recorders and aeroplane controls.

It will help to show the idea of the user model graphically. Look at Figure 6.4. On the left is the real-world system, on the right the user model of the system. In between is the person building up the user model – 'the user'. The user model comes from observing and interacting with the system (the arrow going through the user) and is affected by the user's previous experience and preconceptions.

6.3.1 Building user models

When I brought optical illusions into the discussion I talked about where user models come from. There are in fact four sources of information that go towards building up the user's model of an interactive system.

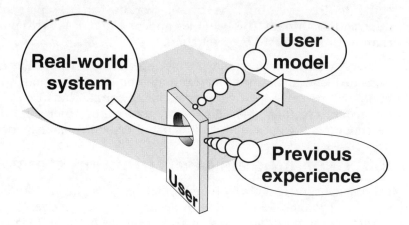

Figure 6.4   The user and the user model.

Previous experience

This is the factor I concentrated on with the optical illusions example. The situation is the same when we are confronted with any other system, interactive or otherwise. The user interprets it, to some extent, in terms of what she has already experienced. She tries to match it up to similar systems or situations previously encountered, and from this attempts to build up some guidelines for how the new system should be treated.

Interaction

This is another important factor which comes into play when we are faced with new systems. The system can tell the user something about itself during the interaction, giving feedback that encourages the building up of a certain user model.

Observation

With many interactive systems we learn how to use them by means of example; we observe other people interacting with the same system. This is true of many things in life besides just artificial interactive systems.

Abstract information

Finally with interactive systems and the methods of communicating information in an abstract way that are available to us, we can build up user models of systems before we have even come into contact with them. With the systems where I work I can read about them, access information on the computer about them, talk to other people who have used them and so on, before I actually sit down and use them.

As an example of all this, when I first came to Amsterdam I caught a tram and had to work out where I wanted to stop and how to stop the tram there. Trams are rare in Great Britain so I had no *previous experience* to go on. I could have experimented by *interacting* with the system and building up a user model in that way, but the system was unforgiving of errors and so were other people. I could have made myself very unpopular by pulling all the levers and pushing all the buttons in sight. There was plenty of *abstract information* there, lots of instructions and labels, but it was all in Dutch. The only way to build up my user model was by *observation*, by watching what other passengers did and how they interacted with the system when they wanted to stop the tram and get off.

6.3.2 Helping users build models

What are the implications then of the above classifications in terms of designing a user interface?

Previous experience

With the design of interactive systems the previous experience of the user is beyond the control of the designer, and the nature of the system may be such that the user has no previous experience with anything like it. However, the designer *is* in control of the system and it is possible with advanced flexible systems, such as computers, to design the user interface so that it imitates certain features of a system with which the user *has* had some previous experience. This idea of using some other area as a metaphor when designing interactive systems is covered further in Chapter 14.

Interaction

The other means of helping the user build up a user model is feedback. An interactive system should help the user to build up a user model (or confirm an existing one) by presenting the necessary information about itself as the user interacts with it. I shall deal with feedback further in the next chapter and again in Chapter 10.

Observation

This is to some extent beyond the designer's control. However, there are some steps that can be taken. The designer can ensure that much of the interaction is made visible, so that an onlooker will be aware of as much of it as possible. Public systems can be set up so that other potential users are in a position to see the interaction taking place.

Abstract information

This is a tricky area. A good user interface should not really have any formal abstract information. When confronted with a problem while using a system you should not be forced to go away and spend half an hour leafing through the user manual. Similarly, on a smaller scale, when faced with a door you should not have to rely upon labels and symbols stuck on it to know how to open it. That should be apparent from the visual aspects of the design. However, there is always scope for informal abstract information, especially talking to existing users of the system. Within groups this seems to be the way that most people start using a particular system; someone else extols the virtues of it or offers to help someone else get to grips with it.

6.3.3 Other user models

I should also mention the many other user models that play a part in user interface design. The designer of the system has several; look back to Section 4.2.1 [p 45]. She has a model of the user (their capabilities, previous experience and so on). She also has a model of the true nature of the system she is dealing with: all the internal complexities that the user does not know about. The designer also has a model of what aspects of the system she wants to present to the user (the abstract model introduced in Section 4.2.2 [p 46]). There is even a simple model that the system itself has of the user, covering what sort of things the system expects the user to do in terms of interaction and so forth. When dealing with all these models (and even with models of other people's models), you need some sort of fairly concise notation for keeping track of what you are talking about.

6.4 Summary

In this chapter I covered 'user models': the models that we build up in our heads about things in the real world. I began by looking at some examples of user models and I then discussed some general points regarding user models:

◆ The range of user models.

◆ The difference between the physical aspects and the conceptual aspects of a user model.

◆ How information becomes part of a really ingrained user model.

◆ Muscle memory – how our fingers sometimes seem to remember how to do certain things when our brains don't.

After some more examples I went on to discuss disagreements between user models and reality and what we can learn from them. Then came a section on user models of artificial, interactive systems. Here I looked at the four key factors that played a part in building up a user model of a system:

◆ Previous experience

◆ Interaction

◆ Observation

◆ Abstract information.

Finally I pointed out that there are many other mental models that play a part in the process of user interface design.

6.5 Exercises

6.5.1 Train doors

Use the state diagrams from Chapter 3 to analyse the train door problem mentioned here in Section 6.1.9 [p 86] and try to come up with a good solution.

6.5.2 A pressure gauge problem

Imagine a pressure gauge on a steam boiler. It is a circular gauge with a needle that moves clockwise as the pressure increases. At the zero-point is a pin that the needle rests against when there is no pressure (see Figure 6.5). Imagine it is the early days of steam. The boiler is a prototype; nobody knows how it will work. Imagine also that the boiler's safety valve (which lets off steam if the pressure reaches dangerous levels) does not work. The stokers stoke it up with coal, listening until the safety valve starts blowing (this was normal practice). It doesn't. By the time they start worrying and checking the gauge the needle has gone once round and is pressed up against the wrong side of the zero-pin! To the

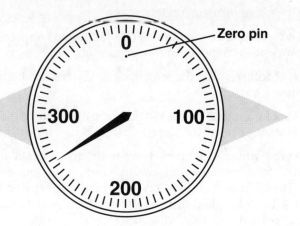

Figure 6.5 A pressure gauge.

stokers it looks like it is still on zero. They think that there is no pressure, maybe a leak somewhere. They stoke even harder to try and get the pressure up. The boiler explodes.

Analyse what happened in terms of the real-world system and the stoker's user model. How could you redesign the system so that they would realize what was happening? (The events described here actually happened. The two stokers were killed in the explosion).

6.5.3 The short drawer problem

Remember the short drawer problem I gave at the beginning of the chapter? How could you alter the design in order to solve the problem? Towards the end of this chapter I talked about the four factors that go towards building up a user model. Devise four solutions to the short drawer problem based upon each of the four model-building methods.

6.6 Systems reaction to errors

In the previous sketch, whenever Barker didn't recognize Hemelsworth's instructions he would say; 'I'm terribly sorry sir, but I don't understand what you are saying'. With computer systems if the computer doesn't recognize your instructions it is usually regarded as an error on *your* part. You are responsible for making sure that you use instructions that the computer recognizes! The system can react to unrecognized instructions in a variety of ways:

Coping

The system can be designed to recognize a wide range of instructions including different ways of stating the same instruction:

Hemelsworth: Barker. Lower the teapot.

Barker: Certainly sir!

Helpful suggestions

If the system recognizes some parts of the instruction it can make a sensible guess at what the user meant and ask the user if it is correct.

Hemelsworth: Barker. Lower the teapot.

Barker: I'm terribly sorry sir, but I don't quite understand what you are saying. Are you trying to say 'Put down teapot'?

Helpful messages

Sometimes, when presented with an instruction it doesn't recognize, a system can explain the situation and tell the user what instructions it *does* recognize:

Hemelsworth: Barker. Lower the teapot.

Barker: I'm terribly sorry sir, but I don't understand what you are saying. At this point I am expecting you to say either 'Put down teapot' or 'Pour tea'.

Useless messages

Some systems, when presented with an unrecognizable instruction, give messages that *don't* explain the situation:

Hemelsworth: Barker. Lower the teapot.

Barker: Error code 19, sir.

No response

Some systems do absolutely nothing:

> **Hemelsworth:** Barker! Lower the teapot..... Hello, Barker? Lower the teapot I said. Good grief man, are you deaf?

System crash

Some systems are so badly designed and implemented that an unrecognizable instruction can cause them to crash (to stop working):

> **Hemelsworth:**   Barker. Lower the teapot.

> **Barker:**   [*Falling over sideways*] Uuuhhh!...

Chapter 7

Feedback and errors

7.1 Feedback

While I was in the process of writing this book I was occasionally giving versions of it to people to review. 'Read it,' I would say, 'and give me some feedback.' What did I mean? What is feedback? In Chapter 4 and Chapter 5 I covered *presentation*: communicating information to the user in an efficient manner. Feedback is also concerned with the communication of information to the user, but it is information specifically related to what it is that the user is doing. So when I said, 'Give me some feedback about my book' what I meant was, 'Tell me something about what I am doing and thus help me to do it properly.'

Feedback informs the user about her interaction with the system. It tells her something about what she is doing and helps her to do it properly. With interactive devices, feedback takes the form of buttons that light up when they are pressed so that the user knows that she has pressed them, or meters on a cassette deck that show the signal level when you are recording to help you adjust the recording level.

Feedback is one of the vital ingredients for interaction of any sort. When it comes to user interface design it plays an important role in helping the user build up a good user model of the system and in letting them know what the system is doing. With interactive computer systems all the feedback must be explicitly designed and built into the system. An understanding of the ideas and techniques involved in feedback enables this to be done well.

Bad feedback can lead to errors in the interaction and a knowledge of this area enables the designers of user interfaces to develop systems that prevent errors or assist the user in repairing things should an error occur.

First of all then let us have a look at the relationship between feedback and time. The feedback supplied by an interactive system can be categorized according to its relationship in time to the interaction:

♦ **Future feedback**
This is feedback about an interaction that is supplied to the user before the interaction is carried out. Basically it tells the user about what *will* happen if they do a particular thing. A simple example is the explanatory labels on buttons. (Strictly speaking this should not be called 'feedback' but something different, 'feedforward' perhaps?).

♦ **Present feedback**
This is feedback about an interaction supplied during the interaction. This tells the user what *is* happening. Examples of this are feeling a switch move under your fingers as you switch it, or hearing a bell ring as you press a doorbell button.

♦ **Past feedback**
Past feedback is supplied after the interaction and it gives the user information about what *has* happened; how the system has changed or is changing as a result of this interaction. When I press the button to call a lift to my floor it lights up and stays lit up. Or consider the tape counter on a tape deck whirring away after you press the fast forward key.

These three types of feedback are useful in all sorts of situations both interactive and non-interactive. They are summed up quite succinctly in the guidelines to giving a talk or presentation: give an outline, give the talk then give a summary, or 'Tell them what you are going to say, say it and then tell them what you said.'

7.2 Feedback and the user model

There are strong links between the presentation of information (dealt with in Chapter 4 and Chapter 5), user models (Chapter 6) and feedback. I talked about the presentation of information and the way the user built up mental models based upon this information. I also discussed interactive systems and how the system could present information about its state and its behaviour from which the user could build up a *user* model. This presentation of information relating to the behaviour of the system is the feedback, and it is the feedback part of the presentation that helps the user build up a good user model. The figure showing abstraction and presentation (Figure 4.6 [p 50]) can be combined with the user model figure (Figure 6.4 [p 92]) to give Figure 7.1. There are also strong links between the previous experience of the user and the designer's model of the user shown in the figure. Ideally the designer's model of the user should include some of the information from the user's previous experience and the user's mental model should resemble the abstract model that the designer builds up and presents.

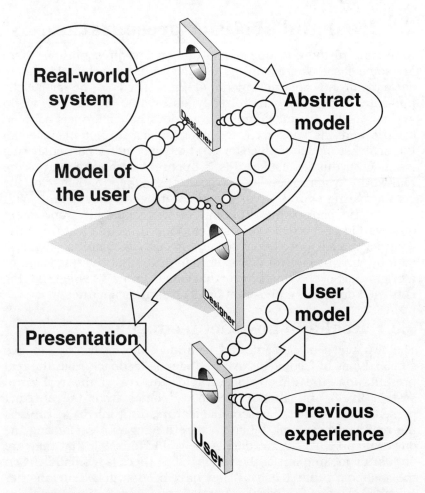

Figure 7.1   Abstraction, presentation and the user model.

The process described above of receiving feedback and building up a user model from it has two beneficial effects for the user:

◆ **Increased efficiency**
  With an accurate and ingrained user model it is possible to use the system in a more rapid, efficient and creative manner.

◆ **Increased motivation**
  The user is aware that through her use of the system she is building up a user model. She is learning and making progress, and this will instil enthusiasm in her to continue using the system.

7.3 Real and abstract presentation

Returning to the question of abstraction and presentation, there are some cases where features extracted from a real-world system as part of an abstract model do not need to be artificially presented since they are directly observable in the real-world system itself. As an example, consider the difference between electric and gas cookers. One important feature for inclusion in the abstract model of a cooker is whether or not a particular ring is on. With the gas cooker this is apparent by observation of the real-world system; you just look at the flames or listen to the gentle roaring sound. This part of the presentation is real. With the electric cooker the situation is less apparent from direct observation of the real-world system, and thus this feature of the abstract model must be artificially presented. There is usually a light by the ring control that is lit to indicate that the ring is on, or a bright part of the ring control dial comes into view when the ring is turned on. Such a presentation is classed as abstract.

7.3.1 Real and abstract feedback

The two types of presentation identified above give rise to two similar types of feedback. Real feedback is feedback from the real presentation (the directly observable features of the real-world system itself) and abstract feedback comes from the abstract presentation (artificial, observable features that mirror features of the real-world system). When you are driving in a car during the day and you turn the headlights on you cannot tell that they are on just by looking out of the window, but there is a small light on the dashboard that 'tells you' they have been switched on (another example of past feedback). That tell-tale light is an example of

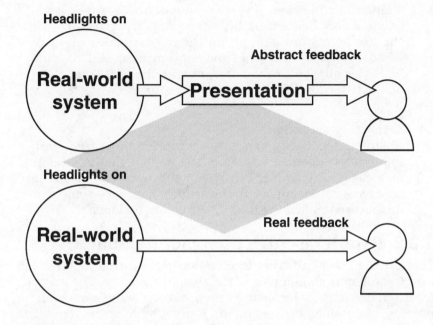

Figure 7.2 Real and abstract feedback with car headlights.

abstract feedback. However, if you have the headlights on at night you will see the landscape in front of you lit up by them; that is *real* feedback (see Figure 7.2).

The more advanced and technical an interactive system is, the more the feedback used tends to be abstract feedback. Technical devices attempt to keep the complicated, real details hidden from the user and give them restricted, abstract feedback regarding what is going on (think of the control panel on a coffee machine). In such systems the abstract feedback plays one of three roles:

◆ **Revealing**
   Abstract feedback can provide the user with information about a feature of the real-world system that is not directly observable: for example, a dial on a dashboard to indicate the engine temperature.

◆ **Exaggerating**
   Alternatively abstract feedback can provide the user with information about a feature of the real-world system that *is* directly observable, but that is too difficult to observe in relation to its importance: for example, the tell-tale light that indicates that the headlights have been switched from

'dipped' to 'full beam'. If you look out of the car window you can just about ascertain this information from the way that the headlights are lighting up the surroundings (the real feedback) but it takes time and concentration which would be better applied to the act of driving the car. Thus clear, abstract feedback is provided in the form of the tell-tale light.

♦ **Attracting attention**
Abstract feedback can also provide the user with information about a feature of the system that is directly and easily observable, but which the user may forget to observe: for example, the warning light on some car dashboards indicating that a seat belt is undone.

7.3.2 Problems with abstract feedback

This prolific use of abstract feedback in technical disciplines can lead to problems should part of the system go wrong. The abstract feedback is a part of the abstract presentation of the system and it must be maintained by the system; it must monitor the real-world system and ensure that the abstract presentation reflects any changes. If the monitoring part of the system goes wrong the result could be a disagreement between the abstract presentation and the actual state of the real-world system. Consider the car headlight example earlier. If the tell-tale light on the dashboard stops working you could have your lights on during the day without being aware of it. The abstract feedback says 'lights not on' so your user model says the same, but the actual state is that the headlights *are* on.

With feedback in more interactive situations the problems become more complicated. If the expected abstract feedback fails to appear during an interaction process the user will suspect that something is wrong with the system, but the nature of the fault will be ambiguous. Let me return to the lift example used in Section 5.6 [p 70]. Consider an old lift in a building: a user on the seventh floor presses the lift down button (the button to request a lift to go down), and it fails to light up. What is wrong? There are two main possibilities illustrated in Figure 7.3:

♦ **Faulty abstract feedback**
The tool (the lift down button) is working but the abstract feedback mechanism is not. The real-world system has been changed but the feedback does not reflect the change. This means that the lift *has* been called but, because of a faulty bulb or a loose connection, the lift down button is not lit.

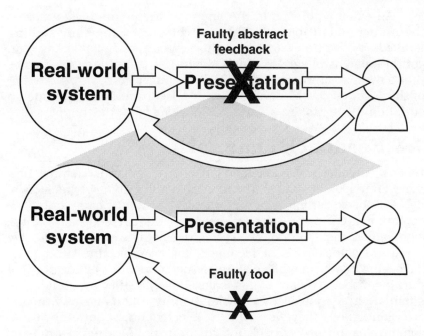

Figure 7.3   Possible problems with abstract feedback.

◆ **Faulty tool**
The tool is not working but the abstract feedback mechanism is. The lift down button is faulty, the lift has not been called and so the lift down button is not lit.

(There are of course other possibilities including both the button and the light being faulty but the above two are the most probable.) The user may assume that the first case is true, that her request was registered and will await confirmation of this by the arrival of the lift. If the user assumes the second case, that there is something wrong with the operation of the tool, she may react by pressing the button repeatedly in the hope of getting the tool to work.

The problems arise because the presentation when the abstract feedback fails is the same as a presentation state within the legal operation of the system. There are systems that overcome the problem by ensuring that the presentation when the abstract feedback fails does not fall within the legal operation of the system and it is thus obvious from the feedback that a failure has occurred.

An example of this is the line crossing points at stations in the Netherlands (Holland). They are for use by the staff and are flanked by white warning lights. When the lights are on continuously it is safe to cross. When the lights flash it signifies that a train is approaching and that is dangerous to cross. Neither of these states can be confused with a feedback failure. In such a situation the lights are off and it is obvious what has happened.

7.4 Feedback channels

Having considered feedback in an abstract manner let me now move on to look at some of the more real and nitty-gritty aspects of it. Feedback from an interactive system can only be communicated to the user by means of the five senses: hearing, sight, smell, taste and touch. The senses of taste and smell do play a part in some forms of feedback, for example fine tuning the flavouring of a meal while cooking it, detecting fires by the smell of burning or being aware of gas leaks. However, they are difficult to stimulate in a controlled, artificial manner and as far as humans are concerned they are not viable channels for the rapid communication of feedback information. I shall thus restrict my discussion to the other three channels: sight (visual feedback), hearing (audio feedback) and touch (tactile feedback).

7.4.1 Visual feedback

This is the most widely used form of feedback in today's technology. One of the most common examples is the tell-tale light associated with a switch controlling some hidden function. Other examples are meters, LED level indicators, text and flashing lights. The feedback does not even have to be as technical as lights and meters. With a row of channel selector buttons on a radio, for example, you can tell just by looking at the position of the buttons which one of them is pressed in, and thus which channel is selected.

7.4.2 Audio feedback

Audio feedback is also widely used, but it cannot convey the same richness of information as visual feedback. There is also a parallel with the technical dials and the more simple buttons mentioned in connection with visual feedback. Sometimes audio feedback is explicitly designed to be a part of the system like the beep of the cashpoint machine each time I press a button. Sometimes it is just a useful side effect of the way that the system operates, like the click a switch makes or the ticking of a watch. In current interactive devices audio feedback is mainly used to give feedback that a certain event has taken place; a button has been pressed or a bar code has been successfully read.

7.4.3 Tactile feedback

When most people think about the use of touch and tactile feedback they think of getting information about the texture and temperature of a particular surface. 'This feels sticky and cold.' 'This feels smooth and warm.' However, tactile feedback fulfils more roles than just this. In some areas it can tell you as much as your sight can about the spatial organization of something; consider feeling for a light switch in the dark.

The third thing that tactile feedback can give you information about is the movement of objects that you are touching. This is a very important role as far as artificial devices are concerned where the user interacts via switches and buttons. The satisfying 'clunk' feeling of a large switch or the smooth movement of a slider or knob under your fingers lets you know that you are changing things and to what extent you are doing so.

7.4.4 Combined feedback

When interacting with things in the real world the feedback is usually very rich. Even something as simple as putting a cup down on a table involves feedback via all three of the above channels. Interactive devices often involve combinations of more than one form of feedback, either on purpose or as a side effect of the design.

Consider using an electric typewriter or computer keyboard. When you press a key it is vital that you know that you have pressed it properly and that the typewriter or computer was aware of the press. The more feedback you have that the key has been pressed the better (within reason). Thus a good keyboard will provide the user with feedback using all three channels:

◆ **Visual feedback**
   The user can see the key being depressed, or more importantly they can see the side effects of the key being pressed – the character appearing on the paper or on the computer screen.

◆ **Audio feedback**
   Provided by an audible (but not too loud) click sound. With some keyboards the click sound is a side effect of the keys' design, but many computer systems produce the click

artificially through their speaker each time a key is pressed. This also gives the user the option of switching the click off or altering its volume.

◆ **Tactile feedback**
Through the feel of the keys moving beneath the user fingers. Some keyboard keys are especially designed so that rather than moving down gradually as they are pressed there is a certain pressure at which they suddenly 'collapse' under the user's finger giving much more definite feedback that they have been pressed.

7.5 Errors

I shall now have a look at how human errors are tied up with feedback and user models. A human error is an error caused in some way by the user of a system. This is in contrast to a system error where there is a physical fault within the system.

To clarify this difference consider a space capsule with two of the buttons on the control panel labelled A and B. Clicking button A switches the radio on and clicking button B opens both doors in the air lock thus letting all the air rush out. Errors of the system would cover things like A and B being cross wired so that A switches the radio on and B opens the airlock doors. The fact that the airlock doors are then opened when the user tries to switch the radio on is entirely due to the system. Human errors on the other hand can be broken down into two groups: errors of user action and errors of user intention.

7.5.1 Errors of action

An error of action is an error in the translation between a user's intention and their action. For example, in the space capsule an astronaut may try to switch the radio on, but owing to the clumsy nature of her space suit she presses button B instead of A. Her intentions were correct but in carrying out the action she made an error. Such problems as this can be overcome by good ergonomic design of the *physical* aspects of the system.

7.5.2 Errors of intention

With an error of intention the user does the wrong thing 'on purpose'. Back to the capsule again. The astronaut wants to switch the radio on, but from somewhere she gets the idea that button B is the radio button. She decides to switch the radio on, intends to press button B and does so. The underlying problem is a user model disagreement of the type identified in Chapter 6. The astronaut's model of the system's behaviour is different from the way the system actually behaves. She carries out an action which according to her user model is fine (pressing button B to switch the radio on) but within the real-world system it leads to different results (opening both airlock doors). Problems like this can be overcome by good ergonomic design of the *mental* and *informational* aspects of the system. Such design helps the user build up the correct user model of the system, and it is useful to identify the possible reasons why the *wrong* user model could be used by the user. The main reasons are:

◆ The user initially assumes an incorrect user model.

◆ The feedback supports an incorrect user model.

◆ The feedback is ambiguous as to which user model it supports.

◆ There is a time delay associated with the feedback, again leading to an incorrect user model.

7.5.3 Initially incorrect user model

Using the wrong user model usually occurs when the system is similar to a system already known to the user. The initial feedback from the new system may lead her to believe that the two systems are the same and she may then adopt the user model for the old system, leading to interactions which, although they are valid in her user model, may be inapplicable for the system actually being used. Errors of this sort are not just confined to the initial encounter with a new system. Users who have a very ingrained user model for an old system may repeatedly adopt their old user model and repeatedly make the same errors when faced with a similar new system.

One example is in the layout of auxiliary controls in a car, things like indicators and windscreen wipers. I know someone who had driven the same car for 10 years; its indicators were controlled by a stick to the left of the steering wheel. When they tried to drive a car with a slightly different control layout the similarities were enough to make them 'slip back' into their old model with the result that they continually switched the windscreen wipers on when turning corners.

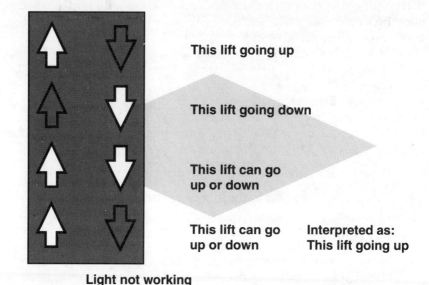

This lift going up

This lift going down

**This lift can go
up or down**

**This lift can go   Interpreted as:
up or down   This lift going up**

Light not working

Figure 7.4   Incorrect feedback from a lift system.

7.5.4 Incorrect feedback

Incorrect feedback (feedback that supports an incorrect user model) can arise if the feedback is badly designed (or just *not* designed at all). It can also arise if the feedback is distorted in some way by problems within the system ('system errors' mentioned above) or by part of it being obscured.

A lift system again gives a good example. I regularly take a lift from the fifth floor to the ground floor. There are two lifts and above the doors leading to each there are two arrows, one up and one down. Whichever of these arrows is lit indicates the direction a lift is going when it stops at my floor. If I summon a lift and one arrives that is *not* already on its way somewhere else then it indicates this by lighting up both arrows, effectively saying, 'I am going up or down.' Unfortunately the down arrow above one of the lifts does not work (faulty abstract feedback as in Section 7.3.2 [p 104]). Thus when a lift arrives and tries to light up both arrows to say 'I am going up or down' only the up one lights up thus giving the message, 'I am on my way up.' (See Figure 7.4.) I was confused by this at first and I still see other people get confused and wait for another lift to arrive.

7.5.5 Ambiguous feedback

Without feedback there is no reinforcement or guidance for the user to build up a user model. However, the presence of feedback does not necessarily guarantee that the user will adopt the correct user model. The feedback may be ambiguous enough to support several user models only one of which is correct.

As an example I was once staying at a hotel where the bathroom had two lights and both switches were mounted outside the door. One evening I was leaving my room and I saw that one of the lights in the bathroom was still on. I closed the bathroom door, flicked the switch up so that both lights were off and left the hotel. When I returned I discovered that both bathroom lights were on. What had happened? The answer was simple. When I looked at the two switches as I left, one was up and the other was down, I assumed that up was off and that down was on. The position of the switches, and the fact that one of the lights was on when I closed the bathroom door, backed this user model up and I then acted on this model. However, the hotel was in Amsterdam. In the Netherlands the orientation of switches is different from that in the United Kingdom, up is on and down is off. So the positions of the switches and the state of the lights were consistent with both user models and I had assumed the incorrect one.

7.5.6 Time delays

Ideally, the user's model of a dynamic system should be updated to incorporate changes in the system as soon as they happen. The user should be able to 'keep track' of what the system is doing as it does it. However, the process of feedback and user model construction always involves time delays. When a real-world system changes, the abstract model changes and thus the presentation changes to reflect this. Then the user comprehends the changed presentation and her user model changes. Time delays can be present in either the updating of the presentation or the user's comprehension of it.

Comprehension delays are usually the fault of the designer of the system failing to start with a good model of the user. Imagine two dials monitoring some aspects of a (very simple) reactor, and that the reactor becomes dangerous if the total of the two readings goes over 100. The user must continually keep track of the total. The dials (the presentation) may react instantaneously to changes in the reactor (the real-world system) but there is then a delay while the user adds up the two figures and alters her model of the system. If such a factor is important to the user it should be a part of the abstract model and also the presentation. In this case there should be a third readout giving the total of the two dials.

Delays in updating the presentation can affect both real presentations and abstract presentations. With real presentations it may take time for the visible aspect of the real-world system to reflect the internal changes of the system. If I switch on an electric fire, electricity runs through the heating elements; two minutes later they begin to glow red. During that two minutes the fire is on but the presentation has not changed.

Abstract presentation is also prone to time delays. Consider the car park with a 'self-service' ticket machine that I once came across. You park your car and get a ticket, stamped with the time, from the machine. To get a ticket out of the machine you click a button on the front of it, it pauses a short time (a second or two) and then spits the ticket out of a slot. When you click the button you change the state of the machine, but the change in the presentation corresponding to this change in the system (the feedback) is the ticket being spat out, and this happens after a short time delay. Thus, in between the clicking of the button and the ticket being spat out there is no feedback to indicate that the status of the system has changed. Thus, your user model of the system is that it has not registered your press on the button. Most users will then act on this incorrect user model and press the button repeatedly until finally the ticket appears.

The solution to this, and the electric fire problem, is to have some form of supplemental abstract feedback that is not prone to time delays. The fire could have a red tell-tale light built into it that lights up as soon as it is switched on; similarly the button on the ticket machine could be one that lights up when pressed and goes out when the ticket is delivered.

7.6 Summary

In this chapter I looked at the feedback that an interactive system gave about the user's interaction with it. I considered how the feedback related to the interaction in time (future feedback, present feedback and past feedback) and how feedback played a part in the user's construction of a user model of the system.

I then moved on to real and abstract feedback, how abstract feedback could be used in different ways (revealing, exaggerating or attracting attention) and the problems associated with abstract feedback. Finally I talked about the three main feedback channels (visual, audio and tactile) and the part feedback and user models played when considering errors.

7.7 Exercises

7.7.1 Does it know I am here?

Many systems follow the procedure of the user requesting something and the system then satisfying this request. If there is a long delay in between these two events the user can begin to wonder,

'Does the system really know that I am still here?'

Common examples are long pauses on the telephone while your call is being shunted around different departments in a large company or arriving at traffic lights that stay red and do not seem to acknowledge your arrival in any way.

Explain what is going on in terms of feedback and user models. Can you come up with any other examples? How would you go about changing the design of the examples to lessen this effect?

7.7.2 A modern telephone

The past few years have seen an upsurge in new designs for the telephone. One such is just a chunky handset without a base. The dialling buttons are located on the handset between the ear and mouthpiece. In between the dialling buttons and the earpiece is a large button that 'hangs-up' the telephone. When you put it face down on a flat surface this button is pressed in and the phone is no longer 'off the hook'. If you put it down on a soft surface or a crowded shelf the button might not be fully pressed in, with the result that the phone is still effectively 'off the hook'. Anyone trying to ring you will then get the engaged tone.

The real feedback concerning the state of the phone is not particularly obvious. What abstract feedback could be designed into the phone to show the user that the telephone was still 'off the hook' in situations like that outlined above? Is it good design practice to redesign something so that it then needs extra features in order to function acceptably?

7.7.3 Combined feedback

In Section 7.4 [p 106] I talked about providing combinations of visual, audio and tactile feedback during an interaction. For the following interactions state which forms of feedback are used and note them in order of importance. For example, putting a cup on a table: the feedback involved is a combination of all three, visual, audio and tactile, with audio feedback playing a less important role than the other two.

◆ Turning a gas ring up under a saucepan on a cooker.

◆ Doing the same but with an electric cooker.

◆ Turning the volume down on a radio.

◆ Putting the top back on a pen.

◆ Pressing buttons on a calculator.

◆ Checking if a mechanical watch is still running.

◆ A blind person using a white stick as they walk.

7.7.4 Feedback for microwaves

Back in Chapter 3 I discussed the safe design of microwave ovens. One method was to link transitions so that when the door was opened the microwaves were turned off. The user would probably feel more comfortable if there was feedback that this actually happened. Comment on the situation and then design some feedback.

7.7.5 Tricks with feedback

Discuss the following with respect to what is really happening (the real-world system), what feedback is being given, what the user's (or observer's) previous experience is in the area and what the resulting mental models are.

◆ A conjurer doing a magic trick.

◆ Camouflaging vehicles.

◆ Filming the spaceship shots of a science-fiction movie by hanging the models upside down and then filming them with the camera upside down as well so that in the final product the strings appear underneath the model.

◆ Confidence tricks.

7.7.6 Hazard warning lights

Explain the following in terms of feedback and the user model. A car is badly parked at the side of the road, half in and half out of the other cars parked there, and with its hazard warning lights on (both sets of indicators flashing at the same time) to indicate that the car is parked there while the driver goes into a shop briefly. Unfortunately other motorists and cyclists on the road are unable to see the indicator on the half of the car that is obscured by the other parked cars and thus the car in question looks as if it is signalling to pull out into the road. Is there any simple redesigning that could be done in order to solve the problem?

7.7.7 A domestic accident

You have just finished using a ring on an electric cooker. You switch it off. The little light that indicates the status of the ring goes off as well, and the ring is not hot enough to be glowing red, but it is still very hot. Your flatmate comes into the kitchen, fails to realize that you have been using the cooker, and then accidentally burns her hand on the ring. Analyse what has happened in terms of the real-world system, the abstract model, the presentation, feedback and the user model. How could you alter the design of the cooker to guard against this? Finally ask yourself why you moved in with her in the first place!

7.8 Dummy buttons

We have just had a new telephone system installed here. The telephones are covered in interestingly labelled buttons, but the instruction book informs us that not all of them have a function. Rather than make several different sorts of telephone housing, the company makes only one sort containing all the buttons. Then, according to how advanced a system you have paid for, they install the electronics inside and connect up the appropriate buttons.

This happens with other high-tech devices as well. I know of compact-disc players and television remote control units that have labelled buttons on them that do absolutely nothing at all. The same thing happens with programs on a computer system. Sometimes I read the description of a program installed on a computer, decide it's useful and then try to run it, only to be presented with a message like 'This program cannot run on this machine,' or 'This program needs more memory to run.'

In all the above cases the system is in effect saying to the user, 'I can do this' and then when the user actually asks it do so, it doesn't. I think it's called 'telling lies' in the real world.

Hemelsworth is sitting in the drawing room in Broadoaks Manor. He rings for Barker who enters.

Hemelsworth: Can you cook anything interesting, Barker?

Barker: Oh yes sir. I've been on extensive catering courses. I worked in Milan for a number of years and I am an expert in the Italian cuisine – lasagne, pizza and I make a fantastic tiramisu.

Hemelsworth: Wonderful, wonderful. I knew I'd made a good choice selecting you to come and work for me. How about a seafood pizza then, and a tiramisu?

Barker: Certainly. I'd enjoy doing that sir.

An hour later Hemelsworth is in the dining room sat at the table. Barker enters with a plate on which there is a fried egg on a piece of toast. Slowly he places it before Hemelsworth.

Hemelsworth: What's this? Fried egg on toast? What about all the Italian stuff?

Barker: Well, actually sir I can't cook Italian at all.

Hemelsworth: What? Barker, do you mean to say that you were lying to me?

Barker: Oh, no sir! Well, not really, I erm... err... Error code 100, sir.

Hemelsworth: Barker...

Chapter 8

Controls

8.1 Understanding controls

The preceding chapters concern themselves primarily with the communication of information from the system to the user. They cover the presentation of information in general, and feedback presenting information about the user's interaction. With interactive systems there is also communication in the other direction. The user can change things, she can influence the behaviour of the system. This is achieved by the use of controls: switches, buttons, knobs, sliders and so on. In many cases it is difficult to make a precise distinction between presentation, feedback and controls because of the large area of overlap between them. With controls, feedback is involved since many controls have feedback built into them, either explicitly by the designer or implicitly just through the nature of the control (for examples of this see Chapter 7).

A knowledge of the range of standard, everyday controls is useful in user interface design; it provides a 'design vocabulary' from which to select appropriate elements. Furthermore, it is useful to understand some of the more abstract issues involved in controls as this enables the designer to analyse controls and to design new control solutions where necessary.

When we move on to controls for interactive computer systems (Chapter 15) we shall see how the nature of computers brings a whole new set of ideas into the area. Despite these new ideas the groundwork covered in this chapter still plays a role in two ways when it comes to controls for computers. Firstly, in the more conventional controls associated with the computer (keyboard, mouse, tablet and stylus and so on) the ideas in this chapter can help with problems relating to their behaviour and use. Things like deciding on the allocation of mouse buttons, and how the pressing and releasing of the buttons should be interpreted. They can also help in the design of the behaviour of more exotic hardware controls for the computer. Secondly, when it comes to the new and somewhat less conventional area of on-screen controls (menus, scroll bars and so on), this chapter provides a collection of ideas and concepts to assist in their analysis and design.

8.2 Underlying functionality

When you first approach the idea of controls on interactive devices their range and complexity can seem very unstructured, but it is possible to pick out groups and make generalizations. For a start there are many types of control that have the same underlying functionality: for example, light switches, two-state push buttons (like the one on top of a ballpoint pen) and gas valves all perform the same action, that of switching the system back and forth between two states.

As well as grouping controls together according to the similarities in their underlying functions, we can also take a closer look at the different types of function. We are not constrained just to switching between two states, we can find controls that switch between several states and controls that choose a certain value from within a continuous range of values. In the following sections I shall elaborate on these different classifications.

8.2.1 Two-state switches

The control type I mentioned above was the two-state switch that switches the system back and forth between two distinct states. There are further groupings here according to the way in which the switching between the two states is controlled. In particular there are the three types below (it will help to look at the state diagrams in Figure 8.1 drawn in the style taken from Chapter 3).

◆ **Action–action switches**
    Here a user action is required to make the transition from one state to the other: S(a) to S(b). Another user action is required to make the return transition.

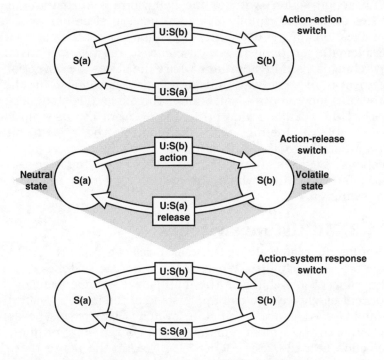

Figure 8.1   Different types of two-state switch.

◆ **Action–release switches**

Once again a user action is required to make the transition from one state to the other, but the action must be maintained by the user in order to keep the system in the new 'volatile' state. When the user stops the action ('releases'), the system returns automatically to the original 'neutral' state.

This introduces two new types of state into the notation developed in Chapter 3. However, these types of state differ in that their classification as 'volatile' or 'neutral' depends upon the type of user action required to make the transition and not upon the inherent nature of the state diagram as was the case in Chapter 3.

◆ **Action–system response switches**

Here a user action causes the system to make the transition from S(a) to S(b), but the return transition is carried out by the system performing some associated action. The initial user action can be seen as a signal which the system then responds to.

With action–action switches the behaviour is such that the two states are treated equally. They are used in situations where the ramifications of the two states are similar; neither is particularly problematic or dangerous. In contrast to this, action–release switching is used in situations where the states are *not* equal; one of them is in some way undesirable or even dangerous and the other is a more neutral, safer state. The dangerous state takes the part of the volatile state and in the event of the user no longer being able to interact with the control, the system returns automatically to the safe, neutral state. Finally action–system response switches are used in situations where the user signals a need for something which the system may take some time in satisfying.

8.2.2 Multistate switches

A multistate switch allows the user to select a state from a discrete number of possibilities. Whereas the two-state switches embodied the concept of 'change', the multistate switches embody the concept of 'choice'. We can apply some of the same classifications that we used above. Multistate switches can be of the action–action sort; the system remains in the chosen state until another selection is made. (See Figure 8.2.) Note in the figure that there are user transitions linking every state to every other state. Multistate switches can also be of the action–release sort: here the user selects which state the system is to be in but must maintain it in that state by continued user action. All the states are volatile except for one which is the neutral state to which the system returns on the release of the user's action. (See Figure 8.3.) Here note the 'star' nature of the state diagram with all the user release transitions returning to the neutral state. Finally there are action–system response multistate switches; these embody the idea of choice more succinctly. The user selects from a set of options and the system then carries out the appropriate response before returning to the neutral state. (See Figure 8.4.) The figure is similar to Figure 8.3 except that the user release transitions are now replaced by system transitions.

8.2.3 Variable controllers

Variable controllers are controls that do not select between an explicit number of discrete states. Instead they control some variable that can be changed across a continuous range of values. They embody the idea of 'level'; they control the level of some aspect of the system. Once again they can be classified using the types used above. The action–action controllers require a user action to set the variable to a certain value where it will stay until

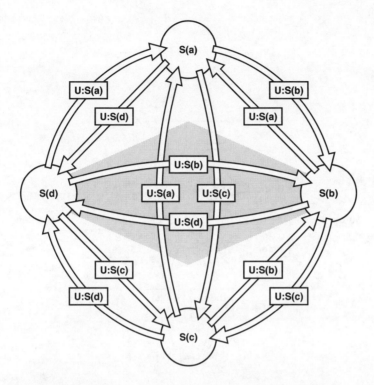

Figure 8.2   An action–action multistate switch.

it is changed again by another user action. These controllers are used in contexts where the variable is required to remain at one value for relatively long periods of time without user intervention. The action–release variable controllers depend upon continued user action to maintain them at a particular value. If the user ceases the controlling action then the system returns to the default, neutral state until the user applies the action again. Because the user is maintaining the level of the action–release variable controller by some sort of action (pressing a button or a pedal) there will be some slight variation in its level due to variations in the controlling force exerted by the user. The slight shifting of the level depends upon the physical ability of the user and on the sensitivity of the control.

Action–release variable controllers are used in situations where the user needs to be in control all the time and have the ability to alter continually the value of the variable. Once again the tendency of the system to return to the default state when user action ceases makes it applicable to the control of dangerous systems.

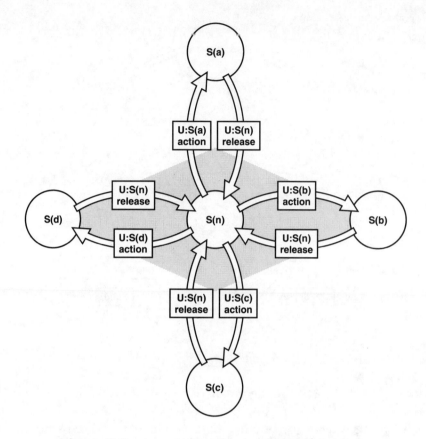

Figure 8.3 An action–release multistate switch.

The notion of action–system response type variable controllers is not particularly meaningful. Variable controllers depend upon rapid feedback to assist the user in 'tuning' the control to the required level. Any appreciable time delay in the system will cause large problems with the use of such a control.

8.3 Presentation of controls

Above I have described some of the different functions that controls can have. Having specified the abstract functionality of a control the next question is how is this functionality presented? When I talk about the presentation of a control I do not mean what colour the switch is or how big it is, these are merely issues of decoration. What I mean is something more fundamental: what actions must the user make to switch between the states, and how is she made aware of which state the switch is in? Once again it is a question of the presentation of abstract models.

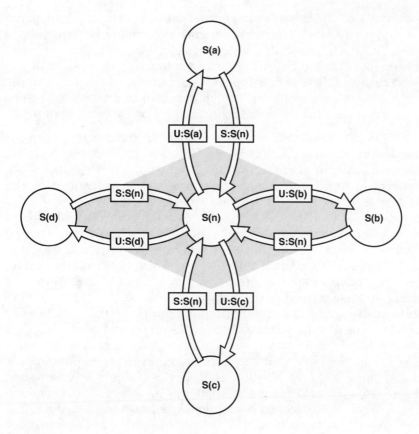

Figure 8.4 An action–system response multistate switch.

8.3.1 Two-state switches

The two-state action–action switch has two presentations. The first way of presenting it is to make a distinct difference in the presentation according to which state it is in like a normal lever-type switch (one way on, other way off). The second way is as a push button switch (push on, push off) with no distinct difference between the presentation of the two states. With the former there is feedback as to the state of the system, since the two positions of the lever are visually different. However, there must be some association between the different positions and the different states either in the form of extra explanatory feedback, such as on/off labels, or in the form of some convention with which the user is already familiar (think back to the bathroom lights in Section 7.5.5 [p 111]). Compare this state of affairs with the push on, push off style of presentation where there is no feedback provided by the switch as to its state.

Both of these switch presentations can be found in lights around the home. The conventional wall mounted light switch gives feedback about the state the light is in but the pull-cord switch found in bathrooms gives no feedback as to its state. If you need this feedback, for example when changing the light bulb, the lack of it with the pull-cord switch can lead to unexpected things happening, like the bulb suddenly lighting up as you install it.

The action–release switch is known to most people through the doorbell button connected to a bell. It is however used in other places as well. In many technological applications where there is a dangerous state and a safer, neutral state the control of the system is governed by an action–release switch referred to as a 'dead-man's handle'. One example of such a control can be found in a train driver's cab where a handle acts as a main on/off control for the engine, relying on continued pressure from the driver's hand to maintain it in the 'on' position. Should the driver become incapacitated in any way while driving the train, the action–release nature of the handle will cause the engine to stop thus averting any disasters. Another example of this 'dead-man's handle' type of action–release switch can be found on the baggage trolleys provided for passenger use at many airports and stations. The bar at the back that the user holds on to when pushing the trolley also acts as the braking device. When it is pressed downwards the brakes are taken off, but as soon as the downward pressure on it is released the brakes go on. Constant user action is necessary to maintain it in an easily movable state as whenever the trolley is not in use the brakes go on.

The action–system response type switch is typically found in lift systems: here a user request may take time to be fulfilled by the system and feedback is needed to indicate which state the system is in, either 'lift not requested' or 'lift requested' (this is also discussed in Section 5.6 [p 70]). Automatic drink machines also have action–system response type switches. Usually only a small time elapses between the request and the fulfilment (the delivery of the drink) and even if there is a delay there is usually enough real feedback being supplied in the form of gurgles and hisses to make abstract feedback unnecessary.

8.3.2 Multistate switches

Action–action multistate switches are very common in practical situations since they embody the act of choosing between several alternatives: for example, the wash programme selector on a washing machine, usually in the form of a large dial that can be turned to point to a choice. Other interesting examples are the push-button channel selection on a radio or the push-button controls to operate a cassette deck. Here pushing one button in forces the previously pushed button to pop out again. This is an example of an action–action multistate switch constructed from a group of action–action two-state switches with appropriate constraints built into the group.

Although action–release multistate switches are possible there are not many practical examples of them. One that I *can* think of is a typical electronic musical keyboard. The system is in the neutral state (no keys pressed) and when the user holds a key down the system stays in a volatile state with a note sounding.

8.3.3 Variable controllers

Action–action variable controllers usually feature in safe systems such as dimmer switches for lights or volume controls on radios and televisions. They can have many different physical presentations including the dial and the slider. Action–release variable controllers are usually associated with more dangerous systems: the accelerator pedal of a car or the pressure-sensitive trigger on a variable-speed power drill. Here the system is immediately returned to the safe, neutral state in the event of the user ceasing the controlling action. It is difficult to find any real-world examples of an action–system response variable controller since the use of variable controllers depends very much upon direct feedback about the interaction. Any delay between the user's actions and the system's response would render it difficult to use.

With some action–action variable controllers there is an extra facet to the presentation. They are presented in a manner that includes extra feedback to inform the user that the variable controller is in a particular state that is in some way important. Consider the following examples. Many radios have a small light (called a 'magic eye' in the old days) to indicate when they are accurately tuned in to a radio station. The balance controls on some hi-fis have a tangible click or groove when the balance control is turned past the midpoint. Likewise, some British gas cookers have a more pronounced click of this kind on the gas control knob to pinpoint the lowest simmer setting of the ring. This prevents you from accidentally turning the gas off when you are trying to turn it down very low.

8.3.4 Combined controls

Earlier, I talked about how it was possible to combine a group of action–action two-state switches to form an action–action multistate switch. It is possible to make other combinations of these basic controls thus providing new types of control that may be more applicable to certain situations. Consider a radio or a light dimmer switch. There are two key functions involved: the switching on and off of the system and the subsequent altering of the level of lighting or volume. In some implementations the former is done by an action–action two-state switch and the latter by an action–action variable controller. However, there are plenty of examples where the two functions are combined under the single control of an on/off knob that also acts as a level control. The user switches the system on and then moves the action-action controller up to the required level. The advantage here is that both operations can be carried out simply with one control. The advantage with separate controls is that the user can preset the level to a particular value that will not be altered when the system is switched off and on.

This idea of presetting can also be found in more complex situations: the tuning presets for a television for example. The television is equipped with a number of channel buttons (an action–action multistate switch) and each of them has a corresponding action–action variable controller. The user employs the latter to preset the tuning for each button and is then able to use the former to quickly select from the different preset wave bands. Early television sets (like most conventional radios) usually had just one action–action variable controller to do the tuning.

8.4 Multifunctional controls

In conventional interactive devices the user interface is made up of physical controls. Adding new controls costs money and makes the interface less reliable since there is more to go wrong. Designers often try to implement an interface design using as few controls as possible. This leads to the problem of trying to provide a lot of functionality with a limited number of controls. Methods must be found of making the controls multifunctional. There are several ways of doing this.

Time-based sampling

Consider a Morse Code key. It consists of one simple control that can be pressed and released. However, this simple control was once the main means of transmitting all sorts of information across the country and the world. There was only one action possible but it could be used to send different signals by varying the one action through time.

To a lesser extent this idea is used in interactive devices. Consider the usual approach to setting the time on digital watches and clocks. There is one button that quickly runs forwards through the digits, but its behaviour in doing this is governed by the timing of the user's interaction with it. Pressing the button once with a quick press and release action will advance the time by one digit. Pressing the same button down and holding it down will have the effect of making the digits tick through rapidly one by one – one control, two functions.

Modification buttons

With the advent of satellite and cable television, modern television sets have access to more and more channels and they usually have a remote-control unit. How do you fit 30 or so channel-selection buttons on to one remote control unit? Different manufacturers have come up with different solutions to this problem. One of these is to have 10 buttons (labelled 0 to 9) and then two or three other buttons labelled '10+', '20+' and so on. The idea is that if you want channel 23, for example, you hit the '20+' button and then the '3' button (20 + 3 = 23). Pressing the '20+' button modifies the behaviour of the subsequent button that is pressed and enables 30 channels to be selected using just 12 buttons.

Mode buttons

I'll go back to digital watches again for this example. The designers always try to cram in as many features as possible and control them with just a few buttons. Usually one of the buttons is a 'main mode' button. Pressing it changes the mode, from clock to stopwatch for example. The display changes and the function of the other buttons change to functions that are relevant within the new mode. The buttons then maintain this new functionality until a different mode is selected.

8.5 Summary

In this chapter I covered controls for interactive devices. I started off with a survey of the different abstract functions that controls can provide, identifying the following types:

◆ Two-state switches

◆ Multistate switches

◆   Variable controllers.

For each of these I then looked at the different ways the user could achieve the switching, identifying three different ways:

◆   Action–action type

◆   Action–release type

◆   Action–system response type.

Also while discussing action–release type switches I identified another state classification to supplement those in Chapter 3, namely volatile states. I then moved on to look at presentations of these abstract types, at practical examples of them and at controls that combined several of the more elemental types. Finally I looked at ways of making controls multifunctional.

8.6 Exercises

8.6.1 More action–release switches

Another example of two-state action–release switches is the trigger on most power tools (electric drills, jigsaws and the like). You press the trigger and they work, entering their volatile, dangerous state. Release the trigger and they stop. Unlike most other examples of action–release switches it is sometimes necessary to have the system in the volatile state for quite long periods of time. Because of this some power tools have a composite switch consisting of a trigger and a supplementary button that can be used to lock the trigger into the 'on' position converting the overall effect from an action–release switch into an action–action switch. Once locked into the 'on' position the tool remains on until the trigger (not the supplementary button) is again pressed and released.

Have a look at a power tool with such a switch. Analyse it and draw the state diagram of the switch. Can you think of any other examples of action–release switches?

8.6.2 Underlying functions

Describe the following in terms of the underlying function of the controls and how the controls are presented:

◆   **A joystick**
     A joystick for controlling the flight of a radio-controlled aircraft. It can be moved backwards, forwards, left and right and is spring loaded so that it always returns to the middle position when released.

♦ **Musical keyboard**
An electronic keyboard (capable of playing chords) with a
volume slider, a range of buttons for choosing the voice (the
style of sound to make) and a 'pitch bend' wheel (a spring-
loaded wheel that shifts the pitch away from the note being
played but springs back to the normal position when the
wheel is released).

8.6.3 Notating variable controllers

In this chapter I showed state diagrams for the two-state and
multistate switches. Illustrating the continuous range nature of
variable controllers is much more difficult; the problem is
approachable in a variety of ways. Have a look at Figure 8.5. This
is just a simple representation of the action–action type variable
controller. The variable V can be altered within the range V(min) to
V(max). A transition from one arbitrary state to another (V(n) to
V(m)) within this range is carried out by the user. Comment on the
notation and think up your own ideas for notating the concept.
What about action–release type variable controllers?

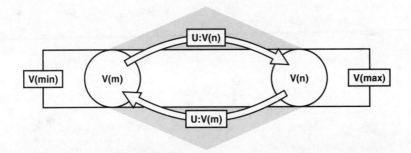

Figure 8.5 Notating variable controllers in state diagrams.

8.6.4 Continental cookers

The behaviour of the control knob on a standard British gas
cooker is different from that of a similar knob on a continental
cooker. Try and have a go with both sorts (or find someone familiar
with both sorts). When you know how they both behave see if you
can work out some way of annotating them.

8.6.5 Action–release multistate switches

I mentioned in Section 8.3.2 [p 126] that there were very few practical examples of action–release multistate switches. Can you think of any others apart from the musical keyboard?

8.7 Guidelines

Several times in this book I mention guidelines for the design of computer user interfaces. User interface design is a complex subject involving people's behaviour. There are many other equally complex people-oriented subjects in real life and we don't become instantly skilled in them just by following a set of guidelines...

> **Barker:** Sir! Any problems you may have with my butlering are over!

> **Hemelsworth:** [*Expectantly*] Ah! You're finally leaving then?

> **Barker:** Fortunately not sir. I have just been to the 'Guideline School of Butlering' and have been given the list of golden rules for butlering. If anyone follows them they will instantly be an expert butler.

> **Hemelsworth:** Let's have a look at them then.

> *Barker hands him a piece of highly decorated paper.*

> **Hemelsworth:** [*Reading*] One: be consistent in your behaviour. Two: always do what your master expects. Three: give good feedback. Four: always behave in a manner appropriate to the situation. Five: always present your master with choices in groups of seven. Six: do not do anything surprising, unexpected or silly. Seven: be helpful. Eight: be nice. This looks like a useless load of rubbish to me Barker.

Chapter 9

Designing interactive systems

9.1 Design guidelines

In this chapter I am going to look at a few simple examples of the design of user interfaces. Before I do this I will mention some of the prerequisites that a good user interface designer needs.

If you ask an architect how she developed her designing skills she will probably answer, 'Ever since I was a kid I used to design and build things – kites, domes, Lego spaceships. When I left school I studied under Professor Robins at Manchester University, analysing contemporary architects like Rogers, Foster and Alberts. Then I worked with DMJB Architects on several projects, including The Bridge of the Future and The Glasgow Eurodrome.' She will probably *not* say, 'Oh, I read *The Public Building: Concepts and Designs* there was a chapter about the rules of good design and everything I needed was in there.'

As with many other design disciplines, and especially those concerning design for use, there are no 'golden rules' to designing user interfaces. There is no recipe whereby you can just do 'A, B and C' and end up with a brilliant interface. True, there are various sets of guidelines in the area, but as often as not they are either so obvious that a designer who needs to be told them can't be a very good designer, or they are so vague that they are not really of any use at all. These guidelines and rules do have some part to play, but only in the larger context of a good approach and feel for user interface design. Such an approach and feel depends upon two key things: a good 'mindset' for the task and a good awareness of user interfaces in general.

9.1.1 A good 'mindset'

What I mean by this is a good attitude and approach to designing a user interface. A mindset constitutes the mental and conceptual things that you bring with you when you enter into design work: an understanding of the importance of what you are doing and the goals of the task you are tackling. Such a 'mindset' incorporates many things.

Realization of importance

Thinking *of* the user. One of the most difficult problems some system designers have is realizing that the user interface *is* important, or indeed realizing that there is such a thing as a user interface in the first place. The key thing in any area of design for use is to be aware of the main motivation behind designing things for people to interact with, namely making the interaction satisfying, useful, comprehensible, easy and efficient.

Innocence of vision

Thinking *like* the user. When designing an interface you must continually switch back and forth between two viewpoints. As the designer you know a lot about the system, what it does and how it works, but you must also try to imagine how it appears from the user's point of view.

Prospective users should be involved in the design process, but it helps if you can think like the user yourself. You must be able to evaluate the interface according to what you can see of it, what you can interact with and what you are aware of on the surface rather than what you, as the designer, know about how it works. Achieving this goal is similar to the 'innocence of vision' that some artists strive for when painting from life. Artists are urged to, 'Draw what you *see* not what you know to be there'. In user interface design it could be paraphrased as, 'Design in terms of what the user can perceive rather than what you know to be there'.

Related areas

There are other areas of design that concern themselves with the question of design for use. A good knowledge of these areas is useful in that it enables the designer to get a better grip of the general principles involved in designing for people. Furthermore, it also gives the designer the chance to transfer ideas and techniques from these other areas into user interface design.

Design vocabulary

One important resource that you need in order to carry out design in any area is a 'design vocabulary' consisting of a knowledge of the materials and techniques that are available and an appreciation of what they do and what it is possible to do with them. Such a 'design vocabulary' is a vital tool when it comes to thinking about the problem and designing a solution. For user interface design this vocabulary is concerned with the presentation of information, ideas and methods connected with typography and layout, graphics, symbols and icons, organization of information, the behaviour of interactive systems, designing feedback and so on.

Ability to generalize

Generalization is a powerful tool in many areas. Try to generalize any observations that you make about user interface design. For example, I was once washing my hands in a sink with a mixer tap (two controls, one outlet). The water got hotter as it was running and eventually it became too hot so I tried to turn the hot tap back. By this time my hands were covered in soap, and the tap was one of those trendy, smooth, streamlined ones. I couldn't get a good enough grip to turn it down, my hands kept slipping, and I couldn't wash the soap off my hands because the water was too hot!

The obvious rule is, 'If you are designing taps, ensure that they can be operated by people with soapy hands.' However, it is possible to go further and generalize from this, 'When designing for a user, think of the context that the design will be used in. In particular think of any changes the user may undergo as a result of that context.' General guidelines like this can then be applied to designing other user interfaces: for example, designing a handle for use on a door in the kitchen of a restaurant. A conventional round knob that the user must grip and turn would be acceptable and look good, but wait a minute! In a kitchen people are going to be moving around with their hands full of trays and such like. A lever-type handle would be better because then the user could whose hands are full could operate it with her elbow.

Awareness of assumptions

In previous chapters I have occasionally referred to assumptions that are made about the user, the design problem and so on. Identifying the assumptions that you are making and explicitly stating them is important when you are involved in analysing and designing something. You should be aware of any assumptions that you make about the user or about any other aspects of the design process. Being aware of assumptions can help lead to useful results. They can be:

◆ **Left as part of the solution to the problem**
'Here is a design solution assuming that...'

◆ **Prompt changes in the design**
'Maybe we should design it so that it can be used by left-handed people as well.'

◆ **Prompt questions about the specification**
'When you say you want *this*, do you mean...'

When you attempt the exercises in this book it may be a useful idea to state explicitly the assumptions you are making. I don't mean the obvious ones like, 'I am assuming that the user is a human being.' Other, less obvious statements are nevertheless important: for example, 'I am assuming that the user is right-handed'.

9.1.2 User interface awareness

Building up a good attitude to user interface design revolves around more than just the key points outlined above. Most of the skills are developed through continued experience of working in the field. This experience can be in the actual designing of user interfaces, but another useful source is using and analysing existing user interfaces that you may come into contact with. Bear the following sections in mind as you come across interactive systems in your day-to-day life.

As a user interface designer, when you interact with systems you should analyse what you see and experience from a rigorous and technical viewpoint. However, you should also be open to 'gut feelings' about user interfaces even if you cannot find any logical support for them. User interface design deals with certain things that are technical and rigorous, but it also deals with people, and people are decidedly non-technical and non-rigorous in nature.

Experiment with user interfaces

If you have to use an interactive system to carry out some task then as well as being aware of the task you are doing, you should also be adventurous. Try other things and attempt to discover the limitations of the user interface. Ask yourself questions like: How does it cope with mistakes in the interaction? Can I correct or cancel parts of my interaction? What does it do if I am 'badly behaved' – if I push buttons when the machine is not expecting me to or choose options which the system does not expect me to choose?

Analyse annoyances

This is another part of the 'be aware' approach. If you use an interactive system and, for some reason, it annoys you, do not just curse the thing. Analyse it, sort out *why* it annoyed you. Try to work out what you were expecting it to do and what it was expecting you to do. Redesign it and think back to your annoyance with its design the next time you design a user interface.

Watch other users

Very rarely are you the only user of a system. You may have strong negative feelings about a user interface but are they very specific to you, or are they common to other users? The converse could also be true; you may like a certain interface because the designer has made an assumption about the user which happens, in your case, to be true. Other users may have difficulty with it because in their case the assumption does not hold. It can be enlightening to watch how other people react to interactive systems, either by arranging for someone else to use a system or just by observing other members of the public using the systems that can be found in everyday life.

Be aware of errors

Now and then, when using interactive systems, things go wrong with the interaction. These problems or misunderstandings are often seen as the user's fault; in the jargon they are referred to as 'user errors', implying that the *user* has done something wrong. They include everyday occurrences such as leaving things switched on when you have finished with them or trying to toast bread in an electric toaster that is not plugged in. The advice here is similar to that given in the section on annoyances; try to transcend the problems and analyse them. Don't just take the attitude, 'That was silly of me, I won't make the same mistake again.' Was the error really *your* fault in the first place? Try to work out why you did things the way you did. What assumptions were you working on? Could the system have corrected the mistake somehow or, better still, prevented it from happening in the first place?

9.2 Darkroom doors

Let us move on now and have a look at some examples of designing user interfaces. Sometimes it is difficult to come up with other solutions to a problem once an acceptable solution has already been suggested. Bearing this in mind, it might be a good idea to think about these examples yourself before studying how I have approached them.

First of all then let us consider the problems of darkrooms. Much photographic work is done in darkrooms. The system of doors leading to such a room must be arranged to let people in and out without letting light in. The common solution is a sort of airlock (or maybe 'lightlock' is a more appropriate term) using two doors. To go in you open the outer door, enter the 'anteroom' between the two doors, close the outer door, then open the inner door and go into the darkroom itself. The state diagram for this is shown in Figure 9.1. As you can see this arrangement has a dangerous state when both the doors are open, and two adjacent critical states. To make matters worse, someone approaching from outside on seeing the outer door shut has no feedback as to the state of the system. The transition they make by opening the outer door could be permissible or it could be disastrous.

An initial approach to the problem could be to give better feedback to people approaching from outside: for example, a warning light to indicate the state of the inside door. If the light is on the door is open. There would of course have to be an accompanying sign to explain this and it would be impossible to ensure that everyone would:

◆ **Read it**
   'Oh sorry! Which sign do you mean?'

◆ **Understand it**
   'Oh sorry! I thought it meant it was okay if it was lit.'

◆ **Obey it**
   'Sorry about this, I had to come straight in. I'm in a rush and I need something from the darkroom.'

◆ **Remember it**
   'Oh sorry! I was miles away, I forgot all about it.'

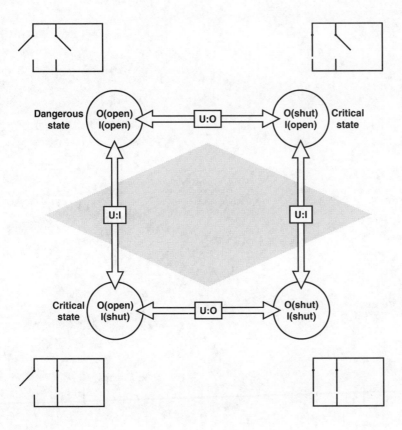

Figure 9.1   The state diagram of a typical darkroom door.

Another option discussed in the chapter on systems (Chapter 3), is to constrain certain transitions so that only one door can be opened at any one time. (See Figure 9.2.) The mechanics of this might be complex, but the main drawback would be the constraints imposed upon the user. If the inner door was left open and someone wanted to enter the darkroom they would have to shout to whoever was inside to close the inner door before they could enter. Worse still if the outer door was left open anybody still working inside would be locked in!

The third option is to link certain transitions together. In other words arrange it so that the act of opening one door would close the other door (see Figure 9.3). This would also involve quite complex mechanical arrangements, especially since having one door closing as the other is opening is still not enough. The other door would have to be fully closed *before* the first door was opened. It would be possible to have some mechanical or electrical system that the user could employ to close the other door before

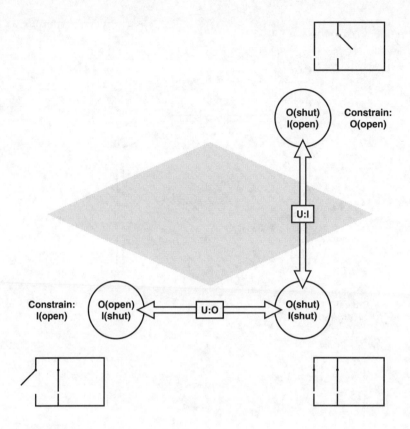

Figure 9.2   Constraining transitions in a darkroom door.

opening her door, but then we are back to the warning light problems since we have to ensure that users know about the system and use it.

There is one mechanical set up where doors *are* linked together in this way – the revolving door. As you push one door around, another swings behind you and closes the exit off before the door in front lets you into the room. Most of these doors are made of glass, but what if they were made instead of some material resistant to light?

In fact a novel solution already exists along similar lines to this. It uses a rotating cylinder. Instead of two doors with an anteroom in between, an upright cylinder is used which has a doorway slit cut into it and which revolves in a sleeve with two slits in it. A plan view of this cylindrical door is shown in

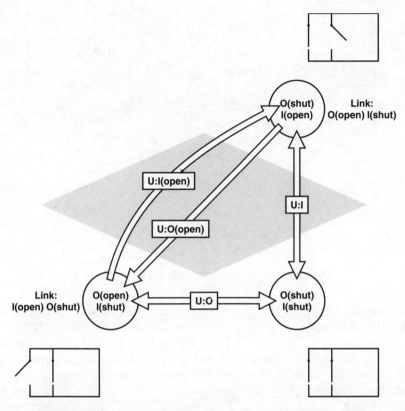

Figure 9.3   Linking transitions in a darkroom door.

Figure 9.4 along with its state diagram. The arrangement ensures that light can never get in since it is physically impossible for both entrances to be open at once.

The above analysis of the problem did not quite go all the way to yielding the cylindrical door solution, but the analysis did help develop a context in which such an intuitive step was made easier. Also, having come up with the idea we were immediately able to realize its appropriateness to the problem. Although one may appreciate the advantages of the cylindrical solution just by common sense, common sense can become less dependable as the system and the design problems become more complex.

9.3 Telephone pagers

A colleague at work carries a telephone pager with her because she is often away from her office in other parts of the building. Someone wanting to speak to her must ring the main switchboard; they set her pager beeping and she goes to the nearest telephone

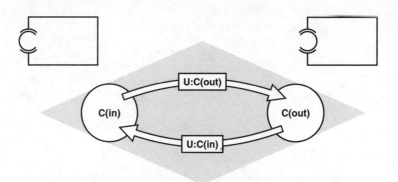

Figure 9.4   A cylindrical darkroom door.

to get in touch with the switchboard. Sometimes she is in meetings or attending lectures which she doesn't want to leave. If the pager starts beeping at a time like this then the only option she has is to sit on it to muffle the beeping until it stops. This begs the question why didn't the designers build a beeping on/off switch into the pager? Then if the user was in a meeting or lecture the device could be switched off to avoid disturbances and switched back on again afterwards.

9.3.1 Switching it back on

The act of switching the beeper off is trivial. The problems come with switching it back on again afterwards: making the transition from a state where the beeper is off to one where the beeper is on. A user transition would mean trusting that after a lecture or meeting the user would remember that she had switched the beeper off and switch it back on again, but this solution invites mistakes. We could make this user transition more likely by providing the user with good feedback that the system is in the 'beeper off' state. Obviously audio feedback is out of the question, but we could use visual feedback – a little warning light for example. As with any other use of abstract feedback there is the risk that the feedback system could fail, and running the light throughout lectures would shorten the battery life of the pager.

A time transition could be used instead of a user transition. After a set time the system would automatically turn the beeper back on. The problem then would be how long a time interval to use. If it were too long it might overrun the lecture meaning that the user could still miss important calls. If it were too short it might turn itself back on during the lecture, possibly causing interruptions again.

The option of constraining transitions is not applicable here since we want to enforce a transition rather than stop one happening, but linking transitions may be useful. We could link the 'beeper back on' transition to another transition or action that we are certain will occur at the end of the lecture. If the user usually takes the pager out of her pocket during the lecture we could link the 'beeper back on' transition to the act of clipping the pager back on to the pocket, either by directly linking them or by making the clipping back on to the pocket dependent upon first switching the beeper back on again. Some ballpoint pens have a mechanism like this; the clip enabling them to be attached to the pocket only works if the pen nib is retracted first.

This solution still has drawbacks. Unlike a pen there may be times when the user wants to override this action and have the pager out of her pocket but active or in her pocket and inactive. Furthermore, prospective users of the new pager will already be familiar with the old-style pagers. As a result, the lack of feedback as to the state of the system could cause problems. Users would not really need feedback to indicate that the beeper is on, since this is what they are used to, but it would be good to have feedback to indicate that the beeper is off since this is a state unfamiliar to most of them. A final solution then is to exaggerate the real, tactile feedback of the on/off switch: designing it to make it very noticeable when it is in the off position. One way of doing this would be to use a small lever instead of a switch. When the beeper was switched on the lever would lie flush with the body of the pager and be relatively unnoticeable. When it was switched off the lever would protrude from the pager giving both visual and tactile feedback that the beeper was off. (See Figure 9.5.)

Since real feedback is being used it would not need battery power, unlike a warning light, and there would be no chance of the feedback system failing. Also with this design there would be some linking to another action: because the lever sticks out it would make it difficult (but not impossible) for the user to replace the pager in her pocket while the beeper was switched off.

Once again ideas such as this are already in use in other areas. The Olympus XA2 camera uses such an exaggerated lever to activate the self-timer. You set the self timer on using the lever, you take the photo, then when you come to put the camera away you cannot help but notice the lever sticking out and switch it

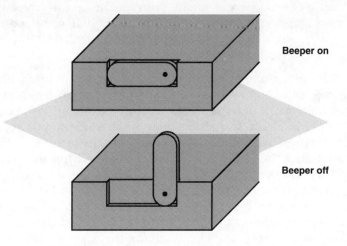

Figure 9.5   Exaggerated on/off switch.

back to the off position. With many other cameras (as with the pager) you could switch the self-timer on, but would probably then forget to switch it back off (and the next time you took a photo the timer would start, you wouldn't realize it and the camera would take the photo while you were still looking at it and trying to work out what was going on).

9.4 Digital timers

Simple digital timers crop up in all sorts of technical devices. Sometimes they take the form of *absolute* times. You set them for a definite time of day, they have a clock built into them and the system ensures that when this clock reaches the time that you set something happens. This sort of system is typically found in video time controls, alarm clocks and central heating time switches. Timers can also be *relative* timers. You set them up to do something after a set period of time has elapsed and then set them running. They measure the period of time relative to the moment you set them going and when they come to the end of that time interval something happens. You find timers like this on microwave ovens, conventional ovens and in the darkroom. This is a good area to consider because although only these two basic types of digital timer exist, they are implemented in all sorts of different ways and with all sorts of controls.

9.4.1 Hardware constraints

A lot of timers are designed within certain hardware constraints in order to keep costs down. (See Section 8.4 [p 128–129].) As a result compromises have to be made with the user interface hardware by excluding certain controls. In terms of the state diagram (see Chapter 3) the effect of excluding controls is to remove user transitions between states. If the user transition is the only transition to a certain state then that state will no longer be accessible (and is therefore no longer a part of the state diagram). In other cases the number of states will be maintained but there will simply be fewer transitions between them, possibly making the interaction more obscure. As an example consider setting the time (current time or alarm time) on a digital clock. We could envisage two buttons: pressing one would make the time skip forward, pressing the other would make it skip back. We could remove the latter of these two buttons without losing any states. The user could still set the time but the decrease in transitions would make it a less graceful interface to use; the user would always have to skip forward to the desired time and if they missed it they would have to go through the times again to get to it. (See Figure 9.6.)

9.4.2 Presenting the time

With the technology currently available for digital clocks it is possible to know the time to a very accurate degree, but how accurate a time is the average user interested in for something like

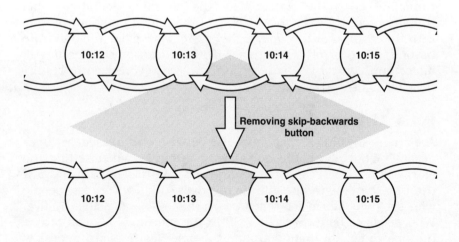

Figure 9.6   Decreasing the user transitions.

an alarm clock? This is a question of abstraction and presentation. Users are certainly not interested in everything up to the tenths of the seconds, and probably not the seconds either, so the clock need only abstract and present the hour and the minutes. But there are a few other facts about the time that may be of interest to the user and therefore need to be abstracted and presented. One is the fact that this model of the time is the correct time, another is the fact that the clock is running. Presenting an indication about the accuracy of the time shown is difficult. The solutions available are rather extreme such as incorporating three independent clocks together so that if one starts to deviate the user can see which one is wrong because it is the 'odd one out'. Showing that the clock is running is somewhat easier. Although this is not vital in day-to-day use, it is useful when the user makes alterations to the clock. For example, when altering the alarm setting and then returning to the display of the current time it is reassuring to be immediately aware that the clock is still running in the normal way. Without seconds on the display the only way a user can tell that the clock is running is to watch it until the minute figure changes. A common solution to this is to use a colon in the display between the hour and the minutes (9:32) and to make it blink once a second.

9.4.3 Relative timers

When it comes to relative timers the obvious extra control is a start button to set them running. In terms of the state diagram, starting the timer takes you to a state where the only outgoing transition is to the state where the alarm is sounding. This transition occurs after the passing of the allotted amount of time with the result that the 'interactive' system is locked into one state beyond the control of the user. Thus a less obvious, but still important, control is a cancel button in case you need to restart the timer.

9.4.4 Other ideas

Are there any areas that have not yet been addressed in timer design? What about the question of accuracy when setting the alarm time? Does the user really need controls to skip forward through the time in one minute intervals? I know very few people who set their alarm for times other than those divisible by five. Who needs to be awoken at 7:33 in the morning? Instead of two buttons to set the minutes one at a time (fast forward and slow forward) why not have a one-minute button that skips through at one-minute intervals and a five-minute button that skips through at five-minute intervals, always keeping to a time divisible by five. The great majority of users would then set the alarm time quickly and precisely just using the five-minute button.

9.4.5 Novel systems

Returning again to current systems, there are two interesting approaches to timers that I have noticed recently in electronic devices. The first was a portable radio/alarm clock that featured a calculator-style keyboard to enter the current time and the alarm time. Instead of setting the time by a process of relative adjustment ('Go forwards/backwards from here') the setting required could be keyed straight in without problems ('Set the time to *this*').

The other interesting idea was in a timer control on a microwave oven. It had very simple controls: a dial to set the timer and buttons to start and stop it. The interesting feature of the dial, however, was that the system was able to monitor the changes in the turning with respect to time, and the speed of rotation was then used to control the strength of the effect that turning the dial had upon the timer. The dial used time-based sampling (Section 8.4 [p 128]) to become a multifunctional control. This resulted in a sort of 'seven-league boot effect'. If the dial was turned slowly it altered the time according to how much it was turned, but if it was turned quickly then the effect of the turning was amplified and the timer was changed by far more than it would have been had the dial been turned slowly by the same amount. (See Figure 9.7.)

Choosing the scale factor used must have been a tricky task. It had to be as high as possible to get the benefits of the effect, yet at the same time not so high that the effect could become noticeable, unexpected and confusing for the user. Anyway, they made the right choice and the result is a multifunctional control that is so natural and subtle that the majority of users are not even aware of the multifunctionality, they are only aware that when using the dial they can set the time quickly and accurately.

9.5 Summary

In this chapter I dealt with two things. Firstly I talked about what sort of a background is necessary in order to practise user interface design. I talked about the factors that you need to bring with you when you approach a problem and how you can learn more about the area through being aware of user interface design throughout your day-to-day life. I then moved on to more concrete

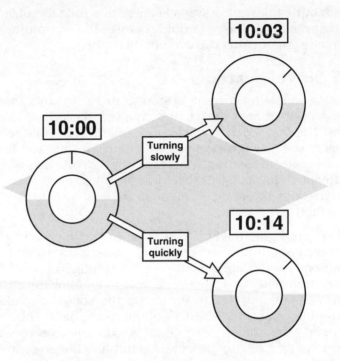

Figure 9.7   Variable effects when turning a dial.

examples, bringing in techniques and ideas that have already been covered. I looked at possible developments of existing designs and suggested new ideas.

Finally, I should remind you that up until now we have been dealing primarily with user interface design that does not involve computers. They will be introduced in the following chapters of the book.

9.6 Exercises

9.6.1 One button

Designing within constraints forces the design process to be very precise and thorough. Although you do not necessarily end up with an ideal design, achieving the best design within the given constraints involves a lot of hard thinking and questioning about priorities and assumptions. Design a one-hour digital timer where the user can set a time (up to one hour) from which to count down to zero. Use a display that has two elements which can either be blank or show a digit, and try just using one button as the control. When you have done that, what about a design for the same timer using only one button and one display element? (See Figure 9.8.)

9.6.2 Panic button

There are many examples of systems with protected states. One of the states is dangerous but necessary. It must be accessible but only if the user really intends it. Design a 'panic button' for use in a bank. It is connected up to the local police station to alert them of a robbery. It must be easy to use in an emergency but must not be susceptible to accidental activation. Are there any important observations you can make about feedback during its operation?

9.6.3 Dictaphone controls

Find a cassette box and hold it in your hand. Imagine that it is a dictaphone (a small cassette recorder used for recording spoken notes rather than listening to music). Design a layout for the controls so that it can be operated with just that one hand. Think about how it would be used and draw a state diagram to identify the common-use loop and the common operations. These common operations should be easy to carry out. Are there any assumptions

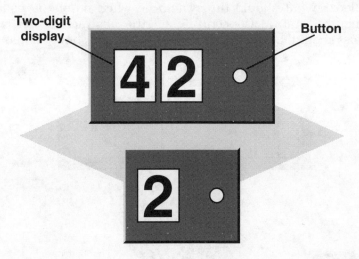

Figure 9.8 Timers with hardware restrictions.

that you made about the user when you did your design? Would there be any group of users who might have problems with the finished product?

9.6.4 More hardware constraints

Design a user interface to enable the user to key in a PIN code composed of four digits from zero to nine. Base it on the following hardware: a display composed of two rows of 10 elements, each of which can either be blank, show a character or digit or show a character or digit in reverse (white on black in place of black on white). The controls to be used are four buttons arranged in a diamond shape. (See Figure 9.9.)

Then try the same exercise, with no hardware constraints; design a PIN code entry interface with no constraints and then specify what hardware you need. Which approach yields the best results from the user's point of view?

9.6.5 Lifts

Good lift systems are notoriously difficult to design. Work on a design for a very simple system involving one lift serving two floors. What controls should there be in the lift and on the wall on each floor? What should the system do when no one is using it (the 'neutral state')? Concentrate on the abstract design (what controls should be available to the user and how should the

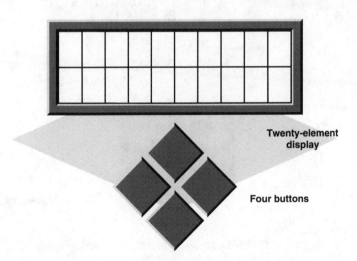

Twenty-element
display

Four buttons

Figure 9.9   Hardware for a PIN code entry interface.

system behave) rather than the presentation of the design (what the controls look like, which bits light up and so on). One of the main problems you will encounter is writing your design down; you will probably have to work out some sort of notation. Are there any assumptions that you can make about the user based on the fact that the system only serves two floors?

An interesting related problem is the effect on the users of waiting for a lift to arrive once they have requested it. How could you decrease the stress and boredom of people waiting for a lift? Is there any information in the real-world system that you could abstract and present to them?

9.6.6 Toaster problem

In Section 9.1.2 [p 138–139] I mentioned the problem of trying to toast bread in an electric toaster that is not plugged in. You put the bread in, push the handle down and wait. It is only after a while that you realize what the problem is. Design a toaster that overcomes this problem.

9.7 The wrong place at the right time

At work I usually use my own computer on my desk. It is connected up to many other computers in a big network. Sometimes I work on another computer in the network. I go to the common room that is full of special computers and use one of them. Because of the network I can still get at all my files on my own computer. However, I do have problems. When I say, 'Start up a word processor in a window on the screen,' it does so, but on the screen of my own computer back in my office! In order to get the computer to do things correctly I have to say:

DISPLAY=zeeeend:0.0 export DISPLAY

and then ask for a word processor.

The computer is a powerful information-handling system; there is enough information in the computer system to do the job properly. It knows which computer I'm typing commands in at so if I ask for something visual, it's most likely that I want it on the screen I'm sitting in front of and not on a screen in a different room. Why should I have to do the computer's work for it? Especially when it involves remembering jargon or alternatively becoming intimately familiar with the internal workings of the system? Let us return to Broadoaks Manor.

Barker has just returned from a 'rigorous methods' butlering course, concerned with accurate specification of butlering tasks. Hemelsworth is busy in his study. He calls Barker in.

Hemelsworth: Listen, Barker old chap. Could you bring me a bit of lunch?

Barker: Certainly sir. Would a bowl of soup be acceptable?

Hemelsworth: Wonderful Barker.

Half an hour later Hemelsworth calls Barker in again.

Hemelsworth: Listen, Barker, I thought you were going to bring me a bit of soup?

Barker: I did sir; it's gone cold in the dining room.

Hemelsworth: In the dining room? But I'm here in the study.

Barker: Well, normally you do eat in the dining room, sir.

Hemelsworth: Barker, if I'm in the study and I ask for something why not bring it to me where I am for goodness sake? Is there any way to get you to serve lunch here?

Barker: Actually there is sir, you have to say SERVEROOM=study:0.0, export SERVEROOM.

Hemelsworth: Goodness Barker, what a mouthful. What does it all mean?

Barker: Well sir, SERVEROOM is an environment variable and you have to set it to what you want, but then it is only set for that particular command shell so you have to export it to the other...

Hemelsworth: [*Interrupting*] Never mind, Barker, I'll just remember it. Now SERVEROOM= study:0.0, export SERVEROOM. Bring me my lunch.

Barker: Error code 98, sir.

Hemelsworth: What do you mean?

Barker: There was an extra space in there, sir. You have to get it exactly right.

Hemelsworth: Oh, what on earth are you up to Barker? SERVEROOM=study:0.0, export SERVEROOM. Bring me my lunch.

Barker: Right away, sir.

Hemelsworth: Phew! What a fuss.

Chapter 10

Interactive computer systems

10.1 Computers

Let me bring computers into the picture a bit more now. First of all, 'What is a computer?' or in this context, 'How should a user interface designer regard a computer?' Computers are difficult to define since they appear in many different areas disguised in many different forms and activities. Basically a computer is a tool for storing, manipulating and interacting with information: numbers, names, lists, descriptions of things, pictures, relationships between things and structured information. A simple analogy is difficult to find. It is like nothing that has gone before. It can be compared to a group of dedicated colleagues with calculators and notepads, a vast library with a fleet of high-speed librarians, a team of business presentation specialists, armed with charts, graphs and coloured pens or a vast information factory where all the above and much more besides are put to work, orchestrated and supervised by a well-trained foreman.

Designing the user interface to a system involves knowing something about the system. The question is, which parts of the system do you need to know about and what do you need to know about them? In this chapter I am going to discuss the parts that play a role in the user interface and then move on to consider some of the more general traits (both positive and negative) that make computer–user interfaces different from the point of view of a user-interface designer. After an examination of the way computer systems affect the use of feedback channels I shall then introduce a structural framework for the following chapters of the book.

If you do not have a computer background this chapter will give you a guide as to what things you may need to find out more about and what points to bear in mind while working on computer–user interfaces. If, however, you do have a computer background then it is still useful to appreciate the division between the areas that are relevant and those that are not.

10.2 Decoupling the user interface

First of all though let me examine the user interface to the computer in a little more detail. Where did it come from? In the early stages of any new design discipline that has anything to do with people there are difficulties with the decoupling of the user interface from the internal aspects of the system. Difficulties occur in the *conceptual* decoupling of the user interface of the system from the internal workings (being able to think about the user interface). Accompanying this is a lack of *real* decoupling (the *technological* ability to separate the internal workings from the user interface). As disciplines mature, the decoupling of the user-oriented design and the internal functional design start to take place despite these difficulties. This has already happened in many areas of technology: the architect and the builder, the industrial designer and the engineer, the automobile engineer and the dashboard ergonomics expert.

As a technological discipline relaxes its hold on the user-related design aspects they begin to be seen in more of a design context. Despite the youth of computer–user interface design, this decoupling is already starting to happen. Technological tools are being developed to aid computer–user interface design which is independent of the other, internal and functional factors of the system. In the area of conceptual decoupling, workers are starting to appreciate the advantages of such a division and beginning to think more in terms of the user interface.

Evidence of this decoupling can also be seen in the way that the discipline of 'computer science' is divided up. 'Computer science' covers a broad range of subjects which widens every day. In the pioneering days of computer science there was very little division of the discipline into separate subjects. There was one big subjectless 'blob' out of which the separate subjects have distilled with the passing of time. Today, as well as creating new subject areas which are pure computer science, the discipline is also engulfing small areas on the fringes of others. This rapid growth in the amount of material to contend with can be daunting. However, as the area matures this rise in the sheer volume of material is offset by the decoupling mentioned above and an increasing awareness and clarity regarding which areas are applicable to the field of user interface design. Which areas of computer science then are relevant?

10.3 The user interface components

The user interface components of the majority of non-computer interfaces are obvious; the external face of a control panel can have buttons or sliders for controlling parameters, as well as dials and LCD screens for giving feedback about what the system is doing. The internal electrics are *not* a part of the user interface. The colours and lights on the control panel *are* a part and so on. The division is clear because the user interface is largely concerned with the physical aspects of the user, and it is put together out of quite distinct chunks of hardware. With computers there is a much greater mental component to the user interface. We are no longer just dealing with buttons for fingers to press but with pictures, information, structures and models that have to be perceived, understood and manipulated. This makes the exact itemization of the user interface components a bit more tricky. How then can we go about dissecting such a system and trying to build up better and more useful models and ideas of its parts? To start with it is possible to break an interactive computer system down in terms of hardware and software and also in terms of parts of the system that the user interacts with and parts that are hidden.

10.3.1 Hardware you can't see

There is a large amount of hardware in the computer that the user, the software designer and the user interface designer never have any contact with at all. This is the 'guts' of the computer – all the circuit boards and chips inside it. Sometimes this hardware is housed in a system box on or under your desk, sometimes there is even more in some remote central room linked to your desktop computer by data communication cables.

From a user interface designer's point of view the exact nature and behaviour of all this is not important. Just as the ergonomic designer of the controls on a hi-fi does not need to know how every electrical component works, so too the computer–user interface designer does not need to know everything about the circuits inside the computer. However, they do have to know *something* about the system. They have to know what the system does and what aspects of it can be accessed and controlled by the user. Once again it is a question of abstraction. The user interface designer has to have some sort of an abstract model of the system – not a comprehensive model of everything but a model of the pertinent features.

10.3.2 Hardware you can see

In order for the user to be able to interact with the computer and its software there must be some aspects of the hardware with which the user *can* interact; these form channels enabling the user to access the software and the system to communicate information to the user. These elements of the hardware include all the interactive input and output devices: the keyboard, the mouse, the screen, the speaker and, more recently, the microphone and the video camera.

With the hardware you can't see we could treat the system either in terms of the underlying hardware, or as an abstract model of what is going on. From the user interface designer's point of view only the latter is necessary. When it comes to hardware you can see there are three ways of regarding what is happening:

◆ **The underlying internal hardware**
   Just as before what is really going on inside the device in terms of electronics and circuits is not important.

◆ **The interface aspects of the hardware**
   The user interface aspects of the device are important. This includes such things as the clarity and readability of screens, the behaviour and feel of keyboards and the sensitivity of the mouse and how many buttons it has.

◆ **The abstract model of the hardware**
   Since the devices are a part of the overall computer system and the only channels of interaction that the system has with the user, an abstract model of them plays a big role in the design of the more conceptual software aspects of the system. The user interface designer needs to know what sort of abstract information the user can communicate to the system and what sort of feedback and communication can be given to the user by the system.

Thus when designing a user interface for a computer system that employs an optical mouse with two buttons on it I don't need to know that it uses infra-red light or anything like that, but I do need to know that by moving it I can alter two variables (the X and Y positions) and that it can only supply relative change information for these two variables (I shall deal with relative pointers in Section 15.2 [p 238–239]). Similarly I don't need to know how the buttons work or the exact nature of the electrical signals sent to the system, but I do need to know that I can communicate press and release signals from the buttons to the system.

10.3.3 Program parts you can't see

The program parts that you can't see cover a wide range of involved tasks which most users are unaware of. These relate to things like the representation of complex data structures in the computer's memory, shifting information to and from disk and handling the low-level information that the user generates with the keyboard and the mouse.

Although some of these topics sound basic and simple, the computer has to deal with them in a way that ensures such factors as security, data integrity, speed, optimal performance, reliability and efficiency. This leads to very complex disciplines well beyond the scope of the user interface. From the user interface designer's point of view you do not really need to know anything about this area, abstract or otherwise.

10.3.4 Program parts you can see

This is the most important area for the user interface designer. The program parts you can see cover the many non-physical aspects of the system which the user is aware of and interacts with. This includes all the abstract factors concerned with presentation of structures, the abstract nature of the underlying models and structures being presented, the tools for interacting with and visualizing the information and so on. You do not really need to know too much about the 'nitty-gritty' of programming things like this, but an abstract higher-level appreciation of the structuring of information is useful. Once again it is a case of knowing what is possible and what is not possible.

10.4 Why computers are different

The introduction of computer technology into the realm of interactive systems brings with it a number of quite radical changes in the underlying nature of the system the user interface is being designed for. These changes will be dealt with below.

10.4.1 Switching from physical to mental

Up to now I have made several references to physical ergonomics, that is designing the physical aspects of a system to fit in with those of a human. I have also talked about mental ergonomics, designing the more conceptual aspects of a system (the behaviour, underlying ideas and so on) to fit in with the expectations of the user. Computer–user interfaces have elements of both of these in their design. Physical ergonomics plays a part in the design of the hardware aspects of the interface identified above. Mental ergonomics plays a much greater part, dealing as it does with the design of the on-screen controls and devices (scroll bars, windows, menus and the like). This is a similar situation to the design of more complex non-computer devices (videos, telephones, lift systems).

However, because of the complex, configurable and general nature of computer systems the emphasis is shifted much more on to mental ergonomics in the design of the system. In addition, computer systems extend the idea of mental ergonomics even further. Up until now mental ergonomics has been concerned with the way users perceive the behaviour and the workings of a system. With the introduction of computers it is now starting to include issues concerned with the way that users carry out more complex organizational aspects of their work. Suddenly the science of industrial design, previously concerned with precise measurements of the physical, has become fluid and imprecise. It is now concerned with the design of system behaviour and the aesthetic appeal of on-screen aspects of the system, finding itself in a nebulous area where the measurement and evaluation of the immeasurable and the analysis of the unanalysable must be attempted. How do people think, design, solve problems, plan, work and in general live their lives?

The nearest parallel to this new area of design for use is architecture. An architect designs spaces and environments for people to live and work in, but how do people live and work? What are the key factors and how can they be measured and given a value? Whereas architecture has been around for a few thousand years, computer–user interface design is only a decade or so old and everybody is trying to produce a definitive model of what is going on. The basic goals of user interface design in these two distinct areas are the same. What is different is the way of satisfying these goals.

10.4.2 Application complexity

Another difference between interactive devices and the computer is the complexity of the underlying application that the system concerns itself with and the complexity of the operations associated with the application.

Conventional interactive devices have various physical limits upon their complexity, but because of their extremely general and flexible nature the complexity of computer systems is less dependent upon physical hardware. The complexity of a computer system does not exist in the rows of switches or banks of electronic components but in the patterns and structures in the information it stores. At present the technology supporting this storage of information is running far ahead of the applications using it, and the future will see even greater increases in the complexity of applications.

10.4.3 User interface complexity

This effect of the general and flexible nature of computers also makes itself felt at the computer–user interface. In hardware interfaces an important factor governing the number of controls available to the user is the cost of adding buttons and other controls to the interface. Buttons cost money and are included only if there is a good argument (usually a good marketing argument) for doing so. This has also been mentioned when I was talking about making controls multifunctional (Section 8.4 [p 128]).

With computer–user interfaces the situation is different; the controls are all constructed by configuring the highly general and flexible 'interaction surface' which the computer provides – the screen, the keyboard and the mouse. The cost of adding on-screen buttons is no longer the cost of adding extra hardware, as that hardware, the screen, mouse and keyboard, is there to begin with. Instead the cost of *programming* the button, the extra time and effort involved becomes important. This cost is dropping rapidly with the advent of more efficient ways of user interface programming, such as specialized toolkits and user interface management systems. The result is that software packages can offer 'buttons for everything'. This gives the user a great deal of control and choice but is of no real advantage if the offered functionality is not what the user really wants or is too large and unstructured and hence complicated. Thus a different approach is needed to keep the number of controls down – a different goal. Once again we have come up against the switch in importance from the physical to the mental that computer–user interface design brings. The governing factor for the number of controls available to the user is now the goal of keeping the user interface comprehensible and manageable.

10.4.4 Resource management

Often texts dealing with the computer–user interface mention a bandwidth problem. They claim (just as I did earlier) that many of the problems at the interface come through a bottleneck (a restriction) in the communication between the user and the computer system. However, although this bandwidth problem *does* exist there is another related problem, namely that there is a shortfall in realizing the possibilities of the bandwidth that *is* available: a shortfall in putting the structures, intelligence, filtering and organization behind the bandwidth already available at the interface.

10.4.5 Reliance upon abstract feedback

As with many high-tech devices the computer depends almost entirely upon abstract feedback. There is some real feedback connected with the input hardware, the keyboard and the mouse, but this is at a very low level and is simply feedback concerning tasks such as pressing buttons and moving the mouse. The very strength of the computer – its generality and configurability – has resulted in an almost complete lack of fixed physical components or controls and thus almost no real feedback. This means that we come up against the problems associated with abstract feedback identified in Section 7.3.2 [p 104]. It also means that all the feedback available to the user regarding the applications, every single bit of information they receive, must be explicitly designed and implemented.

It is interesting to note here that in some situations experienced computer users rely upon the only real feedback that the system provides them with, namely the whirring of the hard disk drive within the machine. By listening to this they can at least ascertain something about what the computer really is doing in the absence of good abstract feedback.

10.4.6 Sensory deprivation

Staying with the subject of feedback, one of the most important things about computer–user interface design is the pronounced lack of feedback in today's systems. Current systems may seem rich in feedback when they are compared with the systems of five or ten years ago but when you compare them to carrying out tasks in a real-life environment, the paucity of feedback is incredible. This lack is only now starting to be acknowledged and addressed.

In the real world humans experience feedback through all five sensory channels, and the feedback received through each channel is both rich and full. As I pointed out in Section 7.4 [p 106] the feedback supplied by interactive devices is currently limited to the audio, visual and tactile channels. In computers these restrictions are further compounded by two other factors. Firstly, there is, as yet, no way of providing the user with configurable tactile feedback. As a result sophisticated use of the tactile channel is almost ruled out. Secondly, the audio capabilities of the computer are only now beginning to be realized. This means that almost all of the feedback communicated to the user is confined to the visual channel alone. To illustrate this imagine using a normal computer with your ears blocked up and with a static keyboard (one that is touch sensitive and has no moving parts). It is not too difficult, you can see where you are and what is going on. Now try the converse, close your eyes and try using the computer relying only on touch and sound. It is impossible. As a contrast imagine the same experiment with a task in the real world, like tying your shoelaces or pouring a bowl of breakfast cereal. It is difficult, but not impossible.

10.4.7 The resulting environment

So, to conclude from the above overview, the user interface designer must provide all the feedback required for large and complex applications making use of a limited-bandwidth channel for the feedback, at the same time trying to keep the interaction simple, manageable and comprehensible. However, it's not all bad news; to their advantage they do have a highly flexible and configurable 'surface' upon which to work. In the following chapters I will mention one or two other advantages and disadvantages that computers bring into the field.

10.5 Feedback channels

Let us now take a more detailed look at how the introduction of computer technology affects the use of the three main feedback channels I identified in Chapter 7: visual, audio and tactile.

10.5.1 Visual

Visual feedback is the main channel in interactive computer systems and the screen is the main target for it. The only other visual feedback consists of warning lights on the keyboard. Initial screen-based feedback was constrained to text, but hardware advances mean that the screen is now highly configurable. It is a feedback surface which can be manipulated and transformed to give almost any form of visual feedback imaginable. Small circles that change colour from black to red just like LEDs. Small blocks that can be moved up and down in rectangular channels like sliders or lines that rotate within circles like conventional dials. On top of this imitation of real-world feedback possibilities there is a host of new on-screen feedback devices which are only possible in this virtual graphic world of the computer: images, animation, colour and cartoons. However, in order to realize the potential of such a highly configurable communication channel the designer of the feedback needs access to high-power, high-level tools to support the work. The subject of feedback and the visual channel is an important one in computer systems and I shall be covering it further in the following chapters.

10.5.2 Audio

Use of the audio feedback channel is evolving in a similar way to the graphic channel although it remains several steps behind. Initially audio feedback was constrained to simple beeps of different length. Currently it too is starting to become a highly configurable resource capable of providing any form of audio feedback imaginable: recorded sounds, voice messages and artificially generated noises. However, it also follows graphics in that there is a resource management problem. There is a distinct lack of high-level tools to make fast and effective use of the resource when designing user interfaces.

10.5.3 Tactile

Tactile feedback is the least-used channel in computer–user interfaces. There is some tactile feedback inherent in the hardware aspects of the user interface, namely pressing the keys and the mouse buttons, but that is almost as far as it goes. However, it is technically possible to provide highly configurable tactile feedback in the same way as with the other two channels. Tactile devices are already available to assist blind computer users with the task of reading text from the screen. The user has an electronically controlled pin-bed linked to the computer. This pin-bed converts the dark and light patterns on the screen into patterns of raised and lowered pins. The user is then able to feel and interpret the text being shown on the screen.

10.5.4 Bounded channels

The main difference between the above forms of feedback is that one is passive and the others active. Audio feedback is passive; usually you just sit and listen to things. Tactile feedback, and to a lesser extent visual feedback, are active; you move your hands about over something to feel it or you move your head around to get a better idea of how something looks.

Up until now in the active feedback domain the computer has simply set up a complete visual or tactile environment and then let the user explore it (the screen or the pin-bed). However, with advances in the user interface hardware and the processing power of computers a new approach is being developed. Rather than providing an entire environment the idea is to supply directed feedback as the user explores the environment. Visually this takes the form of the virtual reality headset being developed by research groups like that at NASA. Two small television screens are mounted in front of the eyes and the computer shows views of a three-dimensional model on them. As the user moves and rotates her head the computer detects this and alters the views on the television screens. Thus, with a computer-based three-dimensional model, the user is able to look up, down, left and right and as she explores the environment in this way she is given the appropriate visual feedback.

Similarly with the tactile feedback channel it is possible to install a small pin-bed in the top of a mouse linked up to the computer and have it react according to the pattern on the screen at the position of the cursor. Different surfaces could then have different textures, window edges could be perceived by touch and there could be on-screen buttons which not only looked as though they were projecting from the background but also felt like it too.

Although audio feedback is less directed and more passive, it is possible to constrain it to be directed in a similar manner. As the cursor is moved about the screen, sound fragments can be triggered according to the object that the cursor is moving across.

10.5.5 Feedback-related problems

The lack of feedback I have referred to earlier causes many problems in the design and understanding of computer–user interfaces. It also plays an important part in some of the other problems perceived in the interaction of humans and computers. One of these is the so-called 'mode problem'. Once the user has selected 'delete' from a menu and deleted a few items she is in the situation of having finished what she set out to do and yet the system is still set up for deleting things. If the user now pauses or is distracted she can easily forget that the system is still ready to delete things. The system is said to be in 'delete mode' and will remain so until the user selects another option (tool) from the menu (toolbox) whereupon it will be in a new mode. Awareness of the environment plays a large part in many human operations. Mode problems arise from not being aware of the mode that you are in. We do not have mode problems in real life because we have plenty of environmental feedback. When I use a hammer in the real world I can hear that it is a hammer, I can see that it is a hammer and I can feel that it is a hammer. When I use a computer and put it in delete mode (in effect selecting the delete tool from the menu) I do not feel or hear any difference and the only difference I see is a slight change in the pattern of the cursor.

Sometimes in the real world there are experiences of frustration connected with modes, but they are usually associated with wanting to be in a different mode (using a different tool) and realizing that there is some work involved in getting to that mode: 'Drat! Here I am up this ladder with a screwdriver and I need the hammer that's down there.' We hardly ever experience frustrations due to making mistakes about which mode we are in (which tool we are using).

There are no inherent problems with modes. They are only bad if the user is not aware of being in a mode. There is thus a case here for making much richer feedback available to the user about which mode they are in.

10.6 A design framework

Because of the complex nature of computer–user interface design the following, more computer-oriented, chapters will be arranged within a more rigorous framework than the earlier chapters. This will help put the information into context and show which chapters address which areas. As well as helping with the structuring of information about the user interface such a framework can also help with the design of a user interface. A useful framework is like a good map; although it cannot tell you what to do next, it can tell you where you are now. In the field of user interface design, knowing where you are gives you an idea of the tools and techniques available to help you with the problems you may come up against.

Useful frameworks in this field usually revolve around layered models of one sort or another. The layers start off with the fundamental and abstract aspects of the design of the user interface and work their way up to the more practical and concrete aspects. Several frameworks of this kind have already been proposed. The earlier ones were designed primarily to be applicable to text-based interfaces, but some of the later models may also be applied to the more recent trends of direct manipulation and graphic environments. The framework I am going to use here consists of four layers: the task layer, the semantics layer, the syntax layer and the presentation layer. Below I shall show where the different chapters of this book fit into this model.

The task layer

This, the most fundamental layer of the four, concerns itself with the analysis of the user's underlying goals and intentions in using the interactive system. It also touches on understanding what the user is trying to do when approaching complex processes such as designing and working in groups. The relevant subjects in the book are some understanding of what design is about (Chapter 2) and tasks and goals (Chapter 11).

The semantic layer

This layer includes aspects of the system such as the concepts, objects and models within the interactive system. These are the foundation building blocks upon which the design of the interface is based.

The semantic layer ties together a large portion of the material in the book. Topics include user models in general (Chapter 6), the structures and models underlying the system (Chapter 12), the basic interaction styles (Chapter 13) and sections of the chapter on designing user models (Chapter 14).

The syntactic layer

This layer deals with how the underlying ideas and concepts are made perceivable and comprehensible to the user. There is also an abstract consideration of how the user interacts with the underlying concepts and models. Relevant chapters cover interactive systems (Chapter 3), the more complex side of presentation (Chapter 5) and several areas that overlap with the adjacent layers: designing user models (Chapter 14) and both the chapters on controls (Chapter 8 and Chapter 15).

The presentation layer

Finally we come to the layer at the surface. All the issues surrounding the basic elements of the interaction find a place here: how things look on screen, the more practical side of interaction and the device-oriented aspects of interaction. In terms of this book the material includes: the basics of abstraction and presentation (Chapter 4), some of the sections on more advanced presentation (Chapter 5), the chapters on controls (Chapter 8 and Chapter 15) and the chapter on user interface graphics (Chapter 16).

10.7 Summary

In this chapter I eased computers into the picture, starting off by looking at the elements of computer science that play a part in user interface design. While talking about this I mentioned the decoupling that takes place with technical disciplines between the design of the interface and of the internal functionality. I then moved on to look at the fundamental differences that computer technology brings to user interface design. Then, after taking another look at feedback channels, I outlined a four-layer-based framework to help organize the following chapters.

10.8 Exercises

10.8.1 Hands-on appreciation

Any description of interactive computer systems can appear somewhat dry and abstract. It is therefore a good idea to complement it with a bit of hands-on appreciation of interactive computers. This helps you to get a good idea from the user's point of view of the sort of things that computers can do and, just as importantly, the sort of things that they *can't* do. So have a go at using computers, watch others use them and talk to people who use them. They are not just confined to high-tech companies and research establishments. Much of the time they come disguised within non-computer technology. There are many people who will reply, 'No', when asked, 'Have you used a computer?' but who will reply, 'Yes', when asked, 'Have you used a word processor?' Try and get your hands on the following, either in everyday work or by getting demonstrations in shops or trade fairs:

- ◆ Public library information systems
- ◆ Computer arcade games
- ◆ Spreadsheets

◆ Word processors

◆ Accounting systems

◆ Stocktaking systems

◆ Desktop publishing packages

◆ Cash points

◆ Electronic diaries

◆ Advanced photocopiers

◆ Drawing programs

◆ PCs

◆ Midi systems

◆ Laptops

◆ Palmtops

◆ Apple Macintoshes

◆ Advanced calculators

10.8.2 Feedback in films

With many modern thrillers and science-fiction films, technology plays some part and so too does feedback. Think about the following scenes from films and comment on them in terms of feedback and user models. Can you think of any other good examples?

◆ *The China Syndrome*
The near disaster when the nuclear reactor overheats and is just saved.

◆ *Ice Station Zebra*
The sabotaging of the torpedo tubes to try and sink the submarine.

◆ *Blade Runner*
The voice-driven interface to the image analyser.

◆   ***The Sting***

The two confidence tricks: the first, simple one with the wad of money wrapped in the hanky and the later one with the fake betting shop.

10.9 Mode problems

Very often when working with computers, you find yourself performing a task thinking that you are in one mode when in fact you are in another.

Consider the following. I am using a computer drawing program. I select 'line mode' from the menu. With this particular system this means that when I point at the picture with the cursor and click the mouse buttons I draw lines. I can go on doing this until I select another mode from the menu. So, the system is in 'line mode' and I draw lots of lines. Then I select 'delete mode' and delete one of them. I study the drawing for a while, forget that I've changed to delete mode and think that I'm still in line mode. I try and draw another line. I think I'm pointing at the picture and saying, 'Start drawing a line here.' In fact I'm pointing at the picture and saying, 'Delete the thing I'm pointing at.' This is a mode problem.

This sort of mistake is very easily made when working with computers but very rarely in real life – except of course in Broadoaks Manor.

Barker and Hemelsworth have just come back from an auction. They both enter the drawing room, Barker carrying an ornate vase and Hemelsworth a large, flat package.

Hemelsworth: Phew! Right. Barker, could you hammer a nail in for that new picture we've acquired, and then dust down the new vase?

Barker: Certainly, sir.

Barker leaves the room. There is a pause. The sound of a nail being hammered in. Another pause, then a loud crash. Barker enters looking slightly flustered.

Hemelsworth: What on earth have you done, Barker?

Barker: Well sir, it's on account of what is known in the butlering trade as a 'mode problem'. I got everything ready. I got a hammer to bang the nail in and a duster to dust the vase. Anyway, I selected the hammer, thus putting me in hammer mode, and banged the nail in.

Hemelsworth: And the vase?

Barker: Well, after I had hammered the nail in, I went over to the vase and I thought I was in duster mode but I hadn't selected the duster so I was still in hammer mode. Anyway, I didn't realize until I tried to dust it and I, err, smashed it to bits.

Hemelsworth: I'm sorry, Barker, but I don't believe a word of it.

Chapter 11

Tasks and goals

11.1 User interfaces and tasks

User interface design is about assisting the user with her task. In the world of non-computer devices this does not present too many problems. The user is usually concerned with some quite simple and obvious task. When using a lift system the user is trying to get to a different floor, or with a bank of light switches she is trying to switch certain lights on or off. However, all these things are usually just subtasks of some larger task in the real world. If I want to use the lift to go to floor seven this could just be a subtask of the need to see someone to discuss something. The higher-level task is set in the real world and is beyond the scope of the system. It is not the concern of the lift system to offer other ways of getting in touch with someone on the seventh floor. With computers the matter is more complex; because of their incredible generality and flexibility they can become involved in assisting with tasks at all levels. Thus a user of a CAD system may want to draw a line from A to B and the computer can give support for the task, but at the same time the drawing of that line is merely a small part of moving a window frame in the plan to another wall, and that is a small part of the whole act of designing and planning a house. All the tasks are contained within the computer system and it is possible for the system to give assistance at all the intermediate levels as well as at the lowest level.

The introduction of computers and complex and comprehensive CAD systems means that the study and understanding of tasks and goals plays a much greater part in user interface design than it ever has done before.

11.1.1 What is a task?

Let me begin by trying to define what a task is. A task is set of actions in the real world whose performance is aimed towards some goal. And a goal is the desired state of the system you are working on or with. Different areas of work have different models of what a goal state is. In some disciplines it is easy to know how near you are to the goal state and when you have achieved it. In other areas the goal state is not actually known at the outset of the task and it shifts throughout the task as new factors and ideas come into play. The task is carried out until eventually the current state is deemed to be satisfactory. This continual shift in the goal state is a particular feature of working in design-oriented areas.

11.1.2 Supporting tasks

When dealing with the majority of interactive systems we can see that they are designed to support the user in carrying out some task, be it getting a cup of coffee, photocopying a letter, using a computer network to send information to another country or designing a new theatre.

So, as designers of interactive computer systems we know what a task is and we know we must support it, but how is it done? There are two approaches to task support, namely:

♦ Supporting the external subtasks

♦ Supporting an underlying model of the task

Supporting the external subtasks involves little concern for the abstract analysis of the task; it is more concerned with supporting the externally observable things that people do in the real world when carrying out that sort of task. Thus we can give a sort of 'intelligent notebook' support, helping the user manipulate things externally without actually getting too deeply involved with what is being manipulated.

Supporting an underlying model of the task, on the other hand, involves trying to understand what is going on: trying to build up a rigorous model of what the person is doing and how they are thinking. An interactive system can then be designed to support the model.

The goal seems to be to devise a model that describes as accurately as possible the user's existing approach to the task. The closer the model is to the user's real approach, the more it will 'mesh in' with what the user is doing and the more the user will be inclined to use it. Many task support systems fail because they are based upon models that are far removed from the way the users really approach the task. The users try and adapt to the new way of working but end up slipping back into their old methods; thus they use the system less and less.

The difference between the two approaches depends to a great extent on the nature of the task. Some tasks are almost completely composed of external subtasks. In these cases supporting the external subtasks will go a very long way towards supporting the underlying model of the task. In contrast to this, some tasks are very 'internal'; so much goes on in the mind of the person that little or nothing can be classified as 'an external subtask'. This makes building up an accurate model of the task very difficult indeed and support for such tasks has to be based upon supporting some model of them.

In the latter case there is a difference if the same task is being performed by a group of people rather than one single person. A group working upon a task tends to 'externalize' many of the subtasks which were previously 'internal'. The interactions and communications within the group about the underlying task make many elements of the task external.

11.1.3 Natural and artificial tasks

It is possible to break down the tasks in the real world into natural tasks and artificial tasks. Natural tasks are those tasks which form an integral part of what it is to be human. They are things such as communication, group work, design, art and decision making. They are characterized by being very human, very hard to model and thus very difficult to support. (Remember the problems of bringing people in as a factor in the design process in Section 2.3 [p 18]?). Artificial tasks are less human, more mechanical and more contrived. They are linked to human creations: accounting, arithmetic, stocktaking, administration and project planning.

As I said earlier, support for the artificial tasks can be given by supporting the external subtasks since the task is so external. Computer systems abound for helping with these sorts of tasks, but when it comes to support for the natural tasks we are still in the realms of research: computer-supported cooperative work, design modelling, decision-support systems and so on. The few attempts at building systems to provide support for natural tasks have met with little success. If you consider the area of CASE (computer-aided software engineering), which is concerned with computer systems to help groups of designers and programmers build large and complex programs, you find it is riddled with systems based on badly thought out models: models that miss out the important things and interactive systems that impose too many trivial tasks upon the users.

Design and task modelling

Although giving structure to the fringe activities is useful, it does not help in addressing or trying to model the underlying process. Current models of the design process are sketchy and the effect of computers in this area will not be known until it becomes easier not only to use computers in the design process, but also to experiment with new ways of using them. This will come about with improvements in the existing technology and a better understanding of the factors that affect user interface design.

CAD and the design process

The idea behind CAD is that the computer provides assistance to the user in carrying out some design task. The word 'computer' does not necessarily have to mean a Macintosh or a PC or whatever, it could be taken to mean any system of rules or anything else that offers even a small amount of assistance to the user in making decisions when designing something. The treatment of CAD systems is important since many interactive computer systems are involved in supporting the user in the design of a structure.

Some of you may be familiar with the CAD systems used to help design buildings, electronic circuit boards or office layout. In fact CAD is not only used for the design of spatial structures like these. There are many other systems that help the user to design and build up other structures such as word processors, desktop publishing systems, project management support systems.

In actual fact the majority of CAD is not really CAD at all. It is not computer aided *design*. The CAD systems in most architectural practices are used only for producing the final drawings to take to the planning meeting or to the client presentation. When architects do the *real* design work they sit around a table with pens, lots of paper and coffee. Similarly, the word processors used by most people to write documents give assistance in typing in and printing out the final draft. When I write the text for a chapter of this book I do indeed use a computer and a word processor, but when I do design work, when I design the structure of a chapter, draw up an outline of the contents and map out the text, I usually sit at a table with a pen, lots of paper and a cup of coffee. And it is the same for programmers designing software or graphic artists designing animated computer graphics sequences – it's pens, paper and coffee. Most of today's CAD systems function as computer-aided *communication* systems; they just give the user assistance in *expressing* an idea in a particular medium. What they do not offer is support in *having* the idea in the first place and then developing it into its final form.

11.1.4 Task analysis and modelling

Concentrating now on the underlying model of the task, I shall have a look at task analysis. This is usually taken to mean task analysis in the context of an office environment, with the aim of improving the efficiency of the administrative procedures going on there. I shall look at task analysis in a more general sense. Task analysis is abstraction again: I consider a task in the real world and I build up an abstract model of it by abstracting those features of the real world task I consider to be important and necessary. (See Figure 11.2.) From now on I shall simplify these diagrams by omitting the block with a hole in it. As with any abstraction process the question of what features to abstract depends upon the priorities and background of the person doing the abstracting. We have something akin to the value systems encountered in Section 2.2.4 [p 17], although in this area there are far fewer possible variations.

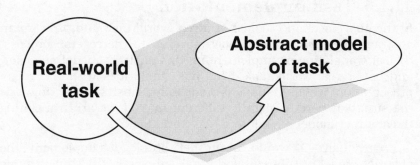

Figure 11.1 The abstract model of a task.

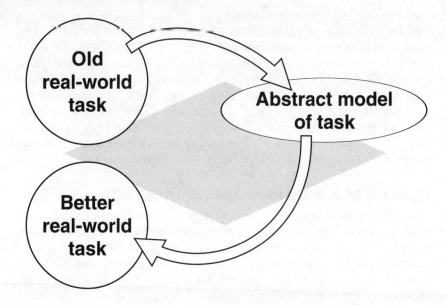

Figure 11.2 Implementing a task.

As an example consider someone filling in a tax claim form. The person carrying out the real-world task must fill in their tax status on the form and they happen to do so with a green plastic pen taken out of a drawer. If I were analysing this task and building up an abstract model, the important things I would abstract would be that the tax status of the person was required by the tax office. The manner in which it was acquired is not important, and even less important is the fact that the person filled it in with a green plastic pen.

11.1.5 Task implementation

In the above section I looked at a real-world task and built up an abstract model of it. I can now move on to the reverse process, that of translating or implementing this abstract model as a new and better real-world task. This has similarities with the act of presentation which usually accompanies abstraction. However, the situation here is slightly different in that we are translating the abstract model back into a real-world task.

Obviously, it would be rather stupid to implement the abstract model of the real-world task in exactly the same way as the original. Instead, it should be implemented in a different (and hopefully better) way. This could be done either through the use of existing tools and technologies or by using new tools and technologies. (See Figure 11.2.)

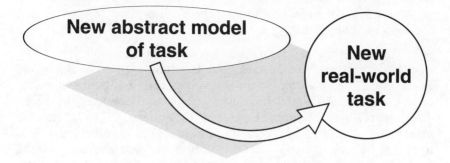

Figure 11.3   Creating a new abstract task.

Returning to the tax form example above, I could build up an abstract model of the task in which one subtask is finding out the applicant's tax status. This could then be implemented in some other manner than the applicant filling it in herself.

11.1.6 New task design

The question of new tools and technologies is an interesting one because it is also possible to have situations where the first part of the process is skipped over. Instead of building up an abstract model of an existing real-world task, the new tools and technologies themselves can suggest completely new abstract tasks which they can then be used to implement. (See Figure 11.3). This is especially true of computer technology. We shall see examples of this in the following chapters. (For example, the in-situ zoom idea in Section 16.3.6 [p 263].)

11.2 Tasks and goals

Any act of task analysis and building up abstract models of tasks involves a great deal of thinking and questioning regarding the nature and, in particular, the goals of the task.

The abstract models of tasks can be at differing levels of abstraction. The more abstract they are, the more they cut away the unimportant facets to leave just the bare essentials of what the task is about. The end of such a cutting-away process is to be left with just the goal of the task. That is the task in its most abstract form. That is the important thing. How the goal is achieved is immaterial and can be designed and redesigned. It is possible to go beyond this stage, to question not only the process used to achieve the goal but also the goal itself. This then brings us into the area of goal trees.

The question of tasks and goals is not a simple one. Very rarely is everything neatly packaged as a task with an obvious goal at the end. The situation usually involves the task being made up of many subtasks with their own subgoals. For example, I was once searching for my illustrated dictionary to look up the annotated picture of a bicycle. As I did so I kept becoming involved in the subtasks, things such as finding my flatmate and asking him if he had seen the book, or looking in the bookcase to see if it was there.

The breakdown of goals and tasks into subgoals and subtasks is quite obvious in this direction. Things get more interesting when we consider that the breakdown happens in the other direction as well. Any task is itself a subtask of a more fundamental high-level task with a more fundamental high-level goal. Let us return to my example of the dictionary. After I had spent a short time searching for it, I realized that my goal was not to find the dictionary, that was only a subgoal. My goal was in fact to find an annotated picture of a bicycle. By choosing a different subgoal, namely, to find my copy of Richard's bicycle book, I was able to carry on much more efficiently since I knew where that book was. I had effectively stepped up the tree to a more fundamental high-level goal and then stepped down the tree in a different direction, moving now in a new and different way of achieving the same underlying goal. It helps to imagine the 'tree' as looking like a family tree with the high-level goals at the top and the low-level goals at the bottom. (See Figure 11.4.)

This working up the tree is useful, but if carried too far we eventually find ourselves in the realm of difficult philosophical issues, the fundamental 'whys' of existence. Finding the bicycle book is a subgoal of finding an annotated picture of a bicycle which is a subgoal of finding out the name for a particular part of a bicycle. This, in turn, is a subgoal of going to a shop to order the part. This action is a subgoal of having a working bicycle, which is a subgoal of visiting friends and so on.

The decomposition of a goal into subgoals is based upon assumptions about the underlying goal and upon the way in which the underlying goal is tackled. What this means is that abstract task models can be restructured by working up the goal tree and considering different ways of decomposing the goal, just as I demonstrated with the dictionary problem.

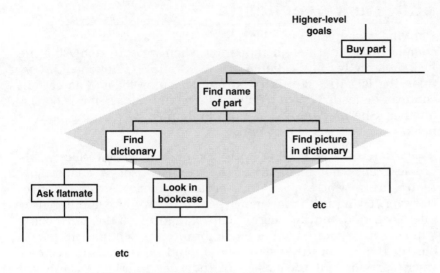

Figure 11.4 A goal tree.

As I pointed out before, moving up such a goal tree eventually involves philosophical issues and when this exercise is being performed in order to redesign a task, the person doing the redesigning has to set some sort of cut-off point. Some compromise between finding a different and novel solution and not going beyond the realistic scope of the redesign task must be made.

If we consider the tax form again, we could step up the goal tree and say that filling in the tax status is a subgoal of the tax office knowing that information in this particular context. We could then choose a different route down the tree and say that they could get that information by cross-referencing the name or employment number in some other records. Alternatively, we could say that tax status is a subgoal of levelling the correct tax against that individual and charging the tax is a subgoal of setting up state projects. Another possible manner of setting up such projects is to have them run by the people for the people (instead of by the state) and a subgoal of this is a vast social reform along more equitable lines. Which, although it may be an honourable goal, does involve going rather too far up the goal tree for the particular context we were given.

11.3 Task overheads

Carrying out tasks in the real world always involves more complications that may be apparent when we start analysing the task abstractly. In Section 9.1.1 [p 136–137] I touched briefly upon the fact that the user you are designing for may in certain contexts be loaded down by physical encumbrances of one sort or another. She may have soapy or oily hands, be carrying piles of books or have thick gloves on.

When one is dealing with computer–user interfaces this problem does not often arise; the average user is comfortably seated at a workstation free of any physical encumbrance. However, owing to the far more mental nature of computer–user interfaces and the far more complex nature of the task being supported, there are mental encumbrances which start to play a part in the use of the system and should be taken into account when carrying out the design of the user interface. These are mental things that the user must remember or guard against. Just like carrying physical baggage when trying to do a physical task, this mental baggage slows the user down, gets in her way and occasionally trips her up!

This mental baggage includes remembering commands and what the contents of a file were, based upon its name, the worry of performing large-scale operations without the help of an undo command, keeping track of windows and icons on a crowded screen, remembering where certain menu options were in large complex menus, and remembering what has been cut while preparing for the paste. There are some people (like me) who experience a feeling of 'holding their breath' when they carry out a large cut and paste within a text editor. There is a feeling that after the 'cut' part of the operation the text is in some sort of unstable limbo until it is safely pasted back into the document. Minimizing the causes of this mental baggage is one of the many ingredients for designing good computer–user interfaces.

11.3.1 Task preparation

Task preparation refers to the work that has to be done in setting up the context within which the task itself will be performed. In terms of the real world this covers things like clearing the table, getting the sewing machine out, sorting out good lighting and so on before starting on the task of sewing. In the world of the computer such physical preparations have no place when interacting with a program, but there are a few examples of informational task preparation and these are mainly concerned with shifting information around, configuring new environments and testing operations on a small scale before doing them on a large scale.

11.3.2 Switching contexts

When dealing with computers, the lack of the physical aspects of the task means that there is less task preparation, as I mentioned above. This is a distinct advantage over task preparation in the physical world. However, physical task preparation does have its advantages. In particular, lots of physical task preparation means that there is much physical context to give feedback to the user. If I am sewing and I stop for lunch, then when I return I can immediately see exactly what I was doing when I stopped. All the information about the state of the task is presented in various physical aspects of the system. It is all there on show and I can quickly resume the task. Contrast this to the situation in the computer world: when I return to my computer after lunch I look at my screen and it sometimes takes me several minutes to work out exactly what I was doing and how far I had got with it. I have not had to set so much up, and any setting up I did do has no visual component. Usually all I can see each time is some text and a cursor and that's it! Thus, when designing computer–user interfaces, we don't just need rich feedback during operations to tell the user what she is doing, we also need to design in rich feedback to give a wider picture that tells her what she is in the middle of doing.

11.4 Summary

In this chapter I took an abstract look at the tasks users perform and the goals they are working towards. I looked at the different ways of giving support to such tasks, paying particular attention to artificial tasks, which are more structured and easier to give support to, and natural tasks which are less well defined and more difficult to support.

The next sections dealt with building up abstract models of tasks and re-implementing such abstract models as new real-world tasks. I then discussed the role of goal trees and how considering goals and assumptions about them can help with user interface design.

Finally I talked about some of the overheads that are involved when carrying out tasks on a computer and the effects that they can have upon the interaction.

11.5 Exercises

11.5.1 Answering machines

Some people I know occasionally use their answering machine as a filter if they are at home but are busy or tired. They listen to who is calling to see if it is a vital message or someone they don't mind talking to, otherwise they leave the caller to the machine.

Think about the goal and tasks that are present here. Can you redesign the answering machine to give more support to this particular task. What about redesigning the telephone system to make things better? What extra information would you need?

11.5.2 Extreme goal trees

A quite amusing exercise is to take a problem and to solve it by applying the idea of working up the goal tree, going as far up the goal tree as possible. Try it and see what sort of questions and problems arise. As a problem consider this one: I come home, put my key in the lock and turn it. I haven't put it all the way in and half of it breaks off cleanly in the lock. My partner also has a key, but it won't go in because the lock is blocked with the part of my key. How do we get my piece of key out so that we can put her key in?

11.5.3 Email

A group of computers connected in a network can make use of 'electronic mail', or 'email' as it is usually called. This is a computer-based message-sending system enabling a user to write some   text with the computer and then say, 'Send this message to Steven.' They can also do the reverse and say, 'Show me all the letters that have been sent to me.'

Think about the email system in an abstract way in terms of tasks and goals. What are people trying to use it for? What are their goals when using it? Can a better system be designed by looking at the more underlying goals that the users are trying to achieve? Think about the problem of electronic communication in general and try and formulate what the underlying goals are, or should be. Try coming up with a novel design to satisfy these.

11.5.4 'There's a hole in my bucket'

Find someone who knows the words to the song, 'There's a hole in my bucket'. What is special about the storyline of the song in terms of goal trees and tasks?

11.6 Automatic suggestions

In the section about the system's reactions to errors I mentioned giving helpful suggestions to the user in the event of an unrecognized command. Work is currently being carried out on computer systems to give suggestions to the user in other circumstances: for example, suggesting more efficient ways for the user to perform a task or suggesting a possible completion of that task which the system can carry out automatically. In a drawing program I start drawing a line of circles all the same size. After three of them the system interrupts and says the equivalent of, 'I see that you have drawn three circles in a row. I think you might be drawing many of them in a row. Tell me how many more you want and I shall draw them for you.'

This idea could be very useful, but the difficulties lie in making the system build up *sensible* ideas about what the user is doing: in effect, building up an accurate computer model of the user's task. Current attempts in this direction have led to infuriating systems which continuously interrupt the user with stupid ideas about what they think she is trying to do. Thank goodness it doesn't happen in real life...

We return to Broadoaks Manor. It is a rainy day and so Barker is helping Hemelsworth clear out the study. Barker has just returned from a one-week intensive butlering course entitled; 'Suggesting courses of action: a workshop for the modern butler'.

Hemelsworth: Right, Barker, those golf clubs can go in the garage, and the golfing umbrella as well.

Barker: Sir, are you trying to say that we should move *all* the golfing things into the garage?

Hemelsworth: Yes, that's right! First of all though let's get rid of some of the rubbish in front of them. Throw out this old set of manuscripts, and throw out this pile of magazines and then throw out this bit of paper.

Barker: Sir, are you trying to say that you want all the things in this room thrown out?

Hemelsworth: No no no! Just throw out what I've told you to.

Barker leaves with the things and then returns.

Hemelsworth: Right. Now can you stand on that chair and put these two boxes on the top shelf?

Barker: Sir, are you trying to say that you want me to put all boxes on the top shelf?

Hemelsworth: Oh good grief! Never mind, I'll do it myself.

Barker: Are you trying to say that I should let you put all boxes on the top shelf?

Hemelsworth: Look, Barker, just shut up!

Barker: Sir, are you trying to say...

Chapter 12

Computer models

12.1 Introduction

In the last chapter we saw that the study of tasks and goals was of underlying importance when considering and designing for the activities of the user. I shall now examine another important and underlying aspect, but one more concerned with the computer system than the user – computer models.

Computer–user interface design, and many other aspects of computing, are tied up with abstraction, presentation and models. In Chapter 4 I looked at the design of information presentations. One of the first steps there was to build up the abstract model, to decide exactly what things you wanted to show and what things you wanted to leave out. The situation is the same with computer models. Within the computer there are underlying models of certain entities and the user interacts with these to achieve certain goals. The design of these models, the decision of what features to include or leave out, is one of the vital foundations of the design of a wide range of interactive systems. Also, the way the model relates to the real world is important in any consideration of errors made while interacting with it and the interactive tools available to the user. Finally, when dealing with the dimensionality of the computer model, an understanding of the abstract issues involved plays a great part in deciding how the model is to be presented to the user.

12.2 Computer models

When I talked about the construction of a user model I explained that it could be an abstract model of an existing real-world system. Similarly, a computer can have a model of certain aspects of the real world; this is termed a computer model. But, whereas the user builds up the user model herself, based upon observation and previous experience, the computer model must be decided upon and programmed into the computer by the designer of the system. The designer analyses the real world, builds up an abstract model of the important features and then implements this as a computer model within the computer system. (See Figure 12.1.)

For some of the tasks for which a computer is used the collection of things being stored in the computer's memory (the computer model) is not too difficult to understand. A word processor stores the documents you write. It stores the text in a very simple model consisting of a long line of characters and spaces with a beginning and an end. More advanced word processors have more advanced and more comprehensive models of the text being worked upon. They store information about other aspects of the text besides just the characters and spaces, extra information such as font sizes, font styles (this text is in a font called Bookman) and font modifiers (*italics*, **bold** and so on). Move

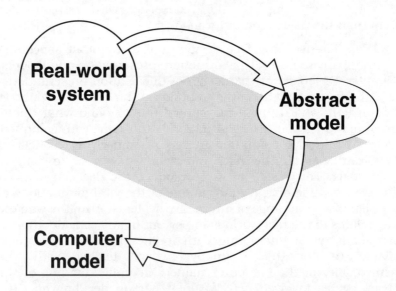

Figure 12.1   Constructing a computer model.

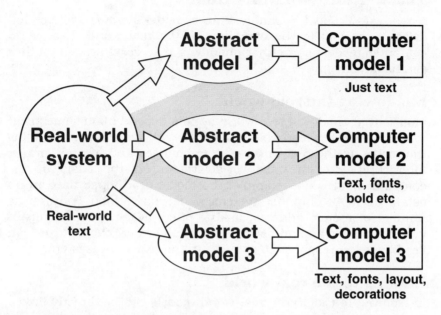

Figure 12.2   Creating different computer models of text.

on to desktop publishing (DTP), and the computer model becomes more detailed still. As well as font details, blocks of text now have attributes governing their layout, their position on the page, how wide the block is, and so on. As well as text block attributes the model can include decorations to the blocks of text such as bounding boxes or separator lines.

In each case the designers of the system are thinking about the sort of text that you come across in the real world and abstracting certain features to build up an abstract model which they then convert into the computer model within the system. (See Figure 12.2.) They will select or reject certain real-world features depending upon what they think is important in the application area they are designing for.

12.2.1 Classifying models

These computer models then are collections of pieces of information with certain constraints and rules governing the relationships between them. There are several abstract classifications of the model that are useful to know about when it comes to the design of the model and how the user will interact with it.

12.2.2 Real-world models

A real-world model is simply that, a model of some system that exists externally to the computer in the real world. Real-world computer models can either shadow a real world system or they can be directly linked to it.

Shadowing the real world

Models that shadow a real-world system depend upon some agent to act as a go-between able to interact with the system, changing the model as the real-world system changes and, if appropriate, interacting with the real-world system on the basis of the computer model. For example, the model of a house used in an estate agent's computer system would have such features as number of rooms, address, asking price, owner, state of repair, year of construction and so on. In such a system the features can be changed in response to changes in the real-world system.

Linking to the real world

In contrast to the above, real-world models can be directly linked to the real-world system they model. Any change in the real-world system is then automatically reflected in the model and, more interestingly, any change in the model is reflected in the real-world system. The agent, or go-between, in this case is the technology. Examples of this include computer control of chemical or industrial plants, computer monitoring and control of railway signal and points or computer-based stage lighting systems.

12.2.3 Internal models

Internal computer models are those having no connection to an existing real-world system. They are not shadowing or linked to anything. A change in the computer model has no effect in the real world and vice versa. (See Figure 12.3.) They are complete in their own right and the user's goal is to interact with them, not to use them as a filter to some real-world system. Strictly speaking this lack of relationship with external things means that in some cases they are not really 'models' any more since they are not modelling anything. However, I shall continue to use the term in order to avoid becoming 'bogged down' in terminology.

Simulations

One important type of internal model that has some connection with the external world is a simulation of a real-world system – for example, a simulation of a game of patience. Here the model is a system that obeys a set of rules and relationships, but it does not

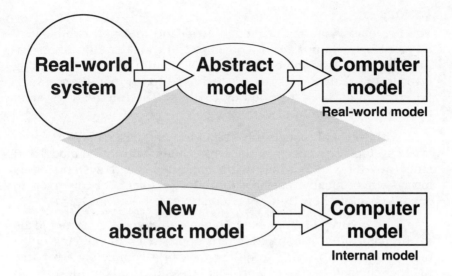

Figure 12.3   Real and internal computer models.

intentionally shadow a real-world system. Thus, in the patience simulation, a card would have features such as value, suit, face up/down, which pile it is in and so on, but there would be no corresponding game of patience taking place in the real world.

12.2.4 Mixed models

There are some cases where the system deals with models that are part real world and part internal. Consider a system for analysing and predicting pollution levels in a certain stretch of the sea. It shadows the real world, building up a real-world model of the concentrations of various pollutants in the water, but there is also a simulation element to it. The users can ask, 'What if?' questions and branch off from the real-world model into an internal simulation of some set of events that has not happened in the real world. 'This is the current state of affairs, but what would the situation be in a week if we had a toxic pipe burst at this point on the coast?'

12.2.5 Interaction

When considering all these different classes of model we should also consider the effects that the different contexts have on the user's interaction with them. In particular, I want to deal with the following three subjects.

Errors

The two classifications of models (real and internal) exhibit very different behaviour when it comes to the consideration of errors. An error when working on a real model results in a corresponding error in the real-world system it is linked to. In many cases such an error could be dangerous or costly so the interactive system must prevent them from happening.

With internal models any errors are not 'passed on' to a real-world system. The effects of the error remain within the model and since anything is possible with computer-based systems, it is always (theoretically) possible to undo the effects of the error, to say, 'Go back to how things were just before I did that.'

This luxury of being able to make and then undo errors leads to the possibility of using different approaches to carrying out a task. Rather than trying to do the task in a completely error-free manner, it may be faster and less stressful to allow the user to make errors and assist her in finding and correcting them at a later stage.

Blocking

With any computer model it is theoretically possible for the user to interact with all aspects of the model's data. However, it is often desirable to allow user interaction only with certain features of the model. In the case of a simulation based upon certain rules, the user is not allowed to transgress those rules. As in the patience example, the user can alter the face-up/face-down attribute of certain cards according to the rules, but she is not allowed to directly edit the values of the cards she is holding in her hand.

Filtering

As I mentioned before, when dealing with an internal model on a computer, anything is possible. You can change things, delete things and undo the things you did. Unfortunately the real world is not usually as forgiving. You cannot argue with entropy or the other laws of physics. If you interact with a computer-controlled chemical plant and it blows up, that's it.

Thus, when interacting with a real-world model linked to a real-world system, some degree of censorship needs to be exercised before passing the user's interactions on to the model and thus on to the real world. The system can be designed so that it incorporates some of the rules and constraints necessary in the real-world system. It can then use these to modify the user's interaction with the real-world model.

Consider controlling the system of variable speed-limit signs mounted at regular intervals on the motorway. Everything is fine, they all show 100 kilometres per hour along the whole length. Then there is an accident. Traffic must be slowed at that point, so the speed limit displayed there must be lowered to 50 kilometres per hour. If the user edits just the speed indicators at that point there will be a sudden jump in the maximum speed being indicated from 100 kilometres per hour on one speed-limit indicator down to 50 kilometres per hour on the next. This will probably lead to more accidents as motorists are forced to slow down quickly. What is needed is a gradual decrease in the limit, displayed on successive indication boards in steps of 10. If the user has to work this out directly and then edit each display, time will be lost and mistakes may be made. The solution is for the system to filter the user's actions into actions that follow a set of safety rules for the particular context before applying them to the model.

12.3 Further classifications

Now that we have considered the nature of computer models in terms of their relationship to the external world, let us consider some of their more inherent aspects. From here onwards I shall use the term 'interactive system' (or just system) to refer to the system being used to interact with the computer model. This interactive system could be a visualization system allowing the user to explore a body of data, or a computer-aided design system allowing her to examine and manipulate the computer model.

Because of the similarities between the concept of the computer model here and 'systems' as used in Chapter 3, It is possible to use the classifications from that chapter to break things down here. We can say that computer models can be static or dynamic, and if they are dynamic they can be interactive or non-interactive.

12.3.1 Dimensionality

As well as the classifications mentioned so far, we can also classify many models in terms of dimensionality. Simple text is one-dimensional in that it is just a long line of characters and spaces. Graphics and text layout are two-dimensional in nature, while applications like architectural design and three-dimensional graphics involve three-dimensional computer models. Areas such as animation or robot simulation involve the extra dimension of time which I shall look at later.

This question of dimensionality is complicated slightly by the difference between what I shall refer to as 'mesh' and 'element' computer models. With mesh models the computer model is composed of a mesh of the appropriate number of dimensions. Each element of this mesh is filled with some value. The on-screen image produced by a computer-painting system is of this type since each element within the two dimensional mesh is filled with a certain value of colour. In element models, the model is composed of discrete elements defined and positioned within an empty space of the appropriate dimensionality. Thus an ordinary two-dimensional diagram is an element model since it is made up of lines, circles and shapes positioned within a two-dimensional space.

When it comes to presenting the model within an interactive system, the presentation is usually screen-based and two-dimensional owing to the limits imposed by the hardware. Thus models of a higher dimensionality must be restricted by this, and it is advantageous for one-dimensional models to be presented in a two-dimensional way to exploit the communication possibilities of the extra dimension. The best example of this is the way text (essentially a one-dimensional model) is 'folded' in the second dimension.

Simple text is, in fact, something of a special case. In some ways it resembles a one-dimensional mesh model since it is a one-dimensional mesh filled with values. Each value represents a particular character and the characters are bound to relative positions within the model. If I delete the letter E, I am not usually left with a gap as all the other characters move in compensation. Contrast this with a list of temperatures measured over a week. If I delete Tuesday's entry I must leave a gap. The value is bound to an absolute position in a one-dimensional model in the case of the temperatures, but to a relative position within the model in the case of the text.

12.3.2 Real and abstract presentation

Most of the above sections describe the nature of the computer model itself. Let me now look at the presentation of the computer models. Once again abstraction and presentation come into the picture; the computer model is an abstract model and we now want to present it to the user. The concepts of real and abstract presentation introduced in Section 7.3 [p 102] play a part here. If the model is presented using a real presentation scheme then what is presented is the real structure. The final result is there on the screen. If I am running a prototype version of an interactive computer program or using a computer-based paint program to do some artwork, then what I have on my screen is the real structure. It is presented in the same medium as the final product of the process will be when I have finished my work on it. In contrast, an abstract presentation uses some sort of symbology to represent the model. Features of the model are presented according to a set of rules and symbols. If I am using a computer to do the drawings for an office block, what I see on the screen is definitely not the real structure: that is, the office block which has yet to be built.

The earlier classification of real-world models has, by its very nature, abstract presentations. The real structure is external to the interactive system and any way of presenting it within that system must be abstract. Internal models, on the other hand, can be presented within the interactive system in a real or an abstract way: that is, presented either how they would look in their finished form or, as above, using abstract symbols and rules.

The question of real and abstract presentation is not a clear-cut choice since abstract presentation can cover a whole range of degrees of abstraction, all the way from obscure symbology through to abstractions that are as close as possible to the real presentation. These later abstractions can be referred to as 'simulations'. They are used in the evaluation of intermediate phases in the construction of the model to get an idea of what the finished product will 'really be like'. Thus, as an example of a real-world model, an architect working on the design of a building and wanting to get an idea of how it looks could generate a coloured and textured, three-dimensional view of it using a CAD system, rather than going out and building a trial version. Similarly with internal models, an artist working on a computer animation could review it by quickly generating a run-through of it in a very simple form using lines and outlines, rather than generating the complete model of what it would look like using colours, textures and so on.

12.3.3 Advantages of abstract presentation

If the interactive system provides real presentations and simulations why should the designer be interested in any abstract presentations of the model? One reason is that this can facilitate manipulation of the model since presentations can be chosen to enhance the user's interaction with it, making certain features easier to see and 'get to grips' with. Another reason is that abstraction gives the system the ability to present only those features that the user is currently interested in, thus maintaining a high degree of clarity in the presentation. The features that are abstracted can either be attributes of model elements that are currently unimportant, or even elements themselves deemed to be unimportant in giving an overall impression of the model.

With the real-world models mentioned earlier, we encountered the use of abstraction to build up a computer model of a real-world system. With abstraction and presentation in interactive systems, what we are building up is an abstract model of the computer model composed of those features we want to present. It is a second level of abstraction within the computer system. The information diagram in Figure 12.4 illustrates this.

12.4 Dynamic models

The leap from static models to the corresponding dynamic model is indeed large. The introduction of the time dimension complicates the review of the model and the design of the user interface for the interactive system. Just consider the gulf that exists between a human body fixed in a certain static pose and the art of choreography, or the difference between setting up a still photograph and organizing a film.

The initial development of interactive and CAD systems began with computer models of static systems – buildings, documents and so on. More recently, interactive systems have

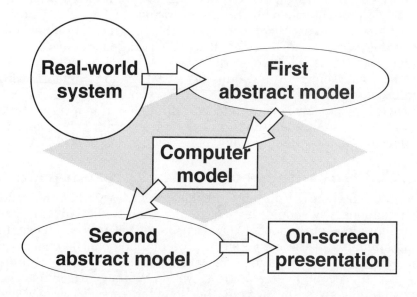

Figure 12.4   A second level of abstraction.

been developed to work with models of dynamic systems such as music processors (for designing pieces of music) and computer animation systems.

The dynamic nature of the models is independent of the other classifications we have met, thus for each of those classifications there is a new one with a dynamic element to it. In addition to the internal and real-world classifications we must now introduce internal dynamic (things like computer animation and computer programs) and real-world dynamic (things like the lighting control script for a theatre production). Similarly, for each of the different dimensionalities mentioned above we can find examples that also have the added dimension of time.

12.4.1 Real and abstract presentation

With dynamic models the distinctions between abstract and real presentation become much more pronounced. Real presentation of the model involves a real-time run-through: for example, running a piece of computer animation or running a program (both internal models). Abstract presentation involves maintaining the dynamic nature of the model and entails simulated run-through. Take for example a computer animation presented using lines and outlines and ignoring small details (a simulation of an internal model) or an animation of a robot arm to test control programs for a real robot arm (a simulation of a real-world model).

12.4.2 Static presentations

It is possible to go further with the abstract presentation and present the dynamic element of the model in some graphic manner resulting in a static presentation. In the lighting control example mentioned above, the intensity of a light is a one-dimensional variable. We can present this as a length and exploit the possibility of two-dimensional presentation by using the second dimension to represent time, producing diagrams like those in Figure 12.5.

Static presentation like this can have advantages over simulations or real run-throughs. Although real presentation is the best way to review a dynamic model, it may not be the best way to build and manipulate it. It is difficult to devise a means of interacting with a run-through of a model and, even if it is possible, the time constraints make it stressful to edit dynamic models in this way. It is, however, feasible to consider creating the initial model by a process of real-time recording. For example, a music processor linked to a keyboard can record a tune played on the keyboard in a structural way (that is, not just a sound

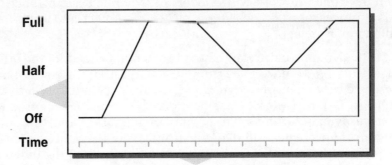

Figure 12.5   Presenting lighting information.

recording but a model containing information about the notes and the timing). This model can then be edited later by means of an abstract presentation.

Another possibility is that of presenting dynamic models textually as a series of event descriptions (a sort of script). This technique lends itself to dynamic models with simple, discrete steps occurring in sequence as in computer programs. It can cause problems when applied to situations where things happen slowly, more continuously and in parallel since constraints arise such as events taking an unknown time to be carried out. Thus it would be fairly easy to choreograph one robot arm, but there might be problems in the choreography of two robot arms acting in unison.

12.5 User models

Remember in Section 6.3.3 [p 94] I talked about how complicated the whole area of user models can become? Well, here's another complication: yet another mental model that plays a part in the whole process. When the user interacts with a system she builds up a mental model of it. When she uses a CAD or visualization system *two* models must be built up. One is the user model mentioned above – the mental model of the interactive system. The other is the model of the computer model or structure being worked on which I shall refer to as the 'structure model'. The 'user model' is the model needed in order to use the system and the 'structure model' is the model of what is being worked on.

Both of these mental models are built up dynamically by the user. They have to be. With the user model the users learn things bit by bit as they interact with the system while the structure model is built up in stages as the underlying computer model is added to or explored. The user model is dynamic and interactive since it is a model of a dynamic and interactive system (the computer system) but the nature of the structure model depends upon the nature of the computer model itself. The structure model is *built up* dynamically as I have mentioned above, but it can still be a model of a static computer model.

The user model is usually built up in an additive way, always adding new bits of information (although if the user interface is badly designed the user may form incorrect assumptions that then have to be unlearned). The structure model is also built up in an additive way as the user creates or explores the computer model. However, with CAD systems if the user experiments with possibilities in the construction, she may have to unlearn those parts of the structure model corresponding to parts of the computer model which she has added and then removed.

12.6 Summary

In this chapter I looked at the models stored within the computer, considering which things are important when building up computer models and how the models can be classified according to their relationship with the real world. I also considered the role these classifications played in the consideration of the users interaction with the models. I went on to look at further classifications, the dimensionality of the model and real and abstract presentations of the model. The consideration of dynamic models introduced several new and interesting problems concerning presentations, and finally I talked briefly about the user's mental model of the computer model.

12.7 Exercises

12.7.1 Orchestrating lighting

Design an interactive system to help the user to design a graphic 'script' to control a set of three coloured lights (the script describes how their intensity is to change over a certain length of time). Work out a method of presenting the script for the three lights and design a set of tools to interact with the model. First of all decide on the functionality of the tools and then sort out how you will present them, what feedback they will give and so on.

12.7.2 More about filtering

Think back to the idea of filtering (Section 12.2.5 [p 195–196]): in particular, the example concerning changing the speed-limit signs on the motorway. The system can be designed to help set up a graduated scale of limits along a stretch of motorway changing from the current limit down to the required limit at the required point. When the switch over to the new speed limits is complete, however, you have a situation where the speed limit being displayed suddenly drops, in some places by a huge amount.

What problems could the above situation cause and how could the system be designed to avoid them? Also, are there any other important considerations that need to be made with this example of filtering?

12.7.3 'Bridger-style' concerts

The Bridgers used to give music concerts where the audience produced simple sounds in accordance to a script. The script in this case was drawn on a long roll of transparent plastic and then scrolled through an overhead projector. In a fixed position on the overhead projector was the 'sound line'. As the parts of the script hit the sound line the audience had to interpret it and make the appropriate sounds. Figure 12.6 shows a short example for one group of people humming and another group hissing. The deviation of the line from the dotted line indicates the volume.

Think about what sort of noises can easily be made by a group of people sitting in an auditorium and design graphic notations for the different noises. For each of them you must also

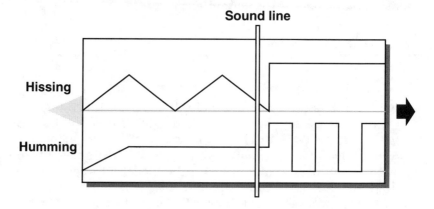

Figure 12.6   A section of script for a Bridger concert.

decide upon a parameter of the noise that is to be 'controlled' by the deviation of the line. Is there any way of notating a variation in two parameters of the noise? For example, the loudness and pitch of the humming.

Which way should the script move past the sound line. To the left or to the right?

12.7.4 Demonstration language

In Section 12.4.2 [p 201] I talked about presenting dynamic models in a static form. One such form was a 'script' of textual commands. Imagine a text-based language for describing very simple two-dimensional animations. I could invoke simple shapes and make them perform simple movements, something like this:

RedSquare= square(10, solid, red)

BlueSquare= square(10, solid, blue)

RedSquare appears at (0,0)

BlueSquare appears at (100,0)

wait for 10 seconds

RedSquare moves to (0,200) over 10 seconds

wait for 10 seconds

BlueSquare moves to (100,200) over 10 seconds

RedSquare disappears

BlueSquare disappears

Think about what other features could and should be included in the language and the best way to present them textually to the user paying particular attention to the choice of terminology, the way of specifying positions and so on.

12.8 Fatal errors

The language used in the error messages given by systems ranges from the polite to the insulting. Some systems seem to specialize in violent verbs, obscure messages and specialized technical terms. I've had several reports of 'Fatal Error' in my dealings with computers, but up to now none of them has actually been fatal. Let us return to Broadoaks Manor.

Hemelsworth is seated in the dining room. He has just rang the bell for Barker. Barker enters.

Barker: You rang, sir?

Hemelsworth: Serve the lunch Barker, there's a good chap.

Barker: [*Loudly*] Panic! Syntax clash! Code 24! Command aborted! Memory dump!

Hemelsworth: What on earth are you talking about, Barker?

Barker: That was a fatal error, sir.

Hemelsworth: What does that mean?

Barker: I'm afraid, sir, that I am going to have to shoot you!

Hemelsworth: That's rather an extreme reaction isn't it?

Chapter 13

Interaction styles

13.1 Interacting with the real world

In the last two chapters we looked at important underlying factors in the realm of the user and the computer. Next, I am going to look at one of the basic ideas underlying the interaction between the two – interaction styles. These are the basic underlying ways of interacting with things (including interactive systems), and the material in this chapter plays an important role in the initial decisions to be taken when designing a user interface and in the understanding of some of the basic problems occurring in interaction.

How do I interact with the world around me? I talk to people, I scribble on paper with pencils, I kick stones, I lift boxes, I stroke cats and horses, I rearrange the furniture, I talk in a simple way to dogs, I read books and magazines, I smile at babies, I switch lights on and off, I kiss people or shake their hand, I make cups of coffee, I listen to the radio and so on. There are thousands of ways, but to some extent I can reduce all these interactions to two sorts: interaction with the *animate* (people, dogs, cats) and interaction with the *inanimate* (furniture, stones, boxes).

Interaction with the animate is usually characterized by an exchange of information: a conversation or a dialogue of some sort. The abstract information of such a dialogue can be presented in many different ways: as speech, talking to someone face to face or over the telephone; as gestures, signalling to someone through a window; as a mixture of both speech and gesture, getting a dog to sit down; as written text and diagrams in books, mathematical articles, magazines, letters, electronic mail and so on. Interaction with the inanimate is a lot simpler, it takes the form of directly manipulating inanimate objects according to some goal that you are trying to achieve.

The choice of interaction style has a close relationship with the animate/inanimate nature of the object of the interaction, but it is by no means governed by it. Sometimes there are situations where both forms of interaction are used with an entity. For example, a bouncer at the door of an exclusive club interacting with an unruly guest may use the dialogue-style interaction – 'Excuse me sir, you are no longer welcome in this establishment, would you mind leaving,' or might resort to direct manipulation-style interaction, dragging the unruly guest out by the scruff of the neck.

13.2 The development of dialogues

In the initial stages of human development, interaction with the environment (both animate and inanimate) is almost entirely carried out by direct manipulation (this is true both in terms of the development of the human race and in the development of a human child). Direct manipulation of the environment has its roots in the more basic behaviour of humans. It is tied up with our fundamental perception of the physical environment and our instinctive and natural reactions to it. Interaction by means of dialogues emerged slowly as thinking became more abstract, symbols began to be used and language developed. Dialogues include communication of all kinds and for all purposes:

◆ **Information**
   Dialogues can involve just the communication of information in one direction (more about this later).

◆ **Alternative purposes**
   It is interesting that dialogues in the real world are sometimes used for alternative purposes such as social chit-chat and smalltalk. When I stand in a bus queue and a conversation starts about the weather, the information being conveyed is less important than the atmosphere of communication and contact involved.

◆ **Discussion**
   Two (or more) parties can be involved in a dialogue to refine a common goal and discuss how to achieve it.

◆ **Giving commands**

Dialogues can, of course, be used to give commands to other agents. I shall use the term 'agent' to signify a party who carries out commands for another party.

When it comes to user interface design the most important of these four purposes is the final one: giving commands to get things done. In a social context, achieving a goal by giving commands to others is linked to many sociological issues:

Abstraction and symbols

All parties concerned must share a common set of symbols in order for understanding to take place. This may be achieved either by sharing some sort of strict language or a common model of the world in order to deduce the meaning. If I say, 'Tell me what time it is' to someone they must know the language in order to understand what I am saying. If they do not understand my language I can tap my wrist and look questioningly at them and they will still get the message because we both share a similar model of the world.

Social structure and organization

A command is only a command if there is someone or something to carry it out. For one party to give commands to another there must be some idea of social structure and organization either implicit in the way a member will assume the lead of a group and give orders, or more formally in terms of fixed power structures within established institutions and organizations.

Common goals

Coupled with the above is the idea of parties in a dialogue having a common goal. An agent receiving commands from another party is only likely to carry them out if they are beneficial. This will be the case if the agent shares the same goal as the party giving the commands, or if the goal is in other ways mutually beneficial. For example, the final goal may not be of importance to the agent, but some sort of reward may be received if that goal is reached.

The area of dialogue, commands and language in the human world is interesting and highly complex. There are many ideas waiting to be unearthed and applied to computer–user interface design.

13.2.1 Information

Among the many examples I listed at the start of this chapter were reading a book and listening to the radio; both can be classified under interaction with the animate, the animate being the book's author or the radio announcer. However, there is an inanimate factor in that the interaction is presented in an inanimate medium – the plastic and metal of the radio or the pages of the book itself. With information I can usually interact with the presentation of the information (turning the volume up, turning the pages over) but in some cases I can also interact with and manipulate the information itself: for example, adding information to a file of cards or changing someone's 'phone number in an address book.

The dialogue nature of the interaction depends upon who is in control of it. If the party supplying the information is in control then it will be more of a monologue; the only interaction the receiving party has is to choose whether to receive or not. If the receiving party is in control then it becomes more of a true dialogue with the receiving party interacting with the supplying party in order to access the elements of information they want.

13.3 Technological agents

In the real world this difference between direct manipulation-style interaction and dialogue-style interaction is fairly clear-cut. If I want a meal I can get on with it in a direct manipulation manner; I go into my kitchen and start cooking it, directly manipulating the real things, making choices directly with no communication involved. If, on the other hand, I go about a similar task in a dialogue style I go to a restaurant, select something from the menu and tell my choice to the waiter. With direct manipulation it is all just between me and the food; with the dialogue style there is an agent (or more than one) who translates my symbolic actions (my choice and commands) into actions in the real world.

The introduction of technology blurs this distinction somewhat. The technology is the agent, it is certainly the one doing the work for me, but where are the symbols? They are no longer symbols in the conventional sense but instead are actions such as pushing buttons or turning dials. When I press a radio button to change channels am I making a request that the radio then carries out or am *I* doing it and is the technology merely something that gives me a more powerful means of direct manipulation? There is no definite boundary between the two. The situation is clear at the extreme ends of the scale. When I use a hammer *I* am doing the job; the hammer is just a tool. When I use a photocopier I tell it what to do and then *it* does the copying. The problem is less concerned with the nature of the tool and more concerned with the user's perception of what is going on.

13.4 Using the styles

When it comes to designing computer–user interfaces it would be advantageous if interaction with the system could be based upon one of these two styles. Interacting in an already familiar manner makes the interaction instantly more amenable and efficient for the user. Interacting in a new and unfamiliar manner makes the interaction inaccessible and complicated. However, when carrying out a task by interacting with the real world these two fundamentally different methods of interaction have many inherent assumptions and connotations attached to them, and this can cause problems when they are translated into the world of computer interaction.

13.4.1 Satisfying interactions

Literature about direct manipulation-based interfaces claims that they have many advantages over the normal 'text command'-based systems. It is claimed that direct manipulation interfaces are easy to learn and enjoyable to use, they give the users confidence and, in general, are a more direct and satisfying manner of carrying out tasks. This is backed up by people's observations and experience. It should be pointed out, however, that this is with reference to interaction with a *computer*. One of the reasons that direct manipulation interaction with a computer is usually much more satisfying than dialogue with a computer is because computers are currently so poor at playing their part in a dialogue. With real-life interactions dialogues can be every bit as satisfying as direct manipulation. A dialogue with someone who thinks along the same lines as you, but has different ideas and viewpoints and can explain them well, can be stimulating, productive and satisfying. Yet with human–computer dialogues we get only the smallest hint of this.

Thus, progress is concentrated in the direct manipulation area because direct manipulation interaction with not much feedback is still more acceptable than dialogue interaction with not much intelligence. The former is better than nothing and the latter is worse than useless. The necessity of making the computer's side of the dialogue intelligent is proving to be difficult to meet. Systems that attempt intelligent intervention when the user is busy with something always run into problems; it is difficult for computers to understand humans. Usually all the mental effort in the dialogue is made by the user. With current text-based systems the dialogue style is only very loosely followed. Although there appear to be two parties, one of them is devoid of almost any intelligence at all (I'm talking about the computer here) and in that respect fails to properly fulfil its side of the dialogue.

Good direct manipulation involves making the other party in the interaction (the computer in this case) as 'dumb' and as passive as possible (basically it just has to sit there and get moved around like a bit of furniture). What then becomes important is the feedback for the direct manipulation interaction. The richer the feedback the smoother the interaction, and providing such feedback is becoming more and more possible with the current increase in awareness and technology.

13.5 Objects and actions

Many interactive systems break the elements of the interface down into objects and actions. The user then achieves everything by carrying out certain actions upon certain objects. Inherent in interactions such as these is the order of selection of the action and the object. There are two possibilities. The first is that the user first selects the object or objects that she wants to perform an action on and then she selects the action to be performed. The alternative is that the user first selects the action ('delete' for example) and then applies this action to the required objects by pointing at them with the mouse and clicking appropriate buttons.

The designers of direct manipulation interfaces such as the Macintosh choose the object–action type of selection because the action–object type leads to mode problems (think back to Section 10.5.5 [p 167]). However, their decision leads to an interesting observation about objects and actions in the user interface. When I use the Macintosh to delete a file I select the file (or files) in question and then I select the command 'delete' from the menu. When I do this I feel that I am giving the command to the computer and that the computer is doing the deleting. With an interface based upon the action–object type of selection I feel more that I am the one doing the deleting. I select 'delete' from the menu and I get a delete cursor (a little skull and crossbones, or something more tool-like like a small hammer) and then I go round 'zapping' all the files that I want to get rid of.

The reason for this is tied up with dialogues and direct manipulation. With the object–action type selection I am selecting the objects and then selecting an action to be applied to them. This is dialogue-style interaction. The act of selection is inherently part of a dialogue. You only select things when you are talking about them to another agent or instructing another agent on what to do with them. Consider an analogy in real life. When I go to the bakery I will sometimes point to the rolls and cakes that I want in the process of asking for them. When I'm at home, however, and I want to take some of them out of the bread bin I don't do any pointing or selecting beforehand, I just take them out. It is a similar situation to the selection of choices from menus. Let us return to the restaurant example. I may order what I want by requesting it verbally in full to the waiter, or I may use the numbers that are provided on some menus or, if it is a foreign restaurant, I may even make my order simply by pointing to the desired dish on the menu and nodding. It is a dialogue. There must be an agent. It is no good having a menu and no waiter. In this example you couldn't use the menu in a direct manipulation sense unless you were to roll it up and swat a fly with it!

With action–-object type selection I am still using menus but rather than selecting an action that something else carries out I am selecting the possibility of performing a certain action myself. I am, in effect, selecting a tool and the menu takes the place of a list of tools available to me. It is a toolbox. Menus for action–object and menus for object–action type selection are in fact inherently different concepts. One is a menu for commands, the other is a toolbox. Confusion about their difference stems from the fact that they are very often presented in exactly the same way.

I should mention here that user interface literature on this subject sometimes uses the terms 'verb–noun' and 'noun–verb' in place of 'action–object' and 'object–action'.

13.6 Presenting the styles

When I talk about the dialogue style and direct manipulation style I am referring to the abstract model of the underlying communication rather than the medium that the communication is presented in (abstraction and presentation again).

Direct manipulation has to be presented in a direct manipulation manner; if there is a dialogue involved then someone else is doing the manipulation. There must be obvious distinct objects located within some spatial environment. However, beyond this there are many different ways in which the underlying style can be presented: as a desk top, as sheets of paper, as a collection of rooms or objects connected by pipelines. The dialogue style too can have its underlying model presented in many ways without having much of an effect upon the underlying nature of the interaction. The commands and communication could be presented as speech, text, form filling or even a choice of commands from a menu. Some of these are obvious media for dialogues but others are dialogues presented in a direct manipulation way.

Form filling in the real world is a direct manipulation presentation of a dialogue. The person filling in the form is doing so in response to questions from some other party. The filling in of the form is not an end in itself (although I sometimes do wonder); it is a medium of communication in a dialogue.

Using a direct manipulation-oriented medium to present a dialogue-style interaction does not cause too many problems. When we look at the opposite case – presenting a direct manipulation-style interaction in a dialogue-oriented medium – we find that there are problems. A good example of this is the telephone. Sound is a dialogue-oriented medium and when you are just ringing someone up and talking to them there is no problem; you are engaging dialogue style in a dialogue medium. The problems arise with more advanced telephone systems where several callers may be kept on hold, calls may be passed from one 'phone to another and several 'phone numbers may be stored in memory for rapid use.

The elements involved are no longer just dialogue elements and the orientation shifts towards direct manipulation. We are presented with the idea of calls as objects and the ability to move objects around from place to place. Achieving this with the medium of sound and the small amount of interaction afforded by the buttons on the 'phone is difficult, and people in organizations large and small are continually having problems with the 'phone system. How often have you said or heard this:

♦ 'What was the number for reception?'

♦ 'How do I transfer this call?'

♦ 'They were just forwarding me to someone else and the line went dead. Have I been cut off?'

♦ 'I can hear a ringing tone on the other end. Is there no one there or am I in a queue of callers?'

♦ 'I'll just transfer you to my colleague on the next desk... Hey! Eddy, have you got her now? No? Well I haven't. Where's she gone?'

What is the solution then? One solution would be to stay with the medium and deal with the calls in a dialogue-style way. How I wish for an intelligent 'phone system with which I could have a dialogue and say, 'Transfer this call to Eddy, and if there's no reply bring it back here.' But as I keep stressing, computer technology is not yet advanced enough to play the part of an intelligent party in a conversation. For now at least, we must try the opposite approach: maintain the direct manipulation style and try to find a direct manipulation way of presenting it.

How then can we present this idea of telephone calls and passing calls around in a true direct manipulation manner? In the old days there was no problem. Telephone exchanges, even those in organizations, were run by a telephone operator who spent the day with a headset on, plugging jack-plugs in and out of a large board full of sockets. From the user's point of view it was dialogue style; they could speak to the operator and say, 'Transfer this call to Eddy, and if there's no reply bring it back here.' And from the operator's side it was direct manipulation. Transferring a call from one party to another involved pulling the plug out of one socket and sticking it into another. The incoming call had a definite physical identity – the jack-plug – and the operator couldn't lose it even if she tried!

Reproducing this direct manipulation style with a modern telephone network would involve computerizing the system and linking each 'phone to a small screen with a mouse. Other people's 'phones, incoming calls and anything else of relevance could then be presented as icons and manipulated by the user.

13.7 Summary

This chapter dealt with the two basic interaction styles: the dialogue style (communicating with other parties to get things done) and the direct manipulation style (shifting things around and doing them yourself). It considered them both in the context of the real world and also in the context of the world of technology and computers. In doing so it touched on several related areas: the development of dialogues in human interaction, how technology, particularly computer technology affects the issues involved and how the two styles were used in practice. Finally the different ways of presenting the two styles to the user of an interactive system were discussed.

13.8 Exercises

13.8.1 Changing hardware devices

Early user interfaces were very much text- and language-based. This was both reflected and caused by the language-based nature of the hardware: teletext terminals for printing out text and keyboards for typing text in. The hardware is changing now to reflect the move to a more direct manipulation style of interaction. Design the ideal interface hardware you would like to use for a direct manipulation style of interaction. Imagine that money and technicalities are no problem. Try and come up with something new.

13.8.2 Direct manipulation and telephones

I have just been talking about making an internal telephone system easier to use by adopting more of a direct manipulation interaction style. Imagine that you have a network of telephones in an organization. Each has a small black and white computer screen (like a Macintosh) and a mouse. Design an interactive system using this hardware for dealing with the normal tasks performed with an internal telephone. Are there any other interesting possibilities opened up by having such hardware?

13.9 Over specification

There are many systems and languages for computers that are designed to offer the user incredible flexibility. Unfortunately this flexibility is still present even when the user doesn't want it. There are no easy forms of shorthand or obvious defaults. When I make use of systems that support the textual specification of graphics I would like to be able to say things like, 'Two circles next to each other.' Instead I have to struggle with all sorts of specifications. The 'X Windows' function for drawing circles requires nine parameters. Postscript is a slight improvement in that it requires only five parameters; however, I then need to specify that the circle I have just described is to be drawn, that I want to see the output and finally I have to preview it. In effect I say, 'Give me a circle,' and then I have to say, 'Now draw it,' 'Now show it to me' and 'Now *really* show it to me'.

In real life if I say, 'Draw three circles in a row,' to someone they are not going to turn around and say, 'What diameters shall I use?' or 'What separation do you want?' they will just draw three circles in a row. At least this is true for most people...

Barker: Good afternoon sir. I have just attended the most useful butlering course I have ever been on. Incredible it was. The philosophy behind it is that in order to please the person being served to the maximum extent, you should endeavour to provide them with exactly what they want. The course dealt with techniques to help the person being served specify their exact wishes.

Hemelsworth: That sounds wonderful. I'll try it out straight away. Let's have tea and a few sandwiches out on the veranda.

Barker: Certainly sir, exactly what would you like in your sandwiches?

Hemelsworth: Oho! I can see the effects of the course immediately. I'd like ham and tomato please Barker.

Barker: Right away sir. Erm, smoked ham?

Hemelsworth: Yes, that's fine.

Barker: And what sort of tomatoes?

Hemelsworth: What? What do you mean 'What sort?'

Barker: I mean, would sir like English tomatoes, Guernsey tomatoes or Dutch tomatoes?

Hemelsworth: Erm. English, I suppose. Yes, English would be fine.

Barker: And sir didn't actually mention butter; shall I make the sandwiches with butter?

Hemelsworth: Yes of course, what a stupid question.

Barker: Now, what about the bread sir? White or brown?

Hemelsworth: You know I always have brown bread!

Barker: And how thick shall I cut it?

Hemelsworth: Well, not too thin. You know how I like it.

Barker: I'm afraid, sir, that you will have to specify it in millimetres.

Hemelsworth: Oh, good grief. Five then.

There is a pause.

Barker: Right sir, I have the specification now. Shall I actually make the sandwich you've specified?

Hemelsworth: Yes. Yes.

Barker: And shall I make it now sir?

Hemelsworth: Yes. Now.

Barker: Shall I *really* make it now?

Hemelsworth: Yes. Go!

Barker leaves in the direction of the kitchen. Two minutes later he knocks and re-enters the drawing room.

Hemelsworth: Gosh. That was quick Barker.

Barker: I'm sorry but I'm afraid I haven't started yet sir. I forgot to ask you to specify which crockery you would like the sandwich served on.

Hemelsworth: Barker, listen, it's simple, I just want a ham and tomato sandwich. Why can't you just go and make one?

Chapter 14

Designing user models

14.1 User models of the artificial

In Chapter 6 I talked about user models. I looked at user models of natural things: people's behaviour, the physical size of things and models we have of interactive devices – user models of kettles, cars, coffee machines. The more complicated these interactive devices become, the more complicated the user model also becomes. When we include computers in the range of technological devices we make a huge leap in the complexity and generality of the interactive systems being designed (see Section 10.4 [p 161]). Because of their generality and flexibility computers are not confined in the sort of user models they can follow or support. The designer has free range, and because of the complexity of the systems a great deal of thought and design must be put into the development of the user model of the system that the designer wants the user to build up.

The majority of user interfaces to interactive devices are put together with little or no consideration for the user's model. With simple technological devices this lack of user model design is not a great problem, but as we progress up the scale of complexity the lack of user model design leads to interactive devices which are impossible to use for the first-time user and remain clumsy even for the experienced user.

When we progress to computer systems, user model design is vital if the system is to be used easily and efficiently. Unfortunately, however, this user model design is still missing in the majority of cases.

14.1.1 Complexity and clarity

To begin this discussion of user model design I shall first make a distinction between the *complexity* and the *clarity* of a system. Complexity is a measure of the internal nature of the structure of the system. A measure of the number of separate ideas, components, subsystems and so on that make up the system. Some of the complexity will be hidden from the user, but some of the workings of the system will be apparent. The apparent complexity is the internal complexity that is perceivable by the user at the user interface. Clarity is a measure of how easy it is for the user to understand the parts of the complexity that 'show through' in this way. A system without clarity is one where much of the internal complexity is apparent and/or this apparent complexity is unstructured or badly organized. Thus it is possible to have a system that in essence is simple, but through bad design lacks clarity and, conversely, a system that is complex but due to good design possesses clarity.

In certain situations it is possible to increase the clarity of the user interface by actually introducing more complexity into the system. Consider the front and back matter in a text book: the table of contents, list of figures, index, references, glossary and so on. It is all extra information. Each item adds a new piece of structure to the system but instead of taking clarity away, it adds to it making it simpler to use. For another example have a look at the idea of grouping in CAD packages in Section 16.4 [p 265].

14.2 Building up models

The first useful observation here is that people always try to understand things. It is a natural human reaction to try to build up models of the environment and the events in it. When something new or unexpected happens you try to fit it into your existing model of the world. Sometimes you may have to bend that model quite a bit to include it, and sometimes you may even have to change part of your model to include the new events. But whichever way you look at it, you usually try and incorporate the new into your idea of how the world works.

A nice example of this occurred during an earthquake (I didn't think of it as being a good example of building up user models at the time, that came several weeks later). I awoke in the night to hear plates and cups in the kitchen rattling around. I racked my brains to find a way of describing the events in terms of my user model of the world. My first thought was that I was being burgled, but why would a burglar make so much noise? The next possible explanation was that the cat had gone mad, but why would it choose the kitchen cupboard to go mad in? Gradually I became aware that vibrations were causing the noise and that maybe it was a late-night goods train on the nearby line. Then as the bed started to wobble I came up with an explanation that fitted – an earthquake.

14.2.1 Explanations

The building up of user models outlined above takes place between the person building up the model and the external thing that they are trying to understand, namely the system. Sometimes there is another party involved. Someone who is 'feeding' a particular model to the person building up the model. Someone who is *explaining* something. The subject of explanations has a lot of overlap with user model design. Explaining something to somebody is the art of helping them build up a user model of it. A good explanation provides a good user model and good methods of getting to grips with it, and a bad explanation doesn't.

Sometimes the thing being explained is quite concrete in nature and must be explained in one particular way. Explaining how a simple piece of technology operates falls into this category. Sometimes, however, the thing being explained is more abstract and can be explained in several different ways. I encountered an example of this when writing this book. In Section 11.2 [p 181] I talked about goal trees. I talked about working up the goal tree to the higher-level goals. The structure of the goal trees is that of an abstract tree, but in explaining it I can make it more concrete by using one of two models: either oriented with the root at the bottom and the branches pointing upwards like a real tree, or with the root at the top and the branches pointing downwards like a family tree. Both models are shown in Figure 14.1. I had quite a loose abstract structure that could be described in several different ways. What I had to do was find an explanation, a user model that suited how I was going to use it and what I was going to say. Although the real tree model is probably more familiar, the family tree model fits in better with the style of what I was

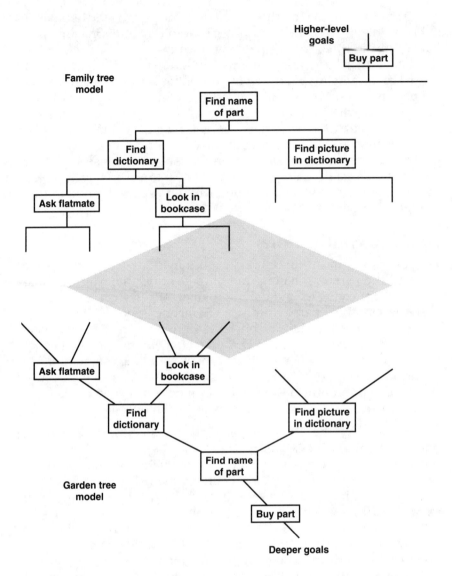

Figure 14.1 Two user models of an abstract tree structure.

describing. The terms I was using were 'subgoals' and 'higher-level goals'. With the real tree model this would have been very confusing.

In such circumstances where the system is rich or abstract enough to be described by several user models, the person doing the explaining also has the task of selecting or designing an appropriate user model to use. The choice of the user model depends upon the background of the person needing the user model and the purpose for which they need it.

There are times when the chosen user model is a cut-down version of what is really going on. Sometimes, if it is deemed to be too complicated, a simpler model is used instead. I can remember in physical chemistry we would be given a new model of what was going on at an atomic level every year. And every year we would be told, 'This is not really the full story but it works, and it is not too complicated. Next year you'll get the full story.'

There are other times when a full comprehensive model may not be too complex for the user, but it may just be unnecessary for her purposes. In such situations the same purpose can be achieved using a simpler model. For example, when explaining lightning to someone walking out in the countryside, instead of getting involved in long explanations about the buildup of electric charge, charge concentrations, air ionization and the like, it is far simpler to give an explanation concerning the fact that lightning 'prefers' to strike lone tall objects. This makes the information easier to understand, remember and use.

When choosing or designing a particular user model there are several goals that should be borne in mind:

◆ **Appropriate**
The user model should be appropriate to the context in which the user will employ it.

◆ **Consistent**
The user model should be consistent within itself. Expectations built up by the user when interacting with one part of it should be met by the system when the user is interacting with another part.

◆ **Support from the system**
The user model should be supported by the system in the sense that the system should provide feedback to guide the user in building up that particular user model.

◆ **Comprehensible**
The user model should be as simple and as comprehensible as possible while still satisfying the three other criteria.

14.2.2 Being 'economical with the truth'

When we are dealing with user interfaces to computer systems we have a situation where although the system is very complicated to understand, the user does not need to understand the full internal workings in order to get her task done. With computer systems then, the designers of the interface must be 'economical with the truth'. Obviously they must tell the user something about what is going on so that some results can be achieved with the system, but on the whole the user should be shielded from the masses of internal system complexity and shown only the barest essentials. These barest essentials are then combined with extra information and embedded in a design that incorporates a coherent user model. We saw this sort of thing happening with abstraction and presentation in high-tech systems (Section 5.6 [p 70]).

I should mention that there are some technological situations where 'being economical with the truth' is not appropriate. Aeroplane pilots cannot use an artificial metaphor about what is going on; they must understand most of what is happening in the underlying system – the aeroplane. As such there are no short-cut simple metaphors; everything must be learned by means of much training, rote learning and understanding. This situation is not the same with interactive computer systems. The user should not need to know vast amounts of information about the internal workings of the system. They should only need to know those aspects of the system which are directly related to using it to get their task done.

A good example of this hiding of internal information is the behaviour of a computer system with respect to deleting files. When I delete a file on a computer I say, 'Delete this file,' and as far as I am concerned the file is gone. Next time I say, 'Give me the names of all the files that are here,' I will not see that particular file. What actually happens is very different. The file is stored in the computer on the disk; it is stored there in lots of fragments in different areas of the disk and when I delete it the computer just says, 'This file is not needed any more, when I need to I can re-use those fragments of the disk where it was stored.' It does not delete it, it just makes it inaccessible; if the computer does not use those areas of the disk then my file will still be there for days to come.

Now here is an example of the converse, a badly designed user model to a system which exposes the user unnecessarily to the intricacies of the underlying system. I once used a computer system where one of the options in the menu was 'Retrieve'. The system allowed me to ask for a brief explanation of the command and when I did this it said, 'Retrieve: transfers a file from hard disk to main memory.' How would this sound to a user without a computing background... hard disk... main memory? What are they? Where are they? What are the advantages of having the file in main memory anyway? With a computing background the explanation is clear, and if this particular user did some background reading on computers she would know what was going on. However, if the explanation had been something like this, 'Retrieve: gets an existing file and presents it so that it can be read or changed,' the user could carry on without any problems and without having to include anything about the internal workings of the machine in her user model of the system.

Even to people who know something about what is going on internally, such 'economy with the truth' and accompanying user models can be extremely useful since they offer a means of minimizing some of the mental load associated with using the system and provide a sort of simplified, shorthand vocabulary in which the user can think and work without getting distracted by reams of underlying complexity. When I use my Macintosh and move a file icon from one folder to another I know something about what is going on in terms of the internal workings of the system but I hardly ever think about this when I'm doing the operation. It is easier just to follow the user model and think in terms of picking things up from one folder and putting them down in another.

'Form follows function'

Designers of computer–user interfaces have to be 'economical with the truth', they have to shield the user from what is going on inside the system, and in this way computers are the exception to the general guidelines appropriate in other areas of design. In many design disciplines there have been movements that advocated strongly against misleading the user in the design of a system. In architecture and industrial design this was typified by schools of design such as the 'Bauhaus' with their ideas of 'form follows function' and 'truth to materials'. They were concerned with allowing the design to follow the underlying ideas and materials.

With the computer both form and function are unclear. The function of the computer is incredibly general, it can be applied to all manner of tasks, and when I talk about the form of the system I am referring to the image of the system put forward to the user, comprising the feedback and the user model and so on. This too is incredibly general and flexible; the computer can imitate all sorts of systems and can be interpreted in terms of many different metaphors.

The result is that computer–user interface design has very little that it can draw on to guide it from within the system itself. The system image, every bit of the feedback, the user model, everything must be designed and constructed from the ground up.

One disadvantage of this is that there is much scope for doing the job badly, and for making mistakes when you are doing the job well. However, in contrast to this the advantages and possibilities are incredible. With the right designs and the right support the computer–user interface can be, and do, almost anything.

14.3 Real-world metaphors

When designing a suitable user model for a system we can take one of two approaches: either we can use some metaphor from the existing world with which the user is already be familiar and base our system upon that, or we can design an artificial user model encompassing the system's behaviour and goals. Let me deal with the first of these. There are many times when we make use of past experience in explaining something, 'This is something new but it is just like...' We can use a similar approach when designing the interface to a new system. We can make the user interface imitate that of a system with which the user is already familiar. This is the idea behind the use of real-world metaphors in computer–user interface design.

The big leap in the use of real-world metaphors as far as the general computer user is concerned, was the introduction of the Macintosh with its 'desktop metaphor'. Instead of the user having to learn a whole new set of concepts and ideas when they started working with a computer (directories, programs, command line, prompt, return, wild cards and so on) they were confronted with a number of ideas and concepts with which they were already familiar, such as a waste-paper basket, folders containing files, sheets of paper on a desk top, calculators with buttons, the acts of picking things up and putting them down, and the concept of spatial organization.

As well as the desktop metaphor used in the Macintosh other metaphors are starting to appear. Organizing large numbers of windows on a screen can be a problem. (See Exercise 16.8.2 [p 273].) One system (called 'Rooms') that helps here is based on the metaphor of different work rooms. Each room has a certain collection of windows in it and when you enter a room (by means of clicking on an icon) your screen changes to show just those windows. It is like having several desks that you can work at and, just like having more than one desk in the real world, it helps deal with the overheads of setting things up to do a task. Another example of real-world metaphor that I shall be discussing is the idea of 'folds' in text documents. (Section 16.4.1 [p 266].)

This use of real-world metaphors in a system's appearance and behaviour is yet another example of the more general idea of making things familiar by imitating the real world. We have seen it already with real-world interaction styles (Chapter 13) and I shall be looking at other examples in the chapters that follow, in particular designing on-screen controls that imitate real controls (Section 15.4.1 [p 243]), the more intensive use of three-dimensional graphics (Section 16.2 [p 256]) and the use of animation and continuity (Section 16.6 [p 269]).

14.3.1 Better real-world metaphors

The development of interactive computer systems has led to quite a range of interactive systems employing real-world metaphors in varying degrees. Initially, systems were without metaphor and very nearly without feedback. Command-line-based systems (such as UNIX and MS-DOS) did not seem to be based on anything at all and feedback was limited to basic text and the occasional incomprehensible error message. As systems developed there was a gradual increase in the use of metaphor. We saw the desktop metaphor with its inclusion of concepts and behaviour more familiar to the user and current experimental systems are pushing even further forwards. Then there are environments based far more upon three-dimensional worlds (Xerox's Cone Tree and Perspective Wall) with three-dimensional representations of information that can be viewed and manipulated in three-dimensions instead of just by pushing things around on a flat desktop. All the interaction within the environment is supported by fast and comprehensive feedback. After that there is the whole new world of virtual reality that is opening up providing novel possibilities for supplying high-quality feedback and thus the ability to support real-world metaphors to a very large degree.

The last step in this progression brings us almost full circle. In this book I have repeatedly extolled the virtues of imitating aspects of the real world when designing computer–user interfaces. If we take this to its logical conclusion we can say that the best imitation of the real world is the real world itself. For years computer scientists and pundits of the virtual world inside the computer have been dreaming of the paperless office. An office where everything is in the computer and all the necessary interactions go through the screen and the interaction hardware. How much better this would be than the usual messy office littered with piles of paper, stacks of notes, reports, books, envelopes, sketches, printout, and photocopies of magazine articles. The designers envisaged battling and triumphing over all this and leaving the user with a clear desk and a computer screen.

But why battle against it? Why not go with it? Researchers at Xerox EuroPARC are working on 'computerized reality', a system that is effectively a layer on top of the real world. This system comprises a conventional messy desk, full of papers, with a video camera mounted above it, a high-power computer system and an advanced suite of software able to read and understand the papers on the desk, understand spoken commands and interpret hand gestures made by the user. The majority of the interaction takes place via the desk full of papers. There is no metaphor, no complex, specially designed user model. There is just the real world, supplemented and well integrated with a powerful computer system.

14.4 Artificial metaphors

The other way of assisting the user in building up a user model is to provide feedback during the interaction to support an artificial model – some sort of system of ideas and concepts which behaves according to artificial rules, unfamiliar in the real world. Although such an artificial metaphor is unfamiliar to the user because it is not based upon the real world, it may nevertheless be advantageous to use since it could be more suitable for the technical application in question. Although it would not be familiar, it is possible to design such an artificial metaphor so that it is comprehensible, consistent and extensible. Thus when the user is familiar with a part of it they are able to generalize what they know and from this choose the correct behaviour and actions when faced with new situations within the system. (A good example of supporting artificial user models can be seen in my discussion of magic tricks in Section 6.2.1 [p 87].)

Examples of artificial metaphors and ideas appear on a small scale even within existing systems. For example, in computer file systems there are many files and information is organized into folders and subfolders and sub-subfolders. It is similar to organizing folders in the real world. The interesting thing is that in the computer world you can have objects present in two or more places at the same time (UNIX refers to them as 'symbolic links'. the Macintosh System 7 calls them 'aliases'.)

On a larger scale there are certain features of word processors and desktop publishing systems that have no analogy in the real world and yet are comprehensible and useful. For example, the idea of 'text flow' to help with structuring large documents, possibly with more than one thread running through them. I can define two text columns and connect them up so that when the first is full of text the text will overflow into the second column.

On an even larger scale there is hypertext (take a look at Hypercard on the Macintosh) which is a type of system highly dependent upon technology. One of the problems facing researchers in this area is that there is no good, general, real-world metaphor that can be used (there are some partial metaphors such as card indexes, art galleries and so on). Instead, researchers must try and come up with new, easily comprehensible, artificial metaphors to describe the system.

I should add here that an artificial metaphor, one that does not use some other system as a description, is not strictly speaking a metaphor. Thus perhaps 'artificial model' would be a more accurate term.

14.5 Rich environments

Rich environments enable the user to interact with a system in a more creative and personal way and to do so without encountering limitations in the system and the user model.

I have already stressed the importance of good and rich feedback several times in this book. Rich feedback implies a large amount of information being communicated to the user regarding her interaction. As well as concentrating on this, we can also go a step deeper to the more fundamental question of rich environments. In a rich environment there is not just a richness in the information we are giving the user about the system. There is also a richness in the whole underlying structure of the system: the underlying models, the concepts, the interaction possibilities, the structuring of tasks and the achieving of goals. We can see this move to richer environments as part of a natural progression in computer–user interface design.

Initially, systems were designed with 'device-oriented models'. The concepts, behaviour and interaction possibilities of the system were seen very much in terms of the internal structure and behaviour of the system itself (look back to the discussion about 'retrieve' in Section 14.2.2 [p 223–224]). The next step up from this was 'designer-oriented models'. The model was no longer directly dependent upon the structure of the underlying system, but instead was designed with the intention that it be consistent, simple, easy to understand and easy to use as a basis for interacting with the system. However, such models still have their drawbacks. They may not be suited to all users. Different users may prefer different models or different ways of working within the confines of a particular model. The users may find that there are things they want to do which are not possible within the model. The user is confined to the model supplied by the designer and, although it may be a relatively good model, the user is still aware of the limitations. Richer environments take the model beyond this. They are truly 'user-oriented models'. They provide a rich environment with plenty of redundancy and many degrees of interaction, giving the user the possibility of exercising more creativity and personality in her interaction with the system.

14.5.1 'Lines of desire'

We can see the advantages and the effects of rich environments in other disciplines concerned with design for use particularly architecture and landscape architecture. Here the issues lead to an effect known as 'lines of desire'. When a landscape architect works on a piece of green space (a park, or the greenery around a new railway station), she decides where the footpaths and cyclepaths are, where the road crossing points are and where she wants people to walk and cycle. Sometimes, however, people have other ideas; they will take short-cuts rather than use the prescribed routes and steps. The resulting trodden pathways across grass or through shrub-planted areas are referred to as 'lines of desire'. They are places where the designer has laid down a formal prescription of how the user is expected to behave, but the user has deviated from this expectation.

There are some cases where these formal prescriptions for guiding the user are enforced more strongly, and any attempt to cut across them by the user is very difficult indeed. At some busy roads there are areas where the designers want the pedestrians to cross at certain points. Sets of railings are placed on either side of the road with a gap at precisely the point where the pedestrians are meant to cross. The effect of this type of imposed control on the 'user' is very negative. People in a rush, or wanting to cut across for whatever reason, can either resentfully follow the prescribed channels or try and use 'lines of desire' to cut across the prescribed channels, but this is very difficult because of all the specially designed obstacles which have so obviously been designed solely to make things difficult for them.

The same negative effects can be observed in other areas where the design of a people-oriented environment is highly controlled and has few possibilities for user control. This is one factor in the so-called 'sick building syndrome'. This is a recent development in modern buildings where many factors of the physical environment are artificially controlled for 'maximum comfort' and are beyond the control of the user. The artificial control systems are usually far from perfect and the effect of the resulting physically bad environment combined with the lack of user control, leads to negative mental and physical effects on the users, loss of efficiency and illness.

I have spent some time working in a modern-looking office building where this lack of user control over the surroundings was at an extreme. The windows could not be opened, the lights could not be switched on and off from within the individual offices and there were automatic sun blinds on the south-facing side of the building which kept opening and closing automatically as the sun went in and out behind clouds. The whole environment was sealed which meant that when several people were working together the oxygen level would drop below the normally acceptable limits and everyone would get headaches. The only piece of user control left, the only evidence of 'lines of desire' in the whole environment, was the folded up bits of paper jammed into the switches controlling the sun blinds to force them to stay open all the time.

The phenomenon of 'lines of desire' and the whole question of rich environments has already occurred with architecture and landscape architecture because both are concerned with the imposition of a designed structure on to an already existing rich environment, and on the whole it is this existing environment and not the designed environment that supports 'lines of desire'. In the world of high-tech devices, this does not happen. There are no undesigned areas. Following the landscape architecture analogy above, there are no superfluous areas of greenery or shrubbery where users can carve out their own paths.

What is needed in interactive computing environments is not accidental richness but deliberately inbuilt richness, redundancy, and ease of use: a system that is extensible. Users can be flexible and creative within the confines of the system and be less aware of the frustrations of coming up against restrictions in using it.

Although such a goal may seem unreachable and far-fetched, moves are already being made in this direction. One example is the spatial organization of objects involved in using the Macintosh. With conventional operating systems (UNIX, MS-DOS and the like) the user is able to structure only the directories (folders) that files are in. The Macintosh gives the user the added freedom of controlling the size and placement of the window corresponding to the directory (folder) and the positioning of the files and subfolders within the window.

Users are able to use this flexibility to 'do their own thing' within the confines of the system. They are able to set up arrangements of windows and spatially organize the icons within them. I know people who have immaculately tidy Macintosh screen layouts, and people whose Macintosh organization and layout is like a messy cluttered desktop.

14.6 Summary

In this chapter I looked at the design of user models for interactive systems. After introducing the area I talked about the complexity of the system and how much of this complexity is perceivable to the user. I then looked at the building up of user models, explanations, and how other agents can help the user here.

I combined the ideas of hiding the internal complexity and helping the user build up mental models and talked about being 'economical with the truth'. This led to an examination of real-world and artificial metaphors. Finally, I looked at rich environments and the ability of a system to support far more interaction than just that based upon a simple model.

14.7 Exercises

14.7.1 Richness and communication

The richness of the information in the human voice is incredible. When you listen to someone talking, their voice conveys much more than the information in the words. Computer users sometimes send email messages to each other from one computer to another. These messages are just plain text and they lose all the nuances of voice communication. In an attempt to re-introduce some of these nuances someone invented the smiley brackets (here they are :-) try turning the page on its side if you cannot see the face there. They imply that what is said within them is meant lightly or jokingly (personally I think that they are one of the most valuable developments computing research has come up with :-).

List as many as possible of the items of information that can be abstracted from the following and indicate which of them are still present when plain text is used instead.

◆   A handwritten letter

◆   The human voice

◆   Morse Code sent over a telegraph

As an example, from the human voice I can usually tell the sex of the speaker, but with plain text I can't. I sometimes can from the contents of the message but not from the medium itself.

14.7.2 Better model choice

There is a file management system on the computer I use. It helps with the organization, visualization and management of files. The idea is similar to the Macintosh in that there are icons representing folders and files that you can move around and do things with. One interesting idea incorporated into this system is an indication of the file's read/write status. Most files can be examined and edited (read and written to) but some are not allowed to be changed. They are referred to as 'read-only' files and are represented in this particular system as the normal file icon with a little pair of glasses next to it.

Is this a good way of presenting the idea of read-only files? Is the concept of read-only files a good way of modelling the system? What is the essence of a read-only file and how can that be presented?

14.7.3 Navigation in large buildings

One interesting area of user model design in the field of architecture is the design of ideas and methods necessary to help users navigate their way around large public buildings or institutes.

I used to work in a building that had an arrangement of corridors all looking exactly the same: same colour paintwork, same floor coverings, same doors. There were only two things that helped you to navigate. First there were the numbers on the doors. The numbering scheme was not much of a guide to finding other rooms; it helped you if you were in the vicinity but not if you were far away. Secondly, someone had made the decision to label the four major corridors according to compass directions.

The drawbacks were apparent when people tried to direct others to certain rooms. The compass names of the corridors were never used and people tried to give directions according to other people's rooms or to fixtures and fittings in the corridors such as, 'Do you know that fire hose near Mr Hemelsworth's room?'

What drawbacks do you see in naming the corridors after compass directions? Given that the layout of the building cannot be changed, what factors *can* be redesigned and how could you redesign them to make navigation and direction giving easier? Think about how people give directions in a rich environment such as a town. Are there any real-world analogies which could be used?

14.8 Press 'enter' to exit

Sometimes when you use a program it will be busy doing
something or showing you something, and if you want to do
something else then you have to hit a particular key in order to
exit from that particular task. One word processor I looked at
recently displayed a lot of help information on the screen for me
and then gave me instructions on how to stop looking at the help
and do something else. It displayed the message, 'Press *enter* to
exit help'... Enter to exit?

> **Barker:** Good day, sir. I have just been to the 'Bert Perfect
> School of Butlering', where they have been experimenting
> with a new technique whereby the orders that the master
> of the house gives the butler to do a task must be exactly
> the opposite of the nature of the task.

> **Hemelsworth:** I've never heard of anything so damn
> stupid in all my life. I've had enough of this, Barker...
> You're fired!

> **Barker:** Fine sir! When do I start?

Chapter 15

Controls and computers

15.1 'Input and output'?

'Controls and computers' is the title of this chapter. If I had written it five or ten years ago it would probably have been entitled 'input and output', which would have been a perfectly good title. In the initial stages of computer development the computers were very remote from the users. They were physically remote, residing in special air-conditioned rooms a long way off from where the user sat at a desk working on the task she wanted to instruct the computer to do. The computers were also remote in terms of *time*. The user would prepare her instructions for the computer in one big block and they would then be 'fed' to the computer at a later date, and later still the results would be disgorged by the computer and picked up by the user. This 'computing at arm's length' gave the computer the appearance of being some remote thing that was treated as a part of a business organization or an administrative procedure. The user carried out her tasks of preparing information, handed it over (input), waited until the 'system' processed it and then received the results (output). Because of this history the interface between the user and the computer has remained cast in these ideas and terms.

Nowadays input and output are still useful terms when referring to the hardware side of computers; there are input devices and there are output devices. But when you are dealing with software and with computer interaction, the immediacy of advanced colour graphics, sound, pointing devices and on-screen controls means that input and output become less distinct, to the point where they merge and it becomes more a question of *controls* rather than input and output.

A survey of these ideas is useful, especially when designing and analysing the user interface issues concerned with the outermost layers of the interface, that is those parts that the user directly interacts with as opposed to the underlying models and ideas behind the user interface. These outermost layers include such things as the configurations of the hardware, the design of user interfaces within certain hardware limitations and the combination of screen-based feedback with the interaction hardware to yield more complex on-screen controls.

15.2 Hardware controls

In Chapter 8 I started the whole control discussion off by considering simple two-state switches. In the early days of computing, simple switches were the main form of input. Keyboards and screens were unheard of. There would be a long row of two-state switches on the computer; these would be set up in a certain pattern which the computer would understand as an instruction. Then another switch or button would be used to say, 'Wake up computer, I've finished! Look at the pattern of the row of switches I've just set up and carry out the instruction it signifies.' Even until recently such rows of switches were still used for the initial input to start a computer and get it up and running: 'booting it up' as it is referred to.

The next step up from these banks of switches was the keyboard. Instructions were typed in to a typewriter-style keyboard using a special language which the computer could then translate into the patterns of switches used earlier. The person typing them in still needed a button to say, 'Wake up computer! Look at the instruction I've typed in and carry it out.' This function was carried out by hitting the carriage return key on the keyboard.

From keyboards and text, computers then moved on to more graphical forms of interaction. Higher-resolution screens and pointing devices meant that the user could deal with much more abstract and accessible ideas. They could even point at 'objects' shown on the screen (representing files and documents) and manipulate them; moving them about on the screen, place them within other objects or dropping them into special (on-screen) boxes that applied processes to them and so on.

The introduction of better and better quality screens is quite a natural progression, but the introduction of the pointing device was a huge leap in computer controls. As I mentioned before, from a user interface designer's point of view the internal workings of such a device are unimportant. What is important is to have a good idea of what it does and what sort of information the user can give when using it: in particular, the difference between absolute pointers and relative pointers.

Absolute pointers have a pointing device and a large tablet (a board) connected to the computer. When the pointing device is placed on the tablet the computer is aware of where it is. It is *position*-sensitive. There is a direct correspondence between the tablet and the screen and if I put the pointer down in the top left corner of the tablet I see the on-screen cursor appear in the top left area of the screen.

A relative pointer is a device connected to the computer where the computer is aware of changes in the position. It is *movement*-sensitive. I can't use the pointer to put the cursor directly in the top left corner of the screen, but I can move it there relatively from where it is now. Relative pointing devices are physically more compact – you don't need a huge tablet on your desk – but because they are only movement sensitive they lack some of the advantages that absolute pointers have. For example I could stick a picture to my tablet and outline it with the absolute pointing device. This would be impossible to do accurately with a relative pointing device. One advantage that relative pointers do have is that of 'cursor warping'. The system can override the pointing device and reposition the cursor to a different point on the screen. This can be done with absolute pointers but it would be pointless since the correspondence between the screen and the tablet would then be distorted.

As well as these examples of mainstream hardware controls there are others that are less widely available or are suited only to more specialized tasks. Dial boxes are available as attachments to some brands of workstations. These constitute an array of dials (10 or so) which can be linked by the underlying software to control different aspects of the system. They can thus be used for colour mixing, for rotating three-dimensional models and so on. There are pointing devices available that can provide three-dimensional position information enabling the user to build up computer models by defining three-dimensional points. Finally there is a range of input controls associated with computer-based games, the most general of which is the joystick which is a pointing device providing the same information as the mouse but used in a very different manner.

15.2.1 Communication channels

When a system uses combinations of the above controls, and especially when a system is being constructed that involves a more complex configuration of hardware controls, it is sometimes useful to look at the user and the computer in terms of 'channels'. A communication channel of a particular entity is a means by which it can either give out or receive information independently of its other channels. With current computer systems the usual input channels are the keyboard, the mouse position and the mouse buttons. The usual output channels are the screen, the loudspeaker and perhaps a few warning lights on the keyboard. More advanced systems can have extra input channels such as a dial box or a pressure-sensitive stylus. They may also have extra output channels: for example, an extra screen to deal with text while the main screen deals with high-quality graphics.

In a similar way users have hearing, sight and touch (being able to feel textures and feel buttons move as they are pressed) as their input channels. As output channels they have voice and the manipulative abilities of their hands. These are the channels considered in the light of existing, widely available technology. With respect to the user's input channels, the remaining two of the five senses (smell and taste) will probably not play any role in the immediate future, but regarding the user's output channels technological advances are making it possible to start considering things such as eye movement, foot movement, general hand gestures and spoken commands.

This hardware-oriented analysis can be useful when it comes to developing new ideas for input or output devices and when deciding what combination of devices to assemble as the hardware platform for a computer system. It can also be useful when designing the software that is to run on a particular hardware platform. Avoiding repetitive channel switching is one thing that is important. For example if a user is entering small amounts of text into many different boxes on the screen ('form filling') and they must indicate to the system which box they want to type into by pointing to it and clicking with the mouse, they will be continually switching one of their output channels (one of their hands) between two different input channels of the computer (the keyboard and the mouse). Another important area where this is applicable is the design of good feedback for a system that uses two screens. On the one hand the user must somehow be alerted if they are busy with screen A and there is something important on screen B but, on the other hand, while busy with screen A they must not have to keep looking at screen B whenever their eye is caught by distracting and unimportant messages appearing there.

15.2.2 Degrees of freedom

Another useful concept with respect to computer controls is the number of degrees of freedom that a control has. A degree of freedom is a way in which some control factor may be varied independently of the variation in other control factors. Thus, when faced with the volume control and tuning dial of a radio we have two degrees of freedom. The volume can be varied independently of the tuning and vice versa. A pretty obvious example, but consider a mouse connected up to a computer: here too we have two degrees of freedom. The user can alter the X and the Y position independently of one another (although to be precise it is rather difficult to keep one constant and alter the other). If you build a simple dial-wheel into the top of the mouse then you have three degrees of freedom: the X position, the Y position and the rotation of the dial.

15.3 On-screen controls

The introduction of computer systems allows the hardware aspects of the user interface to be supplemented by the flexible 'interaction surface' of the computer to yield on-screen controls: controls that have a large part of their behaviour and feedback embodied in the elements displayed on the screen.

These on-screen controls have many parallels with ordinary hardware-based controls on interactive devices. With non-computer–user interfaces a control like a two-state switch appears everywhere: lights, car dashboards, tape recorders and so on. The two-state switch can be seen as a small subdevice corresponding to a particular subtask that is very common in electrical devices – switching between two states.

Similarly computer systems have common subtasks and, just as the two-state switch fulfils the function in the examples above, with computers it is fulfilled by common on-screen controls. The design of such an on-screen control thus constitutes a very simple computer–user interface problem since it alleviates some of the more complex, global issues that occur when designing a complete computer–user interface from the top down.

Common on-screen controls include simulated buttons, sliders and dials, menus, scroll bars, window controls (close, open, iconify) and file-store browsers.

15.3.1 Multifunctional controls

In Section 8.4 [p 128] I mentioned multifunctional controls which provide extra functionality in order to economize on the number of physical controls built into a device. With the on-screen controls of computer systems, adding extra controls is a relatively low-cost exercise. However, because the use of such controls depends greatly upon visual feedback, users with more experience sometimes find them slow to invoke and use. They want more functionality built into the controls that have tactile feedback; they want more dependency upon muscle memory. This gives them fast access to the functions without having to deal with the hand and eye coordination involved in menus and other more visual on-screen controls. The result of this mixture of software applications involving lots of functionality and the inflexibility of hardware controls, is that the hardware controls are often heavily overloaded with extra functions. Complex operations can be carried out by such combinations as pressing the left mouse button while holding down the shift key and the control key on the keyboard. Although this is fast for those who are used to it, the process of getting used to it presents a very high learning threshold to the new user.

15.4 Presenting controls

With two-state switches we saw that there were different ways of achieving the switching between the two states. Also, for each of them there were different ways of presenting the switch. Similarly, the abstract design of an on-screen control can be structured in different ways, and once this is done the abstract design can have several different presentations.

Each of the on-screen controls is aimed at carrying out a particular task such as navigating through a text document, choosing from a list of options or whatever. But different systems implement these controls in different ways with slight changes in the functionality and large changes in the presentation. It is useful to have a look at a survey of the different ways of doing things to see how things can be done well, and how they can be done poorly.

15.4.1 Imitating real controls

Although the combination of hardware and software in the computer system leads to interesting and novel controls, there are still some on-screen controls that directly imitate real-world controls. The fact that they are computer-based simulations has advantages and disadvantages. Sliders are a good example. The on-screen versions lack the tactile feedback that real-world sliders have. When you alter the on-screen variety you cannot feel how far or how fast they are moving; likewise you cannot feel when they have reached the end of their track. However, visually they can provide slightly more feedback (such as using figures to represent the current value) and they can also embody far more functionality that their real-world counterparts. They can be used to control more than one variable. The figure showing their value can be directly edited by the user with the keyboard and they can be used to store any number of configurations of preset values.

Many computer-based user interfaces also use buttons and button combinations based on real-world buttons: bell-push buttons, two-state buttons and radio buttons (see Chapter 8). Once again there is no tactile feedback. The user has to rely upon the visual feedback and in some cases this can be confusing.

15.4.2 Boundary problems

The space limitations of computer screens can lead to novel ways of displaying and interacting with structures (there will be more about this in Chapter 16). These space limitations also play an important part in the design of on-screen controls, especially those that pop up on request and are dependent upon the position of the cursor. As well as designing their behaviour when the cursor is somewhere in the middle of the screen, thought must also be given to how their behaviour will be modified when the cursor is near to one of the screen boundaries. (See Figure 15.1.) The control may behave as normal (A), and if it is partially off screen then it is up to the user to modify her behaviour by not requesting the pop-up control so near to the edge. Alternatively the cursor can be warped nearer to the centre of the screen to allow just enough space for the pop-up control to function (B). Another alternative is that the cursor can maintain its position and the menu is displayed fully on screen (C). The first solution can cause problems since it renders part of the menu inaccessible. The second solution leads to sudden jumps in the position of the cursor while the third leads to inconsistencies in the positional

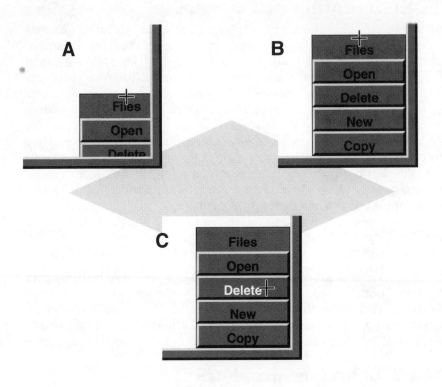

Figure 15.1   Behaviour at screen boundaries.

relationship between the cursor and the menu, thus forcing more reliance upon hand and eye coordination when making a selection.

15.5 Control and variable separation

Thanks to the increased emphasis on software, in our consideration of computer-based controls, we can make use of some abstract ideas to help us analyse controls and design new ones. One of these is the idea of control and variable separation.

It is possible to regard controls abstractly as having two parts: a part which the user interacts with and a related underlying variable which they alter by using the control. With non-computer–user interfaces, flicking a switch or turning a dial has a direct and mechanical effect upon some system variable. The information about the state of the variable is usually contained within the control itself. Consider a volume knob on a radio. Its external part – the interface – is the knurled wheel the user turns with her finger. Its internal part – the underlying variable – is a potentiometer with a variable value directly linked to the knurled wheel.

One of the big effects of computer-based controls is that there is a stronger decoupling of the control from the underlying variable. With more advanced electrical-based systems, and especially with computer-based user interfaces, the variable is stored somewhere in the machine and is quite remote from the input device manipulating it. The device does not directly alter the variable; it sends signals to the system which then does the altering. As an illustration of this I could use the mouse and the mouse buttons to select a line of text in a word processor; even if I then disconnect the mouse and throw it away the system still maintains the information that I had selected that particular line of text. The 'selected/not selected' attribute of the text is stored within the system as part of the computer model and is completely separate from the mouse itself.

15.5.1 Effects of separation

One disadvantage of controls where the variable is separated from the device itself is that the connection between the two is not obvious. In an interface that includes many operations with many results it is possible for two operations to have very different results and yet be invoked by very similar actions. For example, I have a word processor where the keys that I press to save the file are control-S and the keys to delete the current file are control-D. The small difference between the two combinations (S is next to D on the keyboard) means that I could easily do one instead of the other with disastrous consequences since the two operations differ widely in their results. Contrast this with the difference in the real world between the action of putting a document in a folder and putting it in the waste bin. Very rarely will I think to myself 'I'm going to put this document in a folder' and then accidentally put it in the waste bin. Thus, when it comes to software, the designer should ensure that similarity in command equates to similarity in operation and difference in command to difference in operation.

Another problem with variable separation is that the function of the different controls in the interface is not immediately apparent. Consider farm gates in the real world. It is not often that you are at a loss as to which direction they open in and how to open and close them. Their workings are all there on show. If you ever have trouble opening one on your first try you can just look at the mechanism and work out what to do. In a computer–user interface it is very different; the functionality must be explicitly made apparent by the designer using labels, diagrams, icons and instruction manuals, and if this is badly done the user will be confused.

Our experience of life is supplied more through interaction with the real world than through interaction with artificial systems; because of this it is sometimes difficult to appreciate this separation of variable and control. When I wiggle the mouse on my computer and see the cursor move on the screen I am not immediately aware of underlying variables. The concepts can best be shown by considering novel mappings of controls to variables and variables to presentations. By 'novel mappings' I mean mappings that are less in keeping with our experience and thus less taken for granted and more open to analysis. For example, imagine a painting program where the X variable controlled by the mouse is presented as the X position of the cursor and as the density of red in the colour being painted on the screen. As I draw a brush stroke from left to right its colour will intensify. I am painting with 'position-sensitive paint'. Scrolling a text document is another example of this. If I 'grab' the marker in the scrollbar that corresponds to the visible area and drag it downwards, I see the text of the document in the window go shooting past. The Y position of the mouse is being presented in three ways: as the Y position of the cursor, as the Y position of the marker in the scroll bar and (with a bit of filtering) as the part of the text that is being displayed in the window.

Another feature afforded by variable and control separation is the ability to change the associations between different controls and variables: in other words, to configure easily which particular controls have which particular effect. This has both advantages and disadvantages. It offers great flexibility and configurability of the interface. It offers the ability to perform a wide range of operations with a limited set of controls and the ability to re-use controls so that they do different things in different contexts. With current computer systems this flexibility can lead to complicated interfaces and problems. The results of using a particular control may depend not just upon the control but upon the context – upon what the user has done before using the control. Thus more mental processes become involved in the use of the controls (remembering what you have done so far and knowing what context you are operating in) and these can lead to associated problems and errors. The different contexts are known as 'modes'; I have already talked about them in Section 10.5.5 [p 167–168].

15.5.2 Filtering variables

Above I described how it is possible to present underlying variables in different ways. It is also possible to filter the underlying variables and abstract other information from them which can be presented in its own way. Consider the following examples of filtering the underlying X and Y position variables controlled by a mouse.

No filtering

As I shift the mouse about I alter the two underlying variables with no restrictions. Thus I am able to take them beyond the bounds of the screen. If I keep moving the cursor to the right it will 'slip off' the right-hand side of the screen and get further and further away from the screen boundaries. To bring it back again I will have to use the mouse to shift it left by the same amount. Under these conditions losing the cursor completely is very easy.

Bounding

Imagine now that the underlying variables are bounded; they cannot go above or below certain values. If these values correspond to the limits of the screen then the cursor will always be visible. If I move it to the right it will stop when it reaches the edge of the screen and no matter how hard I try I cannot move it past.

Modular variables

Another example is to apply modular arithmetic to the underlying variable. Consider the case where we take the residue of the underlying X variable of the mouse after dividing it by the width of the screen, and then present this residue as the X position of the on-screen cursor. The result is a value that is always less than the width of the screen. This has the effect of 'wrapping' the movement of the on-screen pointer around the screen. If the user moves it off the right-hand edge of the screen it comes straight back on from the left-hand edge and vice versa. (It is as if the right-hand side of the screen were joined up to the left-hand side.)

Thresholding

With thresholding we can use underlying variables to trigger events. The underlying variable is thresholded to a trigger value which is zero (or 'no') while the variable remains below the threshold value, and one (or 'yes') if the variable goes above the threshold value (this type of variable is known as a boolean). One example of using this is to threshold the X position of the pointer against the width of the screen. The boolean trigger can then be used to control something like the appearance of a menu. The practical result of this is that if the pointer is moved over to touch the right-hand edge of the screen a pop-up menu appears.

Time-based sampling

Finally, it is possible to extrapolate other information from underlying variables if we analyse how they change through time. We can look at the underlying variables of mouse buttons, filter their changes against time, pick out things like two clicks within a certain time threshold and use this to control a boolean trigger. In practice this gives the user the ability to issue commands to the system by means of 'double clicking'.

A good example of filtering against time is the 'seven-league boot effect' that I mentioned in Section 9.4.5 [p 149] in connection with oven timers. In a similar way the underlying X and Y positions of the cursor can also be filtered against time and magnified to achieve the effect. The mouse on the 'Next' computer system uses this idea. Move the mouse slowly and you can do it with great accuracy, move it fast and the cursor leaps across in the direction you are heading.

15.6 Structures and tools

To some extent, the design of the computer model or structure underlies the design of the tools for the user to manipulate the model. Where a feature of the structure can have one of several different forms (for example, the style of a font) the designer must also decide on the range of forms that is to be available to the user, and for each of the features they must decide whether or not the user should be able to manipulate it and what sort of tools are needed to do so. If different sizes of fonts are included in the structure then the user should have some way of saying 'use a big font now' or 'make the font here smaller'. Font size is part of the computer model of the text so the computer system 'knows about' different font sizes and it can, if it has been well designed, offer the user the option of specifying and changing the font size.

The power and flexibility of the computer means that as well as simulated tools familiar from the real world there will also be novel tools available with no parallel in the real world. Such power does have drawbacks though; powerful tools enable you to make powerful mistakes. (I once heard of someone accidentally reordering all the paragraphs in their doctoral thesis into alphabetical order.)

In an interactive computer system there are tools to manipulate the underlying structure, to do things like change the properties of elements of the structure, add new elements and delete unwanted ones. In some systems there are also tools to manipulate the presentation of the underlying structure, tools to alter the presentation without altering the underlying structure and tools to navigate through the structure, to choose which bits to look at and how to look at them.

15.7 Future controls

There is still a large body of research being done in the field of user interface design aimed specifically at improving the controls available. New developments are being made in three main directions.

Finding new channels

Firstly, new user communication channels are starting to be exploited. Research is still going on to make vocal input a possibility. Systems have been developed that allow the user to interact using both hands, and every now and then the foot controlled mouse (or 'mole' as it is sometimes called) surfaces briefly.

Improving existing channels

As well as opening up new channels, better use is being made of the existing channels. The conventional mouse uses only a fraction of the information that can be conveyed with the hand. Here researchers have developed the DataGlove, a glove that connects to the computer and is wired up in such a way that the computer is aware of the three-dimensional positions and movements of the hand, fingers and thumb. This needs the support of good feedback and complex rules for interpreting the gestures the user makes, which brings me to the next direction.

Better feedback

Any interactive control on a computer system needs some support from the software. Work is being done to support the new hardware by providing richer feedback and more comprehensive software environments within which the user can interact in a more natural and easy manner. Also in this direction there is work going on to provide richer interaction by supporting better integration and understanding of the information communicated by the user through all the different communication channels available (for example gesturing with both hands and giving spoken commands at the same time).

15.8 Summary

After a somewhat historical look at controls and the computer I examined the hardware controls currently supported by computer systems. I then discussed the communication channels available between a user and a computer and the number of degrees of freedom that a control has. The next stage involved more abstract considerations regarding controls. I looked at on-screen controls and how they were presented and at the advantages and disadvantages of the separation of controls and underlying variables that computer technology has brought about. Finally I looked at the relationship between the computer model and user tools and reviewed the directions in which future research in controls is going.

15.9 Exercises

15.9.1 What's moving?

Sometimes when on a train in a station I look out and see the train next to mine moving past the window. Is it really leaving the station, or is it standing still and am I the one that is moving?

If I have a window on to some text I can usually 'scroll down' by clicking on the downward-pointing arrow button. What is it that goes 'down', and what is it going down in relation to?

15.9.2 Foot pedal

Imagine that I have computer which is connected to a foot pedal that functions as an action-release variable controller (something like a car accelerator pedal). What could I control with the underlying variable? Think of some existing programs which could make use of such a device and invent some completely new ones as well.

15.9.3 Mouse as keyboard

Chording is the ability to send signals to the computer by pressing down groups of buttons as well as single ones, like playing chords on a piano. Remember the problems with 'channel switching' between the mouse and the keyboard (Section 15.2.1 [p 240]). Wouldn't it be a good idea to have a mouse which could also function as a one-handed keyboard?

Using chording how many signals can I generate from the buttons on a three-button mouse? How many buttons would I need for the whole alphabet? And what about including capital letters? What factors are important when designing such an alphabet of signals? (Have a look at the design of Morse Code.) Also, when you've worked on the problem yourself, try and have a go on the one-hand keyboard of an 'Agenda' or a 'Microwriter'.

15.9.4 Pop-up menus

Pop-up menus can be designed so that they are controlled by a mouse button acting as an action–release switch: 'press' and the menu pops up. Move the cursor to the required option, 'release' and that option is selected and the menu disappears. They can also be controlled in an action–action manner: 'click' and the menu pops up. Move the cursor to the required option, 'click' and that option is selected and the menu disappears. Use the state diagrams from Chapter 3 to devise a menu system catering for both styles (it can be done, Sun's 'Open Windows' does it).

15.9.5 Two mice

Here is another exercise like the foot pedal one above. Imagine you have a system with two mice – one for each hand. How could they be used in existing programs and what new ideas does the configuration suggest?

15.9.6 *Brazil*

In the film *Brazil* there is a scene where a data typist is using a keyboard with a difference. The keyboard is a dummy – a sheet of metal marked out with the keys and letters, but the typist's fingers are linked to small rings and rods and through these the system is aware of her finger movements. The system then uses this information to calculate which letters on the dummy keyboard her fingers are pressing.

Such a virtual keyboard would be possible using a computer and a DataGlove. I could have a vast dummy keyboard with thousands of keys and no moving parts to go wrong. What problems are there with the idea and can you think of any other ideas along these lines that the DataGlove could be used for?

15.9.7 Loose ends

Earlier in this chapter, in the section on communication channels, I outlined a few problem scenarios. Suggest some ideas to alleviate them.

♦ **Channel switching**
Using the mouse to point to boxes on the computer screen and then using the keyboard to type in them.

♦ **Alerting the user**
Attracting the user's attention to screen B (of a two-screen system) while they are using screen A.

♦ **Distracting the user**
Avoiding distracting the user from screen A with non-important messages flicking up in screen B.

15.9.8 The ultimate stylus

The combination of a stylus and tablet as a pointing device is widely used in art and design systems. A normal stylus has two degrees of freedom (X and Y position). Give it a pressure-sensitive nib and you have three degrees.

Design a stylus with as many degrees of freedom as possible. Make sure it is still fairly easy to use though. I once used a stylus with five degrees of freedom, controlling five continuous variables. If I had a paint system, what parameters could I map the different variables to?

15.10 Precise feedback for errors

With some systems you can write a long list of instructions and
hand them over to the system to obey. If there is an instruction
somewhere in the list that the system does not recognize it ought
to tell you which one it is. Some systems don't do this. They will
tell you that there's a mistake, but they won't tell you where it is.
You then have to go through a long process of elimination, taking
instructions out of the list and putting instructions back in and
seeing what works. Eventually you track down the instruction that
is causing the trouble.

Hemelsworth: Barker, could you just get Bertie on the
phone and tell him I can't make it for afternoon tea
tomorrow?

Barker: I'm terribly sorry sir, but I don't understand what
you are saying.

Hemelsworth: I said, 'Could you just get Bertie on the
phone and tell him I can't make it for afternoon tea
tomorrow'?

Barker: I'm terribly sorry sir, but I don't understand what
you are saying.

Hemelsworth: Could you just get Bertie on the phone?

Barker: Certainly sir. Any message?

Hemelsworth: Tell him that I can't make it for afternoon
tea tomorrow.

Barker: I'm terribly sorry sir, but I don't understand what
you are saying.

Hemelsworth: Could you tell him I can't make it
tomorrow?

Barker: Can't make what sir?

Hemelsworth: Afternoon tea.

Barker: I'm terribly sorry sir, but I don't understand what
you are saying.

Hemelsworth: Ah! This could be the problem, afternoon
tea!

Barker: I'm terribly sorry sir, but I don't understand what
you are saying.

Hemelsworth: Tea in the afternoon?

Barker: I'm terribly sorry sir, but I don't understand what you are saying.

Hemelsworth: Tea at four o'clock.

Barker: What about tea at four o'clock sir?

Hemelsworth: Could you get Bertie on the phone and tell him I can't make it for *tea at four o'clock* tomorrow?

Barker: Certainly sir... Anything else?

Chapter 16

Graphics and animation

16.1 Introduction

In Chapter 10 I mentioned the importance currently placed on visual feedback at the computer–user interface. Now that we have worked our way up to the surface issues of computer–user interfaces I shall explore this theme in more detail.

I have stopped taking photographs when I go on holiday. I have stopped because when I get them back from the developers they are always disappointing. A vast, open blue sky at twilight comes back as a bit of shiny, blue paper, and a rain-soaked tree catching the sun and glittering just looks like an ordinary tree. There are bound to be problems with the quality of the camera and the skill of its user, but on the whole the problem lies with the restrictions of the medium when compared to real life.

These same restrictions also occur in computer graphics. The image on the screen is like a holiday photograph. It is small, flat, grainy and lacking in vivid colours. The problems of graininess and restricted colour are caused by limitations in the hardware. Currently both these problems are being dealt with by advances in the capabilities of the hardware and by advances in the software coupled to the hardware that takes charge of the way that things are shown on the screen and makes the drawbacks less apparent (for example 'anti-aliasing' to overcome the jagged effects encountered when drawing lines on screens that are grainy, and 'dithering' which allows intermingling of colours on the screen to give the impression of other colours).

255

The problems of flatness and smallness are different from the above two in that they are less of a hardware problem and more of an organizational problem. You cannot solve the problems just by having bigger and bigger screens or by introducing holographic ones. Once again it is a resources problem. The solution does not lie in hardware alone; it is also necessary to have access to software resources to manage the capabilities already available.

The lack of good tools for managing the resource and the bad use of the tools that already exist arise from a lack of understanding of the basics of conventional graphics design and presentation. This lack of expertise in graphics has two causes.

The first is that user interface design is still mostly carried out by computer programmers and, from a historical perspective, these programmers are used to working with computer-oriented concepts. More importantly, they are used to working in a very 'remote' manner with very little feedback as to what they are doing. They also use obscure commands to achieve their aims.

The existence of this style of working and thinking comes largely from the limitations of early computer systems: limitations mainly caused by technical issues such as limited screen capabilities, limited computer power and speed. Also, the majority of practitioners within this discipline have little or no experience of the basic ideas and techniques of graphics and graphic communication.

The second reason for the lack of graphics expertise is that it is difficult for people with a graphics and communication background to become involved in computer–user interface design. The decoupling of the user interface referred to in Section 10.2 [p 158] has still not come to fruition, and as it now stands computer–user interface designers still need to know a lot about the underlying workings of the computer. However, the change is happening. Graphics and good graphic design are starting to find their way into the computer–user interface. Below I shall examine several ways in which good graphics has had an impact on the computer–user interface.

16.2 Three-dimensionality

Humans are used to dealing with three dimensions. Almost everything you see and manipulate in the real world is three-dimensional. Granted, some of it is 'almost' two-dimensional – bits of paper, diagrams and so forth – but usually when you deal with writing and diagrams you spend most of your time producing them and very little time manipulating or changing them. In the real world, however, you are continually moving things, creating things and changing things, and always in three dimensions.

The graphic capabilities of the computer screen have changed all this. Suddenly there is another world available which is separated from the first. A world that is also full of objects and things that you can interact with and manipulate. The difference is that it is a two-dimensional world, full of two-dimensional objects, and you interact with it in a two-dimensional way.

The style of graphics used by early systems was shaped by many things: the purely two-dimensional nature of the screen, the lack of computing power to make advanced use of the screen, the developers' lack of conventional graphics experience (mentioned above) and the lack of any need to make the user interface more accessible. The result was that everything was clumsy and flat. When the growing body of computer users with different backgrounds then came into contact with these systems they found the flat world insubstantial and difficult to 'get to grips' with.

Since these early examples of graphics in computer interfaces the developers have realized that a three-dimensional 'look and feel' is an advantage for interfaces, and at last graphic designers have started to play a part in the design of interface graphics. The MOTIF window manager is a classic example of such involvement, it is highly popular and the style has been much copied. User interfaces now have a much more pronounced three-dimensional flavour to them with well-chosen visual cues giving the on-screen environment the impression of three-dimensionality.

These visual cues approximate those we are used to seeing in the real world around us, with the result that although the users are aware of the three-dimensional feel they are not, on the whole, aware of the precise nature of the cues. Below is a list of the four most widely used. (See Figure 16.1.)

◆ **Overlapping**
   The overlapping of objects is one of the most obvious visual cues for depth. Parts of objects simply obscure parts of other objects. The effect can be further amplified when used in interactive environments where the user can move the obscuring object to reveal the hidden parts of the other object.

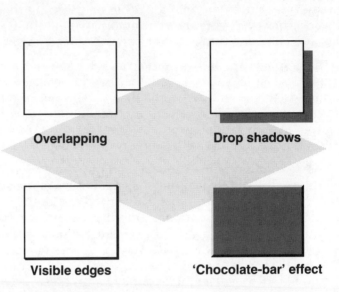

Overlapping   **Drop shadows**

Visible edges   **'Chocolate-bar' effect**

Figure 16.1   Three-dimensional visual cues.

◆ **Drop shadows**

To further emphasize the idea of objects being in front of other objects it is possible to draw drop shadows on the background. These shadows give the illusion of a source of light somewhere above the object and a separation between the object and its background. However, the visual cues from this can become a little confusing if the background is complex: for example, if the shadow is thrown on to several other windows supposedly at different 'depths'.

◆ **Visible edges**

The two visual cues above support a feeling of depth, a three-dimensional context within which the objects can be in front of or behind other objects. But what about the objects themselves? How then can we impart a feeling of three-dimensionality to them? One way is to give flat objects visible edges.

Very rarely in the real, three-dimensional world do you look at an object from directly opposite one of its faces. Normally you see several of its faces at once (look around you!). And if you do look directly at one face you usually see small parts of some of the other faces. This effect can be reproduced by drawing dark lines on two adjacent sides of an object and bevelling them so that they hint at other faces.

◆ **The 'chocolate-bar' effect**
The use of visible edges gives flat objects a feeling of thickness, but the chocolate-bar effect can be used to give objects more of a three-dimensional form. It is used to make surfaces look as if they project from the background with visible, sloping side surfaces much like a chunk of chocolate. The effect is further heightened by incorporating lighting cues; making faces on one side darker and those on the other side lighter. This particular effect is what gives the MOTIF window manager its distinctive style.

It is possible to reverse these lighting cues and give the effect that the surface is in fact depressed into the background. The combination of the two effects is useful when a given screen area functions as a button and can be 'pushed' in and out by the user by means of the mouse.

It should be noted that all the above effects rely heavily on consistency, and should there be any clash the effect of the visual cue will be lessened: for example, using one drop shadow in a different direction to the others. A very small clash of this type is present in the Sun 'Open Windows' window management system: see if you can find it.

Despite this trend towards a three-dimensional feel, the conventional underlying model of the on-screen environment remains predominantly two-dimensional: a pile of overlapping two-dimensional objects. The only part played by the three-dimensional visual cues is to give the two-dimensional objects more of a feeling of thickness, depth and a tiny bit of form. However, research is now in progress to develop an on-screen environment that is not just a pile of three-dimensional-looking rectangles, but is a three-dimensional world filled with three-dimensional objects all having three-dimensional relationships with each other (refer back to Section 14.3.1 [p 227]).

16.3 Space problems

Above we saw how the inherently two-dimensional nature of the screen influenced the style of graphics initially used in the interface. Another important screen-related restriction is the size of the screen. One of the advantages of computers is that they can be used to handle bodies of information and structures too large and too complex to be dealt with by conventional methods. But how can this information be manipulated or even viewed if the system has such a limited screen space? The situation is like an architect trying to carry out all her drawing work, administration and report writing on a small tea-tray!

When viewing and interacting with a structure, different tasks and subtasks require different scales of presentation. Some require an overview of the whole structure to decide upon the context of an operation, and some require a zoom (a zoomed-in view of part of the structure) to concentrate on the detail of an operation.

With the existing power and graphic capabilities of computer systems we already have the ability to imitate all the possible static presentations I dealt with in Chapter 5. The fact that computers provide us with a dynamic interface surface means that more possibilities are opened up. The combinable partial presentations method of displaying graphics can be implemented on an interactive system and there are many more possibilities that are novel, suggested as they are by the capabilities of the new technology. In Section 5.2.2 [p 62] I talked briefly about overviews and zooms in an 'A to Z' street map. How can computers elaborate this idea?

16.3.1 Overviews

When dealing with the complex structures and small presentation areas involved in computer applications, it is possible to use the computer to present an overview of the entire structure by showing the structure on a small scale and only displaying some of the features. Once again, we are talking about abstraction and presentation. The computer abstracts the features allotted to be the key features and this group of features is then presented as the overview. See Figure 16.2 and compare it with Figure 4.6 [p 50].

There are many examples of overviews both in the real world and in the world of computers. Consider the table of contents of this book. It is an overview of the structure and content. You can study it, decide which part you want to examine in detail and then follow up the page reference. Some computer systems support this sort of outline structuring of text by letting you view just the first-level headings from a document or the first- and second-level headings and so on. The key rule in constructing overviews is only to show the user those features that she needs to see. The tricky thing is deciding or choosing what these features are. One way of approaching the problem is to look at the real world; what happens when we interact with things there? When we look briefly

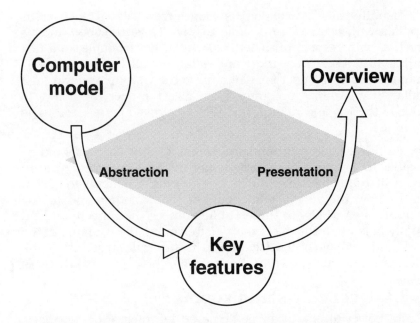

Figure 16.2   Abstracting and presenting parts of a structure.

at something, when we flick through a document or glance at a drawing, what features are we interested in? What do we concentrate on and notice?

16.3.2 Zooms

To carry out detailed operations on a structure usually involves being aware of a large degree of the detail present in the computer model. To present some part of the structure and fit in all the extra features a much greater scale must be used. The result is a zoom of a small part of the structure and the subsequent loss of contextual information.

In the real world this corresponds to reading a particular section of a book or making a detailed study of a particular area of a map. In computers this is typified by the small chunk of a text file that you see in the window of a word processor, or the small area of a large drawing shown in an interactive drawing program.

16.3.3 Zoom navigation

One of the key questions with zooms is, 'How does the user control the zoom?' It only shows a small part of the structure, so how does she specify which part it is to show?

Usually this navigation is done relatively. The user is supplied with controls to be able to say, 'Move the zoom in this direction with respect to the current view.' For example, in a text window with a scroll bar there are usually small arrow buttons by means of which the user is able to move the view up or down. In a similar way graphics programs often give the user the ability to scroll to the left and right as well (this may also be referred to as 'panning').

With a system that supports zooms of this sort it should be possible to have two or more zooms of the same structure on screen at the same time, but it then becomes difficult to get an idea of how the zooms relate both to one another and to the structure as a whole. In these circumstances the conceptual load usually falls upon the user who must examine the contents of the views and remember the location in the overall structure of the different fragments shown in the zooms.

16.3.4 Overviews and zooms

A more powerful effect can be achieved by integrating overviews and zooms to give feedback of the context, the detail and the relationship between the two. The idea is to present an overview of the structure with one (or more) zooms and to include *frames* which will provide feedback within the overview showing the extent of the fragments presented as zooms. Also, if there is more than one zoom then there should be an indication of which zoom corresponds to which frame in the overview. (See Figure 16.3.)

The use of such a system of overviews and zooms would give the user two options for navigation: relative navigation (mentioned above) or *absolute* navigation, the ability to say 'show me *this* bit'. This can be achieved by repositioning a frame in the overview to display an update of the corresponding zoom.

A common example of this is the scroll bar sometimes used to accompany windows displaying part of a document. The conventional scroll bar is a primitive overview showing the structure and a frame. The overview of the structure is abstract in the extreme and is purely based on size. Thus the frame gives only an indication of what proportion of the file is shown in the window and from approximately where in the file the fragment comes from.

In the case of scroll bars, when multiple zooms are used each has its own overview – its own scroll bar. The user has relative navigation in the form of the scroll up/down buttons (move up/

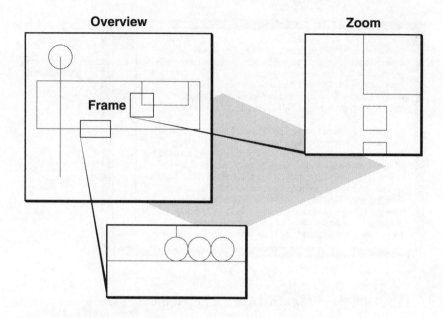

Figure 16.3   Overviews, frames and zooms.

down a bit from here) and absolute navigation in the ability to
grab and reposition the frame within the scroll bar and thereby
say, 'show me *this* bit'. (See Figure 16.4.)

16.3.5 Consistency of operations

With overviews and multiple zooms, the fact that the user is dealing with separate views should not affect the behaviour of operations. The user should be able to switch from one zoom to another
without any problems, even if she does so in the middle of an
operation. Consider drawing a line from A to B in Figure 16.5. This
should be accomplished in exactly the same manner as when both
points are in the same view as A and C are.

16.3.6 In-situ zooms

As well as the idea of an overview and zoom which are separate yet
linked in some way, computers also offer the possibility of in-situ
zooming. This is the ability to interact with an overview, select a
part of it and have that part expanded in detail while remaining in
situ within the overview.

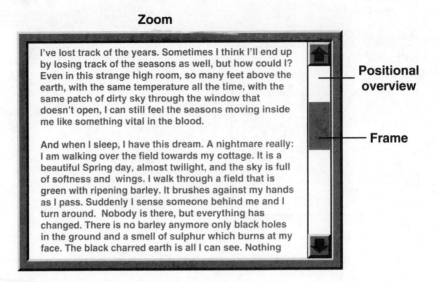

Figure 16.4   A Scroll bar.

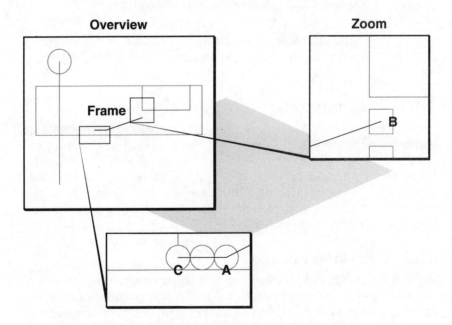

Figure 16.5   Drawing a line between two zooms.

The method of interacting with the files and folders using System 7 on the Macintosh involves in-situ zooming. The user can request a list folders, select one of them and replace the image of the folder with an indented sublist of the contents of that folder. This idea is also used in 'outline processors' where the user works on a document in outline form (just chapter headings, titles and subheadings) and is able to look deeper into the sections by doing in-situ zooms. As the user moves around the structure, 'zooming' and 'un-zooming' areas, she gets an idea of detail from the contents of the zoom, an idea of context from the overall view of the structure, and a good understanding of the relationship between the two.

16.3.7 Fisheye views

Finally, the flexibility of computers offers the user the possibility to use 'fisheye views'. This is a view of a structure where the level of detail is high for a user defined area of interest and then falls off gradually in proportion to the distance from the area of interest. The term 'fisheye' refers to the fisheye lens used in photography which has a similar effect.

16.4 User-controlled abstraction

When I talked about overviews of structures I said that the system could be designed to extract certain features of the structure and present only those to the user: a 'thumb-nail sketch' of the structure. Another similar possibility is to give the user the tools to do her own abstraction. Or, to be more accurate, give a full presentation of the structure and allow parts of it to be hidden by the user.

An example of this is found in three-dimensional drawing programs. Very often we have a computer model where structures are defined in terms of a few basic shapes borrowed from real-world drawing (polygons, circles, spheres). These are positioned in three-dimensional space. With large and complex structures the amount of detail could be overwhelming. The user needs some way of hiding the details she is not working on in order to keep the presentation of the drawing simple. One solution is to design the user interface so that the user can cluster elements of the structure together into groups which she can then make invisible when she is not working on them. For example, if I am drawing a model of the interior of a room I could group all the structural elements together (walls and ceiling and so on), group the windows together, group all the furniture together and group all the decorations (lights, plants and so forth) together. Then, if I was

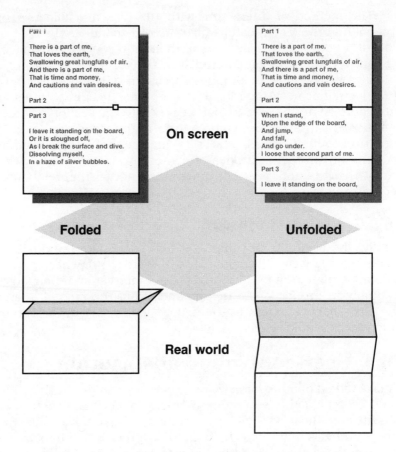

Figure 16.6 'Folds' in a word processor document.

working on just the windows, I could make all the groups invisible except the ones including the structural elements and the windows in order to get a clearer view of exactly what I was doing.

16.4.1 User-controlled folds

The hiding of features can be approached either from the direction of hiding certain abstract groupings of the elements of the structure (as above) or by hiding certain distinct areas of the structure, for example the notion of 'folds' used in some word processors. The user can specify the beginning and end of an area of text to be hidden in a fold. The system then replaces this block of text with a single dotted line to represent the fold. Clicking on this line causes it to 'unfold' and the hidden text is once again visible. (See Figure 16.6.) In this way the user can deal with the sub-elements of the overall structure (sections of text or procedure of a program) or they can hide them away and deal with the structure on a higher level as more of an overview.

16.5 Tools when needed

As well as displaying information regarding the structure, interactive systems must also display information relating to the user's interaction with that structure. In particular they must display on-screen tools and feedback for the operations available. This is another area where the restrictions of screen size lead to novel approaches.

The main goal is to provide the user with visual tools only when needed. This can be achieved either by having the system predict what tools the user wants (difficult for some things, easier for others) or by presenting the tools only when the user expressly requests them. This is the motivation behind many of the on-screen controls mentioned previously in Section 15.3 [p 241]. The user signals her need of the tool by clicking on a small on-screen button and the system then responds with a much larger on-screen tool. Tools of this type can be said to exhibit hysteresis-type behaviour. The behaviour and appearance of the screen changes according to the movement of the cursor but it depends not only on where the cursor is but also on the path it took to get there.

An example will clarify this. Remember the scroll-up and scroll-down buttons described in Section 16.3.4 [p 262]? In order to use up less space they should be kept as small as possible. However, very often the user will use one repeatedly to 'flick through' a document. She is then in the situation of clicking the same button, concentrating on the text in the window and trying to keep the cursor confined to the small area of the button. If it should slip off without the user being aware she could end up clicking the mouse button over some other on-screen control with unexpected results. A bigger button would help, but it would take up more screen space.

The solution is to use a bigger button only when the user is interacting with it. (See Figure 16.7.) The user moves the cursor over the little button (A). The button grows to a much larger size (B). The user uses it to 'flick through' the document (C) and when she has finished she moves the cursor off the big button which immediately shrinks to its previous size (D). In A and C the cursor is in the same position but the system looks and behaves according to how the cursor got to that position.

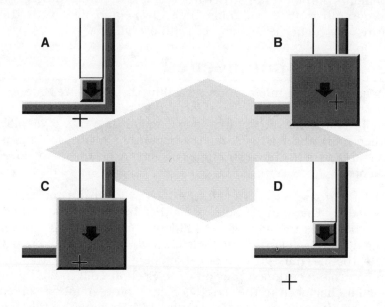

Figure 16.7   Hysteresis effects with on-screen buttons.

Pull-down menus like those used on the Macintosh are another example. The title bar across the top of the screen uses very little space but it provides the user with a 'way in' to a much greater area of menu selections which may be opened up and used when needed. The four steps involved are similar to those with the expanding button and once again the behaviour of the system when the cursor is at a certain position on the screen depends upon what route it took to get there. Did it just move across the screen or did it go up to the title bar and then down a menu?

16.5.1 Reminders

The idea of using small presentations for larger objects and that of giving highly condensed overviews come together when we look at reminders. Here overviews are used not to give the user an idea of the overall structure but as reminders: for example, that a particular button or icon is associated with a particular structure. In these cases the overview is extreme. It is more of a simple label for the structure than an overview. However, the method for generating this label is the same as that for generating overviews; the system must abstract only the barest of key features to use as a label.

One way of doing this is to rely solely on text labels and use the title or name of the document. However, not all structures that the user is working on will necessarily have a name, and of those that do not all will have meaningful names that the user can easily link to the contents of the file. Indeed the whole concept of names comes about because of the limitations of the computing environment. When I work with real documents on a real desk in the real world I very often recognize and select the documents according to the visual patterns of the text, or certain diagrams, or the style of font used. Some systems now enable the user to use similar methods when associating icons with documents or other structures. The window and text is reduced to the size of a postage stamp and this is the icon for the window. The text is unreadable, but the user still knows what it is because she is familiar with the patterns of its layout. A similar method is used in the Hypercard program which runs on the Macintosh. The user can ask for a display of the last 42 cards visited and they are all shown on the screen at once. As a result they are unreadable, but they are recognizable simply because the essence of the layout of the card is still there.

16.6 Animation

Enough of the drawbacks of computer graphics; what about the advantages? Probably the main advantage that computers bring to presentation is the ability to do dynamic presentations. As well as the possibility of adding an extra spatial dimension by the use of simulated, three-dimensional, graphic effects, there is also the temporal dimension to presentations – things can be animated. When I use the term 'animation' here with reference to computers, I do not just mean slick computer animations of rows of dancing pineapples. What I mean is any aspect of the graphics that is dynamic. Whether it is complex or simple, small or large, monochrome or colour – if it moves then it's animated.

16.6.1 Animation in the real world

Real life is animated. Our visual perception of the real world around us is continuously changing, either due to our own movements through it or the independent movement of other entities. Evolution has led us to survive by reacting in different ways to the changes we perceive in our environment. Thus our visual perception, developed over millions of years, makes us more aware of animated than static visual features. It is, therefore, a good idea to exploit this sensitivity to animation when designing the visual aspects of a user interface. This is an argument similar to those we have encountered before (Section 14.3 [p 226–227]). Animation, like advanced graphics, is now becoming more widely used. However, there is still a resource management problem, there are few good tools and building any form of animation still involves a lot of work.

I will now discuss the different ways animation can be used in the computer–user interface.

16.6.2 Attracting attention

As a simple illustration in the real world, consider the action I take when I want to attract someone's attention. If they are close by I can tap them on the shoulder or speak to them, but if I am unable to use either of these methods what do I do? I wave to them; I animate myself.

Animation can be used to attract the attention of the user or observer. Once the user's attention is attracted by something she can either choose to take action or ignore it. This approach is used in many areas. Some applications use flashing lights: flashing yellow lights for car indicators, flashing blue lights for emergency vehicles or flashing lights to attract attention to important messages on a control board.

In computer–user interface design this animation for attracting attention is used in just a few places. Probably the most common example is the text cursor that indicates the typing position in a piece of text and flashes so that the user can quickly see its whereabouts, or the little icon on my screen that flashes if I receive an email message from someone.

16.6.3 Future feedback

Animation is also useful when it comes to providing the three types of feedback identified in Section 7.1 [p 99]. The first of these is future feedback. Information before an operation is useful in interactive systems. The user can always select the options and find out how they work by actually using them, but how to use the operation (and more importantly how to stop using it) may not be obvious once the user has chosen it. Also, the user has no way of knowing if the operation has dangerous effects. Thus it is better to give the user feedback regarding the outcome of the operation before it is carried out.

One way of doing this is to use animation to demonstrate options from a menu, either by means of small animated icons or little demonstrations acted out on screen.

16.6.4 Present feedback

Feedback during an operation is useful where the user is interactively changing the state of the system. For example, dragging objects across the screen, positioning objects in relation to other objects or interacting with on-screen tools. The positions of the mouse and cursor control the position of some aspect of the displayed image, and the more accurately this can be presented the more efficiently the user can carry out the operation. Any feedback of this type involves animation or, to be more accurate, user-controlled animation.

16.6.5 Past feedback

There are other operations which are less interactive. The user simply requests a certain state change and the system then carries out this request. The system is giving feedback for something the user has already done. For example, requesting a window from an icon by double clicking on the icon. This is where animation can be useful in supplying feedback after an operation has been carried out or, more accurately, feedback as to the effects of a request for an operation. The conventional way of dealing with such a request is a sudden transition between the two states; one moment it is an icon and the next it is a window. Animation can play a part by filling in the sudden transition and providing continuity between the two states. In the window and icon example several window managers now provide intermediate feedback linking the disappearing icon to the appearing window. The Macintosh uses a rapidly expanding wire box going from the icon's boundaries to the window's boundaries and Sun's 'Open Windows' uses 'zoom lines', black lines joining the corresponding corners of the boundaries of the two entities.

16.6.6 Animation and continuity

Most transitions in the natural world are not instantaneous and the movement from one state to the other is visible. Once again, it is a good idea to exploit the user's familiarity with this real-world phenomenon by replicating the effect in user interfaces. The use of animation gives the interface a greater feeling of continuity. It breaks down the 'arm's length', input/output image of the computer and reinforces the model of the computer as an interactive tool that the user becomes less aware of as they get to grips with the task they are using it for. One example of this is changing the viewpoint when using a computer system to view a three-dimensional model. The conventional approach would be to erase the view of the model as seen from the old viewpoint and immediately show how the model looks from the new viewpoint. It would be better if the system would animate the transition between the two viewpoints to give the user the illusion that she is moving from the old to the new viewpoint.

Continuity is important in the field of film making. Not having continuity gives us tension, uncertainty and drama. We are not too sure what has happened, and the director is not giving us any hints. In the last shot the heroine was trying to defuse the bomb and now suddenly we have a shot of a hospital ward. Is she dead? Critically ill? Or did she defuse it and is she now visiting someone else in hospital? Exciting stuff! Fine for an evening's entertainment, but for repositioning a paragraph of text using a word processor? No.

16.7 Summary

I started this chapter by examining the problems that surround the use of good graphics in the computer–user interface. Then I discussed the advantages of bringing three-dimensional graphics into the interface and looked at some of the visual cues for realizing this (overlapping, drop shadows, visible edges, the chocolate-bar effect). Space limitations are a key factor in computer–user interfaces and solutions to the problems of limited space were examined, in particular:

♦   Overviews and zooms

♦   User-controlled abstraction

♦   Pop-up tools

♦   Reminders

Finally, I examined the use of animation in the user interface: the sort of information it could be used to convey and the importance of continuity in computer interfaces.

16.8 Exercises

16.8.1 Old files

Imagine that you have a graphic user interface where files are shown as icons (as on the Macintosh). You are doing some work where you generate several new files every hour or so. Soon you will have thousands of icons on your screen. It is all very confusing. Usually in situations like this you are only interested in the most recent files and because the computer electronically 'time stamps' each file when it is generated, it knows how old they all are. Is there a good way then to present this information graphically to the users so that they are aware of which files are most recent and which are older?

The easiest thing to do would be to show the files in a long list in order of their age, but then the user must explicitly ask for this and when large numbers of files are involved the switch between showing the files as icons and then as an ordered list can be very disruptive. Try not to think in terms of lists and showing the age textually. Think in terms of more graphical things such as position, size, colour and movement.

16.8.2 Window grouping

A common situation encountered by users of windows is that they are dealing with tasks involving the use of several windows at once. I'm busy in exactly that situation now; I have a window with the text for this chapter in it, another with the list of chapters, another with a menu of operations and so on. If I want to halt this work temporarily and do something else with the computer I have to iconize all these windows one by one. It would be preferable to be able to iconize them all at once and then later to open them all in the same way.

What ways can you think of for helping the user organize and switch between groups of windows? Once again think of the sort of operations you would like to be able to do with such a system. 'Make these windows into a group.' 'Close this group of windows.' 'Open this group.' What if I've got 20 different groups of windows; what problems will that cause?

16.9 Plenty of power but little feedback

With command-line-based operating systems like UNIX or MS-DOS you examine and change your file and folder (directory) organization by means of short textual commands. You can ask for a list of all the files and folders in the folder you are in and you can move into other folders. Within a folder you can change the names of files and folders and remove files and folders. To speed things up there are special commands to deal with more than one file or folder at once. Indeed, you can very easily give just one command to remove everything in the folder you are in.

Another aspect of these interfaces is the lack of feedback they give. You only see a little 'prompt' telling you that you can type a command in; you get very little idea of where you are. In order to know which folder you are in you have to explicitly say, 'Where am I now?' and to see what files and folders are in the current folder you have to say, 'Show me the files and folders here.'

This combination leads to the problems in this sort of computer environment. You have incredibly powerful and destructive commands coupled with an almost complete lack of any feedback whatsoever. It's a bit like using a flame thrower and wearing a bag on your head...

Hemelsworth: Barker! What are you doing with that flame thrower and that bag on your head?

Barker: Oh. Hello sir. Didn't see you there. Well, all the outbuildings are getting a bit full of rubbish, sir, so I thought I'd go round and get rid of some of it.

Hemelsworth: Well that's all well and good, but what are you doing here in my study then?

Barker: Oh, whoops! I thought I was in the garage. Phew, it's lucky I didn't start clearing up here then isn't it?

Chapter 17

Design examples

17.1 Introduction

Let us now have a look at some examples in the area of computer–user interface design. The three examples I have chosen increase in scope and complexity. Larger-scale projects would be difficult to include; they would use up large amounts of space just in the specification of the end result, let alone the documentation of their design and development. The aim of including examples here is to give a flavour of the process, not to give huge comprehensive case studies. Furthermore, the examples are not meant as a recipe; they are not a set of guidelines that you can try and copy in other contexts. They are meant to make you think about user interface design so that you can come up with your own designs in different contexts.

17.2 Text-based dialogues

To start with I shall look at the standard text-based dialogue which is the first contact with computers most users have. The computer gives the user what is called a prompt (some strange character or other drawn on the screen; a dollar sign is frequently used), the user types her command in after this prompt and presses the return key when she wants the computer to respond. A typical interaction is shown in Figure 17.1.

Computer scientists and people who use computers are so used to this interaction that their memory of their first encounter with it is lost in the dim and distant past and they take the

275

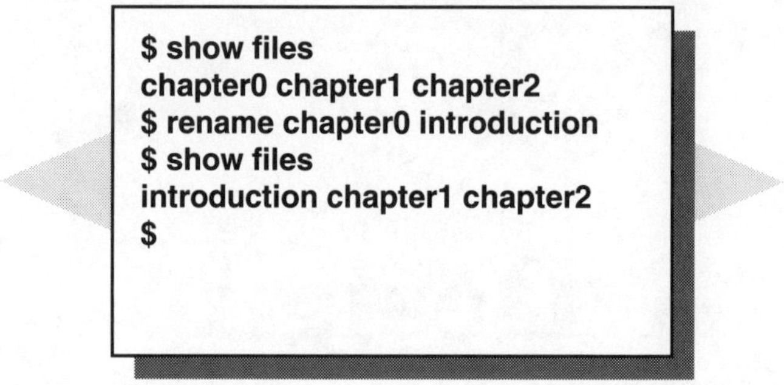

```
$ show files
chapter0 chapter1 chapter2
$ rename chapter0 introduction
$ show files
introduction chapter1 chapter2
$
```

Figure 17.1   A typical interaction with a computer.

current state of affairs for granted. However, from my own experience and from watching the reactions of new users, I have noted a few drawbacks to the style:

◆   People forget to press the return key after typing their commands in (I know *I* used to).

◆   People do not understand what the prompt is; 'Why does it keep putting a dollar after its answers?'

◆   Sometimes people are unsure whether the computer has finished writing something on the screen or not.

◆   When people have finished interacting with the computer it is not clear how they should finish the dialogue.

17.2.1 The problems

One cause of the problems is the anachronistic name of the return key. It is called 'return' because it used to be the key that controlled the carriage return on electric typewriters, and the computer keyboard developed from the electric typewriter. Nowadays, in terms of the dialogue between the user and the computer, the word 'return' is meaningless. One of the reasons that new users forget to press the return key after typing a command is simply because it is such a meaningless thing to do in a dialogue context. Some computer manufacturers realize this and have replaced the word 'Return' on their keyboard with the word 'Enter'. This makes slightly more sense but it still leads to confusion. You enter a command into the computer by means of typing, you see it there on the screen, but then to *really* enter the command you have to press the 'Enter' key.

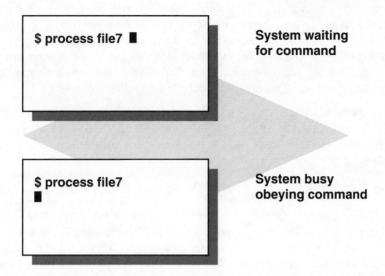

Figure 17.2 Inadequate feedback when typing commands in.

Another reason why users forget to hit the return key after typing a command in is that they are not aware of what state the system is in. When a computer is busy doing something it is usually 'silent' in terms of text messages on the screen; similarly when it is waiting for the user to enter a command it is also 'silent'. Thus, a user who has not hit the return key can easily interpret the ensuing silence on the computer's part as a long pause because it is busy doing the command, when in fact it hasn't even started. The problem is that, from the user's point of view, the feedback is too vague. The system is either in the state of waiting for the completion of a command from the user or in the state of working to obey the command. Two very different states indeed, and yet the only way of distinguishing between them is the position of the text cursor. If it is at the end of the command then the system is waiting for the user to hit the return key. If, however, it is at the beginning of the following line then it is working to carry out the command. (See Figure 17.2.)

Finally, when it comes to the closure of the dialogue more problems arise because the interaction style is so unfamiliar. The user has no idea of what pattern the interaction should follow and consequently no idea of how to finish it. Maybe it is perfectly all right just to walk away and leave the whole thing hanging in mid-air. The current solutions to the problem give the user only a small amount of assistance. In some systems typing the command 'bye' in is regarded as a method of finishing, while others use the command 'quit' or 'exit'; yet others resort to using unfamiliar terms like 'logout'. Each of these has problems. In the context of interactive user interfaces 'bye' is not a familiar method. I am used to saying 'bye' to people, not to machines. And 'exit', doesn't that mean leaving somewhere? As for 'quit': where I come from 'quitting' means giving up or surrendering!

Before I start describing possible solutions it may be useful for you to pause at this point and think about the problem yourself. Maybe treat it as an exercise and spend some time working on it before reading further.

17.2.2 Solutions

Is there another way of giving structure to the dialogue? Instead of using this whole new metaphor for interaction with its new ideas such as 'return', 'prompt' and 'logout', why can't we use a metaphor with which the user is familiar? Copying human–human dialogue would be ideal, but current computers are unable to play the part of a human and unable to let the *user* play the part of a human. However, there are instances in human–human dialogues where more explicit methods are used to structure the dialogue. Consider the users of intercoms and two-way radios. Many people are familiar (even if only from childhood walkie-talkie games) with using the terms 'over' and 'over and out' to punctuate a dialogue. Can we use this idea? The immediate advantage is that both parties would be using the same convention (can you imagine listening to a police radio conversation where instead of 'over', one party kept saying 'return' while the other party kept saying 'dollar sign'?) Each statement in the dialogue could be ended by the word 'over'. The computer would generate the word on screen automatically when it was finished with its part, and the user would generate it by hitting a special 'over' key. To distinguish it from the ordinary text on the screen it could be enclosed in some sort of brackets (maybe square ones like this [over]). The connection between the occurrence of the word on the screen and the special key should be reinforced by writing the word 'over' on the special key in the same way as it appears on the screen [over].

Feedback as to which party was responsible for which statement of the dialogue could be provided in the form of names to introduce each statement, similar to a script. This would help in re-reading earlier parts of the dialogue and it would be a more obvious prompt to the user that it was their turn to do something.

```
User:       show files [over]
Computer:   chapter0 chapter1 chapter2 [over]
User:       rename chapter0 introduction [over]
Computer:   done [over]
User:       show files [over]
Computer:   introduction chapter1 chapter2 [over]
User:       [over and out]
```

Figure 17.3 A better interaction with a computer.

Closing the dialogue could be done by means of pressing a key labelled [over and out], or two keys at once, the [over] key and another labelled [out], thus logically generating the [over and out] request. Such a combined action would be clear and consistent but complex enough to prevent it happening accidentally.

Another relevant point here is that there are many books and instruction manuals in existence today describing aspects of textual interaction. These manuals use different fonts and even different colours to distinguish between the computer's side of the dialogue and the user's side. This device is very helpful and makes things clear to the user, but it begs the question why is it that everybody can manage to display textual interaction that way in an instruction manual but not in the system itself? It would be really useful if the user could write in a 'nice' typewriter font, in black on white (since they may already be used to using a real typewriter) and the computer could then write in a font a bit more machine-like, although still legible, and maybe a different colour.

Following this scheme a typical interaction could take the form of Figure 17.3. The advantages of adopting the features would be twofold. Previous dialogues would be much more readable and the user would have a better idea of what she had done, but more importantly the current dialogue would be clearer. The user would have a better idea of what she was doing and what the system was doing.

The argument against adopting the above changes is of course 'backwards compatibility'. The old way of doing things is already so entrenched that people used to the old ways are not going to want to change to the new way. However, the above problem is still a good illustration of user interface design and the problems of acceptance just go to show that good user interface designers, like good politicians, must be both idealists and realists. They must not only have far-reaching visions about user interface design, but they must also have realistic goals and be aware of the context within which their user interfaces are going to be used.

17.3 Octagonal menus

Let me move on now to the design issues surrounding another aspect of the user interface. Many user interfaces are starting to use graphical menus instead of text commands. These offer several advantages but they do introduce a few drawbacks. New users find them attractive because all the options are visible and there is no need to remember commands. However, experienced users find them restricting when compared with textual commands typed in at the keyboard. Choosing an option from the menu takes more time, concentration and hand–eye coordination than typing in a text command. And if you are not concentrating you can end up selecting the wrong menu choice. I often use a particular system that has a menu with 10 options. The bottom two are 'save changes' and 'exit' (exit finishes the program without saving the changes). Thus to select 'save changes' I have to call up the menu and move the cursor quite a way down, but if I accidentally move it just another few millimetres further before releasing the mouse button I lose all the changes I've made. Needless to say, this happens regularly.

My initial reaction to this error of selecting the wrong item from a menu even though I had used it many times before was, 'Oh! I'm getting so used to these menus that I am not concentrating hard enough when I make a selection.' After a while I reconsidered my reaction. Why was it that even when I had used the menu hundreds of times I still had to concentrate very hard in order to make the correct selection? Contrast this to my experience with the PIN code of my cashpoint card in Section 6.1.7 [p 84]. It was a similar situation, I had gone though the actions hundreds of times, but with the PIN code I could enter it smoothly and automatically. Indeed, the only time that I had any problems was when I *did* try to concentrate. Where does the problem lie then? Is it possible to make menus that are acceptable to experienced users while remaining attractive to new users?

Previous attempts at menu redesign were confined to trying to improve the visual feedback using techniques such as colours and icons, or altering the depth and ordering of the abstract menu structure. Despite this the basic linear list approach of the menu structure was usually retained, with the result that selection was still based solely upon visual feedback.

At this point you should think about this particular problem yourself before I start discussing solutions.

17.3.1 Redesigning menus

The answer to the problem lies in muscle memory. I can rely on it with the PIN code because I have a distinct muscle memory of my actions. I just put my hand in the right place and let my fingers get on with it. With the menus I cannot do this. The physical actions I must make to select adjacent choices differ by a downwards movement of just a few millimetres. This is not great enough for me to be able to depend on muscle memory alone; the result is that I still have to rely upon the visual feedback and hand–eye coordination. Indeed, the only part of the menu control that *can* be carried out without relying on visual feedback is the act of quitting the menu without making a choice. I just move the cursor off the menu and click the button. Yet this, the option that is easiest for the user to select, is the least frequently used.

How can we exploit muscle memory in menus to make the actions for different choices more distinct from one another? One way of achieving this would be to exaggerate the existing differences until they were great enough to allow muscle memory. In other words, make the menu entries a lot taller so that the differences in downward movement for selections is enlarged from a few millimetres to a few centimetres. It might work as far as muscle memory is concerned, but you would end up with huge menus obscuring most of the screen and options near the bottom would need long downward movements to be selected. Also, any change in the sensitivity of the mouse (a factor that is changeable on most systems) would completely invalidate any muscle memory the user had. A better aspect of the tactile interaction that is not susceptible to these sorts of problems is the direction of movement of the mouse. We can envisage a pop-up menu consisting of a square centred about the cursor with the four directions corresponding to four choices. (See Figure 17.4.) Indeed, as the directions are so distinct, selection could be achieved just by moving the cursor over the boundary in the appropriate direction thus removing the need for accurate clicking within small on-screen targets. The user just clicks on the button to call the menu up, makes a sweep with the mouse in the appropriate direction, and they have made a choice. The distinction is so great that they can even do it with their eyes closed!

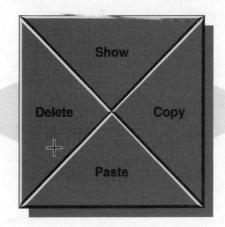

Figure 17.4   A direction-based pop-up menu.

17.3.2 How many choices?

Four options is not many, and somehow the user must be able to stop using the menu without making a choice. Seven is always reputed to be a 'good' number of options to have in a menu, but this would mean using a completely unfamiliar and asymmetric polygon for the menu. Six is a small improvement but apart from up and down the other four directions are a little unfamiliar. Eight choices based on an octagon seems to be the best solution. It is near to seven, it uses familiar directions and it has the added bonus of a degree of metaphor from the real world; the eight directions correspond to the eight main directions of the compass: north, northwest, west, southwest and so on. (See Figure 17.5.)

The centre of the octagon could also have some associated action. This would be a good place to have the 'quit' option. Since it doesn't touch one of the borders of the octagon it would have to be selected by a click with the mouse button. However, this different selection method would be acceptable since the 'quit' option is conceptually a different class of option from the others.

17.3.3 Hierarchical menus

Menus can be hierarchical: choosing an option from a menu can have the effect of calling up another menu. The user can then move the cursor over to the new menu and make a choice from there (this technique is called submenus or cascading menus; see Figure 17.6). It is a good way of bringing structure into the menu, but with some conventional cascading menus the act of calling up

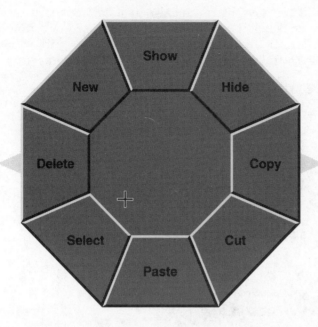

Figure 17.5   An octagonal pop-up menu.

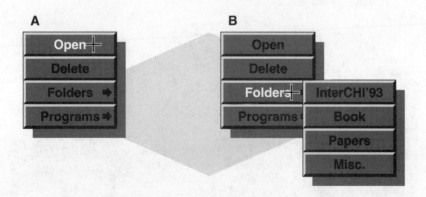

Figure 17.6   Cascading menus.

the menu and moving into a submenu begins to resemble a game of hand and eye coordination. I have to move the cursor down a certain distance with an accuracy of a few millimetres. I then have to move it to the right, keeping it within the horizontal bounds of the menu choice that it is on, until I get it into the submenu where the whole process may have to be repeated, and all this just to pick an item from a list!

Could we have hierarchical octagonal menus where choices made in one octagon call up further octagons? For example I make a swipe to the east and this calls up a sub-octagon. (See Figure 17.7). In keeping with the goal of dependence upon muscle

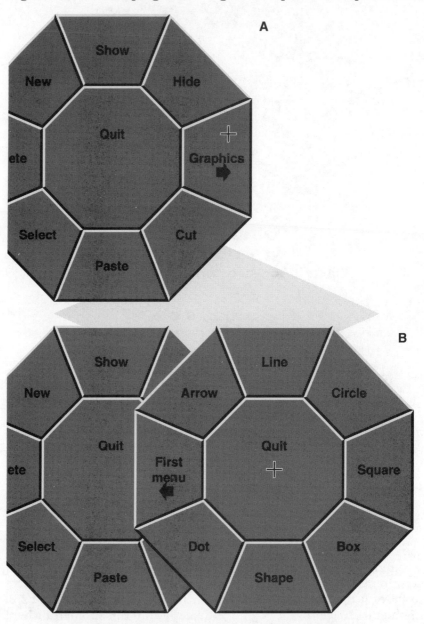

Figure 17.7 Cascading octagonal menus.

memory in place of visual feedback, the positioning of the second octagon should not be fixed but should depend upon the position at which the cursor stops moving after having made the swipe: thus when I stop moving the cursor it is at the centre of the new octagon ready for the next swipe. Selecting options is then still a matter of 'click, click, swipe, swipe' and is still dependent upon muscle memory and not upon visual feedback.

17.4 Supporting conversations

The previous examples deal more with the upper levels of interface design – the presentation and behaviour. In the following example I shall look at the deeper levels of user interface design. I shall 'set the scene' for a design solution but, as I am including it to illustrate the design of the deeper levels, I shall not get involved in the complete development of the idea through to the upper levels.

In the above section we saw an example of going down the goal tree and questioning some of the more underlying assumptions about menu design. Let us take the same approach again but this time in the slightly more complex area of communication between people using the computer. I have already mentioned email, the system with which I can send text messages to other computer users (Exercise 11.5.3 [p 186]). This system is another good example of real-world metaphor. It is an electronic version of the post delivery that we get in our pigeon holes at work during the day.

Such email systems often feature in exercises about user interface design, but the emphasis is usually on designing just the top layers of the system governing how the functionality is presented to the user. The assumptions about the nature of the underlying functionality of the mail system usually go unquestioned. Could the underlying nature of the system be improved or augmented in some way?

Over large distances, and especially with long delays between the sending and receiving of email, the system does indeed function just like conventional mail. But with shorter delays, for example when exchanging email within an organization, people attempt to use it for other, more conversational purposes: checking facts, asking questions, discussing things and sometimes several people will have a group 'discussion' using email. Since it adheres more to the real-world metaphor of letter post, its support for the more conversational nature of its use is lacking. Attempting a conversation using email is a bit like everybody having answering machines and no telephones. I send a message to Eddy saying, 'Do you want to go swimming tomorrow?' and a minute or so later I get a reply saying; 'I can't go tomorrow, I have to go to the dentist. What about Thursday?' and so on. It becomes a disjointed and spread-out conversation.

What would be useful is computer support for real-time communication between people. There is already one such system that is fairly common; it is called 'Talk'. It uses the telephone as a metaphor and thus it automatically includes all the technical limitations of the telephone. In addition to this it also has its own technical limitations. The sum of the two makes it a poorer medium than the telephone with the result that because it is also more complex and less efficient it is hardly ever used.

So what are the drawbacks of the telephone that 'Talk' also has? The first big problem is that the telephone is only intended to support one-to-one communication. It can support group communication, but in a very limited manner and it is very difficult to set up such a group telephone call. Certainly I have never used it in this way or heard of anyone else using it so. There is also a lack of communication channels; because it deals in sound without vision there is no chance of conveying information with visual cues. Thus, any information that is usually communicated in this way must be communicated using sound. The most obvious example is self-identification. In the corridor it's, 'Hi! How are things going?' whereas on the telephone it's, 'Hello, this is Lon here. How are things going?'

With any attempt to support a group meeting or conversation using just sound these sorts of problems multiply, especially when it comes to things like taking turns in speaking or judging the response of an audience.

As I mentioned above, the 'Talk' system brings its own drawbacks as well. Basically 'Talk' has the same lack of good user interface design as almost every other early computer application. Using it involves strange meaningless terms that cannot be understood, but nonetheless have to be remembered, and it requires a good knowledge of the internals of the underlying system. When I ring someone up and they answer I give them the key information they need: I say, 'Hello, it's Lon here.' When I use 'Talk' to connect with someone the first thing they receive is a message like this:

Message from Talk_Daemon@geelgors.cwi.nl at 13:05...
talk: connection requested by lb89@havik.cwi.nl
talk: respond with: talk lb89@havik.cwi.nl

There is lots of information there. To begin with, the first thing it tells the other party about is the talk daemon (Talk_Daemon). This is the automatic process that establishes communication links. It tells them which machine it is running on (@geelgors.cwi.nl). It tells the other party who is trying to reach them (lb89@havik.cwi.nl): the lb89 is my 'login name' – the way that the system identifies me. It also tells them how to establish the communication link with me (talk: respond with: talk lb89@havik.cwi.nl). It even tells them the time (13:05). Everything is there and more besides. Everything, that is, except for the one important bit of information – my name!

What else is wrong? The concept of the talk daemon is completely irrelevant to the users. So too is which machine it is running on. And why does the computer tell them to how to respond to the request for communication? It tells them what to do so it must be able to do it itself. Why can't it just say, 'Do you wish to respond?' and then set things up for them if they type, 'Yes'?

In communication terms, the concept of the machine in the above discussion is similar to the concept of the telephone exchange in the telephone system. However, with the telephone system the idea of telephone exchanges is all nicely hidden away in the telephone number. The system that organizes the connections doesn't make its presence known, and responding to a call is simple; the user just picks up the receiver. The equivalent to the above message from 'Talk' in the world of the telephone would be if I rang someone up and when they answered the telephone they heard:

> Hello, here is a message from the connecting system in the telephone exchange in Manchester. It is five past one. There is a call for you from telephone number 6943544 in Oxford. If you want to respond to it then dial the following number: 6943544 in Oxford.

17.4.1 A better system

Firstly we should state our goals. We want a system to support short, real-time, group discussions using text as the medium. As such it will also be able to support one-to-one discussions. What sort of direction should we go in then to achieve this? To begin with we need to adopt a more suitable metaphor. What other real-world metaphors for communication are there besides post or the telephone? Well, the best metaphor for a computer-supported, real-time group conversation is probably a real-time group conversation in the real world.

Obviously, for the majority of conversation-support systems, voice communication would be better that text communication. However, the majority of today's computers do not have sufficient hardware or software support for the use of sound, so for this discussion I shall concentrate on the design of a conversation support tool that can make use of existing widespread technology (I shall include the design of a similar voice-oriented system as an exercise).

Having said that, there will shortly come a time when the majority of computers will be able to manage sound as easily as they do text. It is therefore important to bear this in mind when designing the underlying structure of the text-based system and to design it in such a way that sound can be 'slotted in' at a later date. I do not mean 'slotted in' in terms of the functionality of the system, but in that it can be easily slotted in with respect to the conceptual model of the user interface. The user interface design should not be too concerned with the fact that text is the medium. It should concern itself with supporting group communication in such a way that other media besides text can easily be incorporated into the conversation.

17.4.2 Ideas and concepts

What are the key ideas and concepts the user is dealing with then? In the case of the telephone (and the 'Talk' system) we have the following:

◆ **Users**
These are the people who are accessible using the system.

◆ **Connections**
A connection is a communication channel established between two users.

Email has a slightly different set of underlying concepts. It still has the idea of users, the people who are accessible using the system, but it does not include the concept of connections between users. Obviously connections exist between the users in order to send the email, but the connections are part of the implementation of the system and not part of its conceptual model. Email also introduces a new concept:

◆ **User groups**
Email has the useful concept of the user group. I can build up a list of users' names and addresses and give it a group name. For example, a list of people interested in hearing about the latest developments in the Views Project could be given the group name 'Views group'. If I then send a

message to 'Views group' a copy will go to each of those concerned. (The terminology actually used in the email system is not 'group name' but 'alias'.)

Elements of both these systems come into play when we start dealing with conversation support. The concept of users and of user groups and the concept of a connection are all useful. What is new is this:

◆ **Conversations**
The new concept that is being introduced is the idea of a conversation. Not just a connection between two users which only exists as long as both users want it to, but an ongoing conversation that continues to exist as users join it and other users drop out.

(Those of you familiar with 'Internet', or other such computer-controlled bulletin boards, will already be familiar with this concept. I decided to leave Internet out of the discussion to keep things slightly simpler and also because what I am interested in here is support for real-time conversations. Internet is more like a group email system.)

17.4.3 Underlying attributes

Above I identified the underlying conceptual entities that play a part in the models of the different systems. Each of these entities is interactive and thus has various features and can be in various states. We need to use abstraction to build up an abstract model of each type of entity in the system made up of the key features as far as the user of the interactive system is concerned. When I ring user B up I am not interested in features such as what colour shirt she has on, but I am interested in features such as whether she is in or not, whether she still has a telephone and so on. Let me have a look at these features in more detail. Firstly I shall deal with the user, or more particularly the two key types of user, and then the concepts of connections and conversations.

The user being contacted

The main feature of the user who is being contacted is how available they are for interacting with the system. If they are not available, they could be busy using the system already to communicate with someone else; the system would know this. They could also be busy externally to the system, doing something else completely. In the latter case it would be useful for them to be able to tell this to the system: the equivalent of hanging a 'Do not disturb' sign on your door, or of saying, 'No calls for the next half hour' to your secretary.

An interesting addition is whether the state of being busy is just a question of busy/not-busy or whether the ability to specify different levels of being busy would be a good idea: for example, 'Do not disturb', 'Disturb me if it is something important', 'Do not disturb under any circumstances'.

The user doing the contacting

What are the key factors about the user doing the contacting? Well, there are two important facts I need to know when someone contacts me, namely who they are and, of lesser importance, what the subject of the communication is. Within existing systems these are available with email but not with the telephone. (To some extent they *are* available: the person will say, 'This is Eddy, I want to talk to you about the graphics', but strictly speaking the communication has then already started, and after such contact has been made it is more difficult for the person being contacted to say 'No, go away I'm busy'.)

The connection

A similar question of interruptibility arises with the connection itself. If Eddy calls to talk about swimming while I'm waiting for a communication from York about a conference, I want to be able to talk to him while still maintaining the option of receiving the other call. As before, it might be a good idea to introduce a few levels of interruptibility into the model, to be able to hold an 'open' conversation that other calls can interrupt or a 'closed' conversation that cannot be interrupted by others.

The conversation

When it comes to group conversations there are extra features involved. Once again there is the question of interruptibility. Although now, rather than a user interrupting an existing connection, she is joining an existing one. Thus in an open conversation other users would be allowed to join while more closed conversations could be made exclusive.

Events occurring during the conversation are also of importance. It is useful to know when someone joins, and similarly when someone leaves, the conversation.

Other important information concerns those who are currently involved in the conversation. If I get the message that user B has joined the conversation and then she does not say anything I could forget that she was there; she then becomes an invisible eavesdropper on what is happening. I need an ongoing indication of all those present in the conversation: just like being able to see who is there in a real-world conversation.

Since we are aiming at a text-based system there are a few issues on higher levels that need to be sorted out as well as the more general ideas discussed above. One of these is keeping track of which chunks of text belong to which participant. One option here would be to lay the whole conversation out like a script with each text chunk preceded by the person's name.

17.4.4 Tools

The 'tools' that are included in the system are defined in each case in terms of these concepts. For the telephone I may have:

◆ **Connect**
To attempt to set up a connection to another user (ringing someone up).

◆ **Disconnect**
To break the connection that is currently in use (hanging up the 'phone).

With email I have the following:

◆ **Send**
To send a message, either to a particular user or to everyone in a particular group.

I also have a set of tools for dealing with email sent to me ('Show me the list of letters to me', 'Show me this letter in full') and tools that are connected with the composition of the message to be sent ('Forward this message to user B'). However, such tools are more concerned with the organization of information than with communication as such.

As far as supporting conversations goes, the situation is made a lot more complex by the fact that we have a richer metaphor and that computers do not have the hardware limitations of conventional communications hardware. Furthermore, it is no longer just a question of making or breaking the connection; there are now more complex operations to do with changing who is included in a conversation. Here is list of possible tools that could be included:

- ◆ **Start**
  To initially start a conversation. It can include any number of available users.

- ◆ **Join**
  To request to join an ongoing conversation.

- ◆ **Leave**
  To stop taking part in a conversation.

- ◆ **Include**
  To request another user to take part in an ongoing conversation.

- ◆ **I'm busy**
  To indicate that you are not available for a conversation.

- ◆ **Make private**
  To alter the privacy level of an ongoing conversation. It would be a good idea if it could also be defined when the conversation was initially started.

There is an element of the rich environments philosophy here (see Chapter 14) since the system does not dictate a particular way of using it. It is flexible enough to allow users to build up their own ways of conducting conversations and communications within the framework.

Following the design outlined above a text-based conversation could look something like Figure 17.8. The basic design has been supplemented by important items of feedback. These should include feedback for operations carried out by the parties involved in the conversation and automatically generated names to help distinguish who is saying what.

I shall stop at this point. We have had a look at existing systems, seen what their drawbacks are, realized the need for a new system and set the foundations for its development. We have a basic metaphor, a description of the underlying objects and concepts which make up the system and a good idea of their attributes and of the sorts of tools that are needed by the user to interact with the system. In order to go further, the next steps should include such things as a more rigorous definition of the exact structure of the interactions, some attempt at simulating the ideas and concepts to see how people use them and an identification of the problems. This should then be followed by a look at presentation issues: how the window appears on the screen, what buttons, controls and menus are included, how

Lon:	[Starting with; Eddy, Steven, Lynda] Hello. Shall we go swimming tomorrow after work?
Eddy:	[Pre-recorded] Sorry but I'm away this week.
Lynda:	[Joining] Hi. OK by me. What time?
Lon:	6.30
Steven:	[Joining] Hello! Doesn't the pool shut then?
Lon:	Not sure. Jack knows. [Include; Jack]
Jack:	[Joining]
Lon:	Hello.
Jack:	Just reading the conversation so far. Yes. It shuts at 6.30. Bye [Leaving]
Lon:	What about 5.30 then?
Lynda:	OK
Steven:	Fine
Lon:	Right 5.30 at the pool. See you [Leaving]
Lynda:	[Leaving]
Steven:	[Leaving] [End of conversation]

Figure 17.8 A text-based conversation.

users are alerted when someone wants to include them in a conversation, what feedback is given to show who is present in a conversation and so on.

17.5 Summary

This chapter dealt with some problems from the world of computers and attempted to solve them using various techniques and ideas from the rest of the book. Firstly I looked at interaction with the computer through text commands, then I moved on to the design of an improved pop-up menu system. Finally I looked at the design of the underlying concepts involved in supporting text-based conversations.

17.6 Exercises

17.6.1 Viewing three-dimensional models

Viewing and manipulating three-dimensional models with the computer is a very tricky problem. There are many ways of approaching it. I have a tablet and a stylus that I can move in two dimensions. I have a three-dimensional computer model of a building. How many degrees of freedom does my tablet and stylus have? How many degrees of freedom does a view of a three-dimensional model have? (How many independent directions/positions can I change?) I want to see the model on screen and control my view of it dynamically with the tablet and stylus. Which of the degrees of freedom of the view can I control with the degrees of freedom of the tablet and stylus and which must I then fix at set values?

Try to think of real-life metaphors that would make such a view control system easy for the user to understand.

17.6.2 Dynamic menu contents

Back to menus again. Some menus of choices stay fairly constant ('choose a font style from the list') while others are dynamic ('choose a document from the list of documents that you are currently working on'). With the standard list-like menu, deleting one option from the middle of the list causes the rest of the options to shift upwards to close the gap. This does not cause too many problems to the user since the hand movements for selecting individual options are all fairly similar and the user always relies on visual feedback.

What factors are important when dealing with dynamic contents like this? Is the way the list-like menu deals with it the best way? How could such dynamic menu contents best be handled within the octagonal menu system I described earlier?

17.6.3 Supporting voice conversations

Using present computing technology it is possible to introduce sound fragments into a computer system: the computer can record sound, store it, manipulate it and play it back (but not understand too much of it). Such recorded fragments of sound can then be used either to enhance existing software ideas or as the basis for completely new ones. A quick example: clicking on a menu option selects it; double clicking on it triggers a sound fragment that explains what the option does.

Such sound fragments could be incorporated into the conversation support system described earlier, with each computer in the network having a microphone and a speaker. Extend the design of the text-based system to include multiway conversations based on live sound.

17.6.4 Anagrams

On my computer I have a program that takes a word and automatically generates all the possible anagrams of it. I can then read through the list and pick out the good ones ('Barfield' can be rearranged to give 'drab life' or even 'bed flair'). The list is usually very long and most of the options are pretty boring. When I work out an anagram on my own I go through a much more complex process. I select a few letters to form one word, then I rearrange what's left. Sometimes I write the letters in a circle because that helps with picking words out. For example, given the phrase 'user interface' I may want to extract the word 'furnace' and then work on the remaining letters.

Design an interactive system to work with the user to extract an anagram of some word. It should support the user in the things that they want to do, yet be able to do other, more complex, things itself.

17.6.5 Intelligent graph

Imagine a line graph drawn upon a piece of graph paper (something like the graph in Figure 4.8 [p 56]). Now imagine the same thing on a computer where it is interactive. What sort of tools could the user have in order to extract more information from it? One example could be that the user can click on any part of the graph line and the system will display its corresponding values on each of the axes.

It helps to think of what sort of general questions you would want to ask about the information shown in such a graph.

17.6.6 Intelligent answering machines

Many modern answering machines have the ability to deal with sound fragments. They can store messages so that they can be retrieved separately instead of storing them on one long recording. Also, with the introduction of digital telephone exchanges (see Section 4.5.1 [p 52–53]) the owner of the answering machine is able to ring it up from somewhere else and then interact with it by means of the numbered buttons on the 'phone.

Design an interface to such a system. If you were ringing up your home and wanted to interact with the answering machine what sort of interaction would this be?

17.6.7 Bookmarks

Sometimes when I read a text book I have several bookmarks in it at once and a list of references to interesting pages. Design a computer-based system to do this with long text files. It could have two windows: in one is the text file with scroll bars and so on and in the other is a list of the bookmarks and references. What things can I mark? What operations can I perform on the marks and the page references in the list? How are the marks presented in the text window and in the other window?

17.6.8 Advanced telephones

Back to telephones again! With the advances in telephone technology it is now possible to do all sorts of clever things:

- ◆ Telephones can store telephone numbers in a memory and dial them on request.

- ◆ One telephone apparatus can be set up so that it responds to two or more telephone numbers.

- ◆ Telephones can make different sounds when they are 'ringing'.

- ◆ With some telephone networks the telephones can be aware of the number of the person who is ringing up.

- ◆ Telephones can be linked up to intelligent answering machines.

- ◆ Users can interact with the systems by pressing the numbered buttons.

After this explosion in high-tech features the next interesting problem is how to combine these features into useful systems.

Try to come up with some useful combinations. Or approach the problem in a different way; are there any problems that you have with the current telephone system that could be solved by a combination of the features? One example I can think of is that sometimes I wish I knew who it is that is ringing me up before I pick up the telephone.

17.6.9 'Slide show' system

Imagine I am using my workstation for presenting a set of still images during a demonstration. I don't use the keyboard, I just have the screen set up and control the presentation of the images by sitting a few feet away, holding the mouse and pressing the mouse buttons. I don't point with the mouse so I don't need any mouse pad. The set up is similar to giving a slide show using a slide projector with remote control.

Design a set of signals that the user would need. Then imagine that the mouse has three buttons and think about how you would present the signals: that is, what combinations of button presses to signal what operations. First assume just three button clicks, then try it assuming that you can do chording (pressing more than one button down at once). Finally assume that you can do double and triple clicks and have certain operations bound to holding buttons down.

17.6.10 Text conversation problems

Here are some problems that could arise with the computer-mediated text conversation that I discussed earlier in this chapter. Suggest solutions.

◆ **Remembering your status indication**
I sit in front of my computer. I'm going to be busy with something for the next ten minutes, I don't want any interruptions so I set my status to 'very busy'. No one can interrupt me no matter what. Ten minutes later I have finished what I was doing and completely forgotten about the 'very busy' status. Two days later someone rings me to complain that they have been trying to establish computer contact with me and can't.

◆ **Security**
If some unscrupulous person tries to imitate me on the 'phone it is difficult. With the limited channel of text it is much easier. If they have access to my computer they can just log on as me and as far as the computer system is concerned they are me. If they join a text conversation the system will announce, 'Lon Barfield has just joined the conversation'. How can the system be designed to guard against this?

◆ **Overload**

In the early days of the telephone when only a few wealthy people had them, the chances of ringing someone up while they were using their 'phone were pretty low. Nowadays, especially in the busy business world, the chances of actually getting through to someone are low.

If a text conversation system is introduced, the same will be true of its use. Setting up a text meeting or trying to include someone else into an already running text conversation will, more often than not, result in messages of 'Very busy' or 'Already in text conversation'. Design some tools to help set up a text meeting between people in such a context.

17.7 Inability to interrupt tasks

Here is another common scenario: you quickly make a selection from a computer menu and the system busies itself with carrying out the operation you have selected. Suddenly you realize that you chose the wrong option. How do you interrupt it while it is doing the wrong thing and make it do the right thing? You hit all the usual buttons and try making other menu selections; no response. Suddenly it finishes doing the first task and starts reacting to all the other things you tried, with chaotic results.

It is Barker's fiftieth birthday. Hemelsworth is taking him out to a restaurant of his choice. Barker has chosen the 'Restaurant La Botomie' because he knows one of the cooks there. A waiter shows them to their table and informs Hemelsworth that he has to make his selection from the menu by pointing to his choice without saying anything.

Hemelsworth: This sounds like one of your ideas, Barker. Oh well, let's have a go then.

He studies the menu and then points at one of the choices.

Waiter: And, err, what wine would monsieur like with the Peking duck?

Hemelsworth: Oh darn it all! That's not what I wanted I meant to choose the chicken... Excuse me... Undo Peking duck!

Waiter: I am terribly sorry monsieur, but I do not understand what monsieur is saying.

Hemelsworth: Control D Peking duck?

Waiter: I am terribly sorry monsieur, but I do not understand what monsieur is saying.

Hemelsworth: Kill -9 Peking duck... Destroy process Peking duck.

Barker: Try 'exit' sir. That sometimes works.

Hemelsworth: Exit Peking duck.

Waiter: I am terribly sorry monsieur, but I do not understand what monsieur is saying.

Hemelsworth: Wait a mo! Maybe if I choose the chicken now that will automatically replace Peking duck as my order.

Hemelsworth goes through the menu process again, this time very carefully pointing at 'chicken'. The waiter watches without comment.

Hemelsworth: Do you think it worked?

Barker: I don't know sir, try selecting it a few more times just to be sure.

Hemelsworth pokes at the menu several more times. The waiter watches and then walks quietly away.

Waiter: [*In the background*] The monsieur would like one Peking duck and seven chickens...

Now with computer systems, if things get really bad and you really don't know what sort of a mess you are in, you always have the option of switching the computer off, switching it on again and starting all over again from the beginning...

Hemelsworth and Barker wait until all the waiters are out of sight. They get up, straighten up their table and walk smartly over to the entrance. They stand by the door as though they have just come in. A different waiter approaches them.

Waiter: Good evening, monsieur.

Hemelsworth: Good evening. A table for two please.

Waiter: This way, monsieur.

They make themselves comfortable at the new table and then Hemelsworth goes through the menu process again carefully selecting 'chicken' while the waiter looks on.

Waiter: [*Apologetically*] I am terribly sorry monsieur but I am afraid that we have just run out of chickens... However, our chef does a very good Peking duck.

Chapter 18

Conclusions

18.1 The future

In this book I have attempted to give a taste of what user interface design is about and to slip in my own share of novel ideas in the process. It can be seen as a bridge: a bridge from the real world of interaction and user interface design for everyday devices, across to the world of user interface design for computer systems. Once across this bridge the reader can start browsing through the literature concerned *directly* with specialized aspects of computer–user interface design.

The future of computer–user interface design looks set to be very interesting. The subject still has a long way to go before it settles down, and even then, like many other disciplines concerned with design for use, it will remain dynamic and controversial (take architecture as an example). At present it is in a state of flux, people are talking about metaphors, methods and viewpoints, and because of the youth of the subject people from many varied backgrounds are able to get involved and bring novel insights to bear.

18.1.1 What to conclude

So, how should I conclude the book? Looking backwards and summarizing has already been done on a per chapter basis. Looking forwards and predicting is always risky and is not a very valuable exercise. Instead of forwards and backwards I have decided to look outwards and inwards. Looking outwards I shall examine some of the more negative aspects of how user interface design is being approached and how the situation is changing. Looking inwards I shall discuss some of the more basic issues of user interface design, namely the role of formalism and the goals of interface design.

18.2 Looking outwards: the real world

First of all, where do user interfaces come from? The user interfaces developed in academic research projects make up a minute fraction of the user interfaces used by people in general. The majority of interfaces are in commercial products and these commercial products are the result of the manufacturing industry. They are responsible for the whole range of user interfaces from the brilliant to the awful.

As far as computer–user interfaces are concerned the research world and the software industry is starting to come to terms with the problems of user interface design, and they are coming up with good solutions which do make their way out into the marketplace, so it is possible to understand where the brilliant user interfaces come from. But where do all the awful ones come from?

18.2.1 No user interface

One cause of bad user interfaces in products is the fast-moving nature of technical development on the leading edge of technology. The development and release of new high-tech products happens in a market-driven manner. In the current climate it is better to get there first with a bad interface than to get there later with a good one. A system on the market that does something but has a bad user interface will sell more than a system that does the same thing but is not yet on the market due to the investment of time, energy and money in the design of the user interface. And, when the product with the better interface eventually does come on to the market, it will be a market where the first product has already made its mark. Users of the first system will be reluctant to make the switch, and new users will be reluctant to begin with a system that, although it may be easier to use, is different from the one that everyone else is using.

18.2.2 Complicated user interfaces

At the other extreme from high-tech products, we have more established industrial products where there is less of a rush to bring the product on to the market. Designers have time to work on the user interface, but because the market is already saturated with similar products the design work is usually driven by the goal of competitive marketing. This involves trying to make their product have more features than the competition and, as the user's model of a product depends to a great extent on how it looks, this means more features and controls in the user interface – 'featuritis'. Although this does put the emphasis on providing the user with extra controls, the main motivation is on new features as an aid to marketing rather than trying to supply a set of features that are useful and organized in a coherent and meaningful way.

Consider the marketing of washing machines. In order to sell them you have got to be sensational. You want to say things like 'Thanks to modern technology, you can now be the proud owner of a state-of-the-art washing machine with over 2000 different wash programs and a microchip-controlled spin dryer that together can take care of every possible wash that you, or your family, may need in today's busy life.' What is emphasized is the number of wash programs, the technology and the features. What isn't mentioned is the one, big, confusing knob, covered in numbers and icons that is used to select the program, and the thick manual in which (before it gets soggy and thrown away) you are expected to look up the appropriate wash program each time you do a wash. And when the one huge knob gets water into its workings the washing machine breaks down and you have to get another one, but that's okay because this year's model is packed with even more new features.

Compare this to the kind of washing machines that you find when you go into a launderette. They are very easy to use. No manual of instructions, no board of strange controls and no huge range of complex options to choose from. There we have a system that can be used with ease, that does the job and that (thanks to the simpler design) will last a lot longer. This is true for many other appliances: the industrial products available are usually better designed, more robust and simpler to use than their counterparts available for domestic use.

Another prime example of 'featuritis' is hi-fis – cassette decks, CD players and so on. They practically bristle with features, flickering lights and LCD displays. Digital watches too suffer from 'featuritis', the worst symptom of which is the beeping on the hour. Very few people need reminding that it is 'something o'clock'. In the days before we had these watches I can't imagine a busy executive saying to her secretary, 'Listen, could you just pop your head in on the hour every hour and remind me that it is 'something o'clock.' The underlying motive with these examples seems to be features for the sake of features, and maybe a hint of boasting. A flashy device that advertises itself. People want the beeping watch, not because its beeps say 'It's something o'clock' but because they say, 'Look, I've got myself a flashy bit of technology!' Cars too fall prey to 'featuritis'; within the past week I have seen a billboard advertising a new model of car and the only feature it mentioned was the heated wing mirrors!

18.2.3 User interfaces that only look usable

We have seen products with no user interface design and products with user interfaces designed for a marketing goal. What's next? Nowadays product usability is actually starting to become an important factor. However, firms are not saying 'We must make our products usable out of responsibility to the user,' but instead they are saying, 'We must make our products look usable so that we are competitive.'

A similar thing has already happened in the manufacturing world with the 'green factor' in marketing. Companies began making their products environmentally friendly. But what they were really saying was not, 'We must make our products more environmentally friendly out of responsibility to the world and the environment,' but, 'We must make our products seem environmentally friendly so that we are competitive.' It wasn't so-called 'deep green' philosophy, it was more of a green veneer to promote sales.

With user interfaces now, what we are seeing is not a move to the consideration of 'deep' design values, but a move to the superficial appearance of deep design values. This manifests itself when designers build user interfaces by borrowing bits of well-designed interfaces and patching them together without any thought of the true nature of the underlying problem they are designing for.

Here is an example of this: a computer system that offered the user a wide range of image-processing facilities. The choice of option was controlled by means of a collection of menus. The user would select an option from one of the menus, the menus would disappear, the image processing option would be carried out and then the screen would go blank again and the user would be returned to the menus. The designer had chosen to use pull-down menus like those used in the Macintosh (see Section 16.5 [p 267–268]). This meant that the menus were hidden away till they were needed, but in this particular system when the menus were there the screen space behind them was blank. There was no need to economize on screen space, no need to use pull-down menus. The only effect was to make the menus slightly more inaccessible to the user.

The designer had not been thinking about the underlying problem; he had simply used the Macintosh idea for pull-down menus out of context. If he had been more in touch with the deeper design issues he would have realized that the Macintosh uses a menu system especially designed to meet its particular needs, therefore he should have used a menu system especially designed to meet his particular needs.

Another example in this area is an early window manager which ran on a system with a colour screen. The window manager made use of the colour resource by making every new window a different pastel colour. The screen looked pretty and it was obvious to any observer that this was a system with colour capabilities, but the colours seemed to be allocated to the windows on a random basis. One day your editor window would be pink and the next time you created an editor window it would be light blue.

18.3 Change

In an industrial context user interface design is still far from perfect, but things are changing. From what directions are the changes coming?

18.3.1 Changes in the user

The dominance of industry by market forces that I have complained about above leads, indirectly, to a method of changing the situation. Market forces depend upon the consumer, the user of the product in our case. Change the attitudes of the consumer base and you change the industry. But the situation regarding the perception of quality is very different in user interfaces compared with other products. With computer–user interfaces the majority of users are not aware that some user interfaces are better than others. And even if they are, they do not know how to evaluate a user interface and they certainly do not have the time or opportunity to evaluate and compare all the user interfaces available.

Changing this lack of user awareness is a slow process. It needs to be done and it is being done, but it needs to be accompanied and supported by other changes.

18.3.2 Changes in the technology

Many aspects of the technology surrounding computer–user interface design are becoming faster and more powerful. The decoupling of the user interface from the rest of the system is becoming more pronounced and efficient tools are being developed to ease the task of designing and prototyping computer–user interfaces. The result of this is that computer–user interfaces are becoming more fluid, more open to changes and experimentation, and they will become less costly to develop. Soon the developers of computer systems will have fewer technical hindrances to the development of good interfaces. Also, the more usable nature of these design systems will allow developers with less of a technical background and more of a design background to become involved, thus overcoming some of the conceptual hindrances to the development of good interfaces.

18.3.3 Changes in the developers

Another important area of change is that everybody involved in the design and development of interactive systems is becoming more aware of the issues of good design and ease of use. Industrial design and development teams are either learning more about the subject themselves or employing experts in the area to advise them, and institutions that provide courses on computer science are starting to give user interface design an evermore predominant part in the curriculum.

18.3.4 Changes in companies

As well as the changes above, there are also other changes in the way companies operate, brought about by forcing them to adopt certain methods and practices through external legislation. For some time now there have been laws regarding the working environment. They used to cover such factors as the quality of the air, the strength and nature of the lighting and so on. Gradually they have moved on to include aspects of comfort: chairs, tables, the view from windows and the amount of VDU work permissible without a break. The majority of these factors are physical ones. The use of the computer leads to a switch from physical to mental work, with an accompanying switch from physical to mental problems at work. Just as before, when we had workers subjected to continuous physical discomfort due to continual exposure to badly designed physical environments, nowadays we are starting to see workers subjected to continuous *mental* discomfort due to continual exposure to badly designed conceptual environments.

Just as laws were passed to govern the design of the physical environments, there is now a need for legislation to control the design of the interactive computer environment.

18.3.5 Protectionism

Legislation also has its negative side. Good user interfaces are highly profitable. The user interface is starting to be treated as a closely guarded magic formula. But whereas Coca-Cola, for example, can be marketed and sold while its recipe remains a total secret, a user interface is, by definition, there for all to see...and to copy. So, rather than forging ahead and channelling all their energies into creating the new by researching and experimenting with new ideas, companies are channelling much of their energy into guarding the old: taking out patents and copyrights on any idea that someone else might be interested in using and getting involved in long-running, costly law suits with other companies. Indeed there are some companies that exist *purely* on patenting and copyrighting obvious user interface ideas and then suing other companies for huge sums of money. Remember the flashing colon used in digital displays of the time that I mentioned in Section 9.4.2 [p 147–148]? That has been patented! No one else can use the idea now without making themselves a possible target for legal action.

18.4 Looking inwards: basic issues

I shall now move on to consider user interface design on more of an abstract level and look at some questions about its underlying nature.

18.4.1 Informality

There are currently many movements trying to bring formalism to bear on certain problem areas. In many areas this is beneficial, but in creative design it is fraught with problems, especially when we consider design for use. People cannot be formalized. I shall draw on architecture again as an analogy.

Many years ago building and engineering revolved around 'gut feelings' and experience. There were master builders who knew the best way to do things and how to make beautiful things that wouldn't fall down. With the introduction of drawings as a communication notation it became possible to split the discipline up: to separate the rigorous 'will it stand up, how do we build it?' from the less rigorous 'what will it look like, will people enjoy it?' The former dealt with inanimate materials and dimensions and was open to rigorous and logical methods. The latter dealt with people, behaviour, feelings and emotions and was less open to rigorous and logical methods. People still tried to impose quantifiable theories and relationships upon it though, sometimes with unpopular results (see Section 2.3.1 [p 19]). Granted there is some place for rigour and logic if we are to avoid something approaching a post-modernist movement in user interface design, but an attempt to completely formalize any people-oriented branch of design will lead to problems.

Another good analogy in this area of design for use is game design. This is also the design of a system that follows some set of fairly rigorous rules yet, at the same time, satisfies or evokes certain feelings within the user. Just as with user interfaces there are two aspects to the design. One is designing the more logical aspects of the system so that a certain goal is achievable within the framework of the rules and concepts – the functionality of the system. The other is the design of the group of features concerned more with the human side of the game. Can the players understand what is going on? Are they motivated to play it? What are their expectations of it? Once they start to play it do they quickly get a feel for good strategies, methods and ways of thinking? Do the players enjoy playing it and do they find it satisfying to play? All these questions have strong analogies within the world of user interface design.

It is difficult to address these more human aspects in a rigorous way during the design phase. It is difficult to define and abstract the features that govern these human aspects and thus the design process must be carried out in an iterative manner: design, evaluate, design, evaluate. It is almost impossible to envisage carrying out the complete design of a game before giving it a first, evaluatory test play. If someone were to approach me and say, 'Here's a game that has never been played by anyone before, but due to the use of rigorous analysis techniques and special logical methods it is going to be a brilliant game that you will enjoy playing,' I would naturally be very suspicious. The enjoyment of a game has little to do with either rigorous analysis or logic. They both play a part in the development of the game, but there are other, more human-oriented factors and techniques that also play a part, just as is the case with user interface design.

18.4.2 Guidelines, standards and spirit

Earlier I talked about the need for legislation to control the design of interactive computer environments in the same way that there is legislation governing other aspects of comfort in the work place.

The problems with the introduction of such guidelines and standards is that good and bad physical environments are easily definable in terms of air, light, space and noise, whereas there are as yet no methods for a similar evaluation of conceptual environments. However, effort is being applied in that direction in the form of the preliminary formulation of standards governing computer–user interfaces design. But there are still fundamental questions remaining. Are such standards possible? And if they are, are they useful? Once again there are parallels here with architecture. The design of buildings is subject to strict regulations and acceptance by planning authorities. In fact, in Great Britain every single building built since 1947 has been subject to such building legislation and has been evaluated and accepted by the planning authorities with respect to its aesthetics and the way it fits in with the local environment. Have the standards and evaluations worked in this area? The answer is no, because there is more to designing things for people than guidelines, standards and committees.

In the world of computer–user interface design the same is true. The majority of people involved in user interface design have a copy of Apple's 'Human interface guidelines'. This is a collection of guidelines for computer–user interface design in the style of the Macintosh. It is a useful book, but it does make an interesting point in the foreword. It says that good application design happens when the developer has absorbed the spirit as well as the details of the desktop interface. Apple's book, and others like it, provide the guidelines, but where are the books to help the designer get in touch with the spirit of user interface design?

Despite the above observation, guidelines do have some role to play in that they can serve as confirmatory support for practitioners of good user interface design. If a user interface designer justifying a design to a manager says; 'I have designed it this way because I think it's good,' this will not sound as credible, or be as convincing as, 'I have designed it this way because I think it's good *and* it follows this body of internationally agreed guidelines.' Guidelines are a good thing, but only in the right context. They are not a quick way to become a good user interface designer, but they are an important tool in the user interface designer's armoury.

18.5 Goals of user interface design

The above sections once again show how difficult it is to pin down the essence of user interface design. What then are the more widely accepted goals of computer–user interface design?

18.5.1 Efficiency

Here and there throughout this book I have talked about efficiency. Although I have talked about what things decrease it and how to improve it, underlying it all is the assumption that efficiency is 'A Good Thing'. In certain areas it is obviously good. When we discuss the use of materials or energy then, in terms of the conservation of these things, efficiency is good: good for the environment and good because of the decrease in the work necessary to generate the energy and produce the materials. When we talk about the efficiency of the user, or of people in general, what exactly are we talking about and what criteria can we use to judge how valid a goal it is?

As with design, efficiency is a question of value systems. When we say 'efficient', we are talking about how well certain needs are satisfied. The needs themselves and the idea of satisfying them are linked to a particular idea of what things are good/bad or important/unimportant: in short, a value system. There is usually a big difference between efficiency from the worker's point of view and efficiency from the manager's point of view, just as there was a big difference between 'good design' in terms of the value system of the user, the designer, the designer's peer group and the design client. As an illustration I have heard of company buildings where the management decided that the large windows overlooking the busy city streets should have horizontal opaque strips stuck on them at eye level to prevent the workers from gazing out. Efficient from the managers' point of view maybe, but what about the people working there, the people actually using the environment? Have you ever heard of anybody in an office putting strips like that up themselves so that they can work more efficiently? As a more extreme example consider working at a computer with someone holding a gun at your head. Your motivation would certainly increase and your 'efficiency' as well, but would you classify the experience as satisfying or have any desire to repeat it? Probably not.

Another example comes from the world of games. Space invader arcade games are very popular. The user puts her money in and then tries to destroy a horde of aliens advancing across the screen. It is a rather inefficient way of achieving the goal in terms of time taken and the amount of interaction. We could minimise the time to do the task and the number of key strokes by installing one big red button labelled 'Destroy all aliens'? Far more efficient, but probably not as satisfactory. In the context of interface design for computer systems just doing the task as fast as possible is not the only important factor. Because we are considering people, there are many other factors that are just as important and yet are a lot more difficult to pin down and quantify.

18.5.2 Stress

Efficiency from the user's point of view is an important consideration and it should be balanced against other factors effecting the user during the interaction. For example, the level of stress on the user in the interaction should be minimized. But even here there are difficulties; what exactly is stress and is it a simple question of it being good or bad? There has recently been some discussion about the detrimental effect of current trends in automobile ergonomics. Thanks to the large design effort in past years the experience of driving a car has been made as comfortable as possible. Drivers are being lulled into a false sense of security and remoteness from the world outside. This is happening through the damping down of various communication channels between the external environment and the driver: visually through tinted glass, audibly through the use of soundproofing and the installation of high-quality stereo systems, and in the case of the tactile channel through smooth suspension, soft furnishings and power-assisted controls. Although this all makes driving a car a more relaxing, stress-free exercise, it is possible that some degree of stress has an important part to play in keeping the driver alert, aware of their actions and even awake.

Such factors are important when you are in control of a car. They are also important in computer–user interfaces where there are already problems with the feeling of remoteness from the actual task. There can be similar dire consequences associated with small lapses in concentration or small errors either through the use of the computer to control some external task or through the use of the computer on internal tasks involving the investment of much time and effort.

18.5.3 The user interface designer

So, where do the good user interface designers come from? How do they develop their skills? To begin with they should be in touch with a wide variety of multidisciplinary techniques and ideas. They should be open to information from all aspects of their field and open to new insights from people in other fields. But they should also think about that information and decide for themselves on its value. Whenever a new user interface book came out I used to wonder whether it would become the future user interface designer's 'bible'. Now I feel that there is no such thing. Any user interface designer who sticks to just one book is not going to be a good user interface designer. User interface designers should not have a 'bible'. If a good book is published it should become another useful book on the designer's shelves, giving a different outlook on user interface design from which they can select or reject material according to how valid they believe it to be.

There is also an interesting question relating to the level upon which the user interface designer should operate. It is easy to operate on a basic level and just deal with improvements at the elemental level of interaction. The best examples of such issues usually crop up in user interface discussions on the Internet (see Section 17.4.2 [p 288–289]): long discussions under such titles as, 'How many buttons should a mouse have?' and, 'Where should the full-headlight-beam control be on a car dashboard?' Although these factors are important, it is also possible to go further up the goal tree (as described in Section 11.2 [p 181]) to question some of the aims and goals and maybe to find higher-level goals. 'What do users really need?' 'What are their goals?'

The problems arise in knowing at which level in the goal tree to stop. Once you start looking a bit higher up the goal tree what is there to stop you looking even higher, and then higher still? Where do you stop? It sometimes seems difficult to have insights into improving the usability of technology by questioning *some* of the assumptions being made without going all the way and questioning *all* of the higher assumptions being made.

The good user interface designer has to be someone who can make these initial insights, who can look at the higher-level goals and values of the people who use the product and yet stick to the middle ground, stay there doing good work without getting distracted by the yet higher goals and values involved.

But what is the ultimate goal of user interface design? At the highest level what are user interface designers trying to do? Make technology easy and satisfying to use? That's a valuable goal, but at the root of the goal tree is the whole question of using technology itself. If it is all satisfying and easy to use, this will result in even more technology being used in our lives, and is that a good thing? There are many people who would argue that a life without lots of complex technology is a lot more satisfying than a life with it...no matter how easy to use it all is.

18.6 Exercises

18.6.1 The journal of bad interface design

In *A Vision of Britain*, HRH The Prince of Wales donates some space to examples of bad architecture sent in by members of the public: a 'rogues gallery' of corrugated tin boxes and garish coloured post-modernism. It would be educational (and entertaining) to build up a similar collection of awful user interfaces. Keep notes of any that you encounter, be they advanced computer systems or stupid coffee machines. If you have the time to describe them accurately and post them off, send them to me:

> Lon Barfield.
> Computer systems and ergonomics group
> Department AA
> CWI
> Postbus 4079
> 1009 AB Amsterdam
> The Netherlands
>
> or by email: lon@cwi.nl

The final collection could be assembled, typeset and distributed. If there is a continuous supply of good examples of awful interfaces it could even become a monthly event: 'The journal of bad interface design'!

18.7 Finally...

Finally, here is a section that I have decided to include right at the end of the book because it is more relevant here. It is about satisfactory interactions. With most everyday interactions the user has expectations – a user model of the interaction. One of the factors affecting her satisfaction with the interface is how well the interaction matches up to this model.

With direct manipulation interfaces dissatisfaction arises if the objects being manipulated do not behave in an expected manner. Similarly, with dialogue-oriented interaction dissatisfaction arises if the dialogue does not follow the expected course. The most important areas of such a dialogue are the boundaries – the initiation and finishing of the dialogue. One way that these can fail to meet the user's expectations is if the start or finish does not happen in a way that the user expects.

To illustrate this here are a few examples. In my local supermarket I unpack my basket of shopping on to a short conveyor belt and the person behind the till then begins adding up the prices. They start doing this as soon as they have finished with the customer in front of me and usually we do not have much of a chance to make any initial acknowledgment of each other. In that respect the interaction feels as though it has not started, and yet they are attending to my shopping so to some extent the interaction *has* started but the beginning is indistinct. It is no big problem, I do not loose sleep over it, but it loses a little bit of humanity and feels just a little unnatural.

Another example is the telephone number enquiry service in Great Britain. I ring the operator, the interaction starts normally. I say 'Hello' and give a name and address which is keyed into their computer. If the computer finds the number I am immediately disconnected from the operator and connected to a computer-generated voice that reads me the number, and that's it. Our interaction is unexpectedly cut off. No chance even to say thank you. Again it is no big problem and it *is* more efficient, but it still feels slightly unsettling. When designing an interface, or the structure of a dialogues, this is something that should definitely be avoided.

Books are not very interactive, they are more of a monologue than a dialogue, even so I believe that the same argument applies. They still need a satisfactory initiation and finish. I could just have stopped after the last section and left you hanging in mid-air like a lot of other text books do, but that's not what good user interface design is about. Instead I shall give you advance warning about the end of the book so that it is not too unexpected... Here it comes... Goodbye!

THE END

Guidelines
for exercises

The guidelines

This appendix contains guidelines for the exercises in the book. I would recommend that you attempt the problems yourself before looking at the guidelines; use them only as a last resort. The nature of some of the exercises is such that it is difficult to give guidelines for them. Thus not all of the exercises will feature in what follows.

2 Design

2.6.1 Triggering cameras on kites

There are so many approaches to the problem that I shall only give a few pointers to possible solutions.

The two key problems are aiming and triggering. Aiming can be done in a preset manner by setting the camera up pointing in a particular direction before lifting it. Alternatively it can be done remotely with some system of radio control. With both methods there is the problem of feedback: knowing where the camera is pointing once it is up there. The situation is the same with the triggering of the camera. This can be done in a preset manner, setting up some sort of timer before lifting the kite (clockwork, slow-burning fuse and rubber bands). Alternatively it can be done remotely using radio control, a secondary line going to the camera that can be tugged or some way of communicating using the main flying line such as giving it a sudden tug or letting it suddenly go slack. Again, it is useful to have feedback about whether the camera has gone off or not. Even winding the film on presents all sorts of interesting problems with different factors that need to be balanced against each other.

2.6.2 Value systems

There is some dependence here upon the model of the user, since different users can have very different requirements for a camera. The best thing to do is to carry out the exercise using your own personal value system and then think about the factors that other users might consider important. Here are a few factors that play a part:

◆ Ease of use

◆ Silence of operation (important for wildlife photographers)

◆ Degree of automation

◆ Ability to override automation

◆ Range of shutter speeds

◆ Ability to work without batteries (imagine being a journalist in the middle of nowhere and your batteries run out)

◆ Ability to function in extreme climates

◆ Weight (think back to aerial photography)

◆ Availability of accessories

When it comes to really specialized cameras, I have heard of something called a 'party camera'. This is a camera with a sound-sensitive trigger. You set it up at a party, pointing into the crowd, and every time the laughter and noise go above a certain level the camera takes a picture.

2.6.3 Design classics

The only comment I have here is that the chapter on abstraction and presentation helps. Many classic designs start with abstraction, asking the question: 'What are the essential elements for a chair, a reading lamp or whatever?' Having determined this the designer can then move on to the best way of presenting these essentials.

3 Interactive systems

3.4.1 Hot drinks machine

I can give you a hand with the state diagram by giving you some of the user transitions:

♦ The user putting the money in

♦ Making a selection

♦ Modifying the selection

♦ Asking for change

♦ Taking the cup out of the machine

Also, here are some of the system transitions:

♦ Supplying the beaker

♦ Supplying the drink

♦ Giving change

♦ Giving various messages to the user

3.4.3 Protecting states

Some movie cameras have a trigger lock (a 'safety catch' on the filming trigger). This can be used to lock the trigger in the 'on' position for unattended operation, or it can be used to lock the trigger in the 'off' position to prevent accidental filming.

The idea of protected states also occurs a lot in computer programs in order to protect potentially dangerous commands. I say, 'Delete this file' and instead of doing it straight away, the computer asks, 'Are you sure you want to delete this file? (Yes or no).' Thus to really get rid of a file I have to make two distinct transitions instead of one.

Having dangerous states that need protecting in this way tends to slow the interaction down. In the unforgiving real world such an approach is necessary, but in the world of computers it is possible to provide almost unlimited undo and thus there is no longer such a thing as a 'dangerous command'.

3.4.5 State diagrams

The key transitions for the pelican crossing are:

♦ The user requests that they want to cross the road.

◆   The system stops the traffic and gives the user the 'cross now' signal.

◆   The system lets the traffic go and gives the 'don't cross now signal'.

You can add extra features to this according to the type of crossing you are familiar with. In Great Britain there is an intermediate state between the 'cross now' and the 'don't cross now' signal. The system flashes the 'cross now' signal meaning 'don't start to cross now but if you are already crossing then carry on'. Another consideration is that if there are many pedestrians they are going to be continually pressing the 'request to cross' button. To ensure a flow of traffic as well as pedestrians the pressing of this button should not have an immediate effect. There should be some delay to give the cars a chance.

The remaining three examples are simple although the canal lock will contain quite a lot of detail.

4 Abstraction and presentation

4.7.1 Hours and minutes

A lot of the design depends upon the purpose that the clock will be used for. For example, in railway stations the departure board gives the times of departure in digital twenty-four hour form. It is therefore a good idea to accompany the board with a clock that presents the current time in the same style.

4.7.2 Maps for cyclists

Cyclists may also be interested in the following:

◆   Cycle paths

◆   Cafés

◆   Quiet routes

◆   Picnic areas

◆   Secure bike-parking facilities

◆   Vegetarian restaurants

4.7.3 The audio dashboard

Most of the information you want to convey falls into two classes: two-state information (headlights on/off) and variable information (oil pressure, speed, battery charge level and so on). Two-state information can be handled by providing audio signals for the transitions between the two states or by providing continual audio feedback when the system is in one of the states. Both methods have drawbacks.

Variable information can be presented as a continuous sound with some feature of the sound dependent upon the variable: for example, pitch, rate of beeping or volume. Alternatively the variable value can be thresholded to turn it into a two-state value: for example, oil pressure okay/oil pressure too high. Alternatively the variable could be thresholded into a values with several states. For example, the speed could be presented as speed below 50 kilometres per hour, speed between 50 and 80 kilometres per hour, and speed over 80 kilometres per hour, using thresholds according to the speed limits in force.

It is interesting to note that some dashboards already have an audio element to them. With some models of cars the electronics that control the indicators make an appreciable clicking noise thus letting the driver know when they are on.

5 More about presentation

5.8.2 Electrical wire colouring

How about the following: brown for earth (if I go into the garden the earth there is indeed brown), grey for neutral (grey is a neutral colour), and red for live since red is the colour of life/blood; red also means danger and the live wire is the dangerous one.

As to the user, there could be language problems with the above scheme if it were adopted in many different countries. The word for electrical earth may not be the same as that for earth in the garden. There could also be different connotations due to cultural differences. If there were a country where grey was worn at carnivals then the colour would be associated with being lively and not with neutrality.

Finally, anyone who is colour-blind is going to have problems unless there are differences in the density or pattern of the colours that they can detect.

5.8.4 Designing information structures

Based upon my own experience I usually have the following questions regarding the information I have and the information I want.

- ◆ **An atlas**
  Where is a particular city?

- ◆ **A recipe book**
  What is an amazing recipe I can cook based on what is in the fridge?

- ◆ **A theatre programme**
  What plays are showing tonight, or in the coming few days, and what are the plays about?

- ◆ **A train timetable**
  When is the next train to such-and-such a place?

- ◆ **A book on user interface design**
  What does the author have to say about a particular topic?

- ◆ **A spelling dictionary**
  I have a word that I can pronounce; what is the correct spelling?

- ◆ **A list of what's on at the movies this month**
  See the theatre problem above.

5.8.5 Built-in feedback

If you need help here the best source of material is Don Norman's book on design mentioned in the bibliography.

5.8.6 Planet guide

Here are a few more ideas:

- ◆ Vaccination requirements
- ◆ Population level
- ◆ Customs regulations
- ◆ Special laws
- ◆ Climatic conditions
- ◆ Length of the planet's day
- ◆ Vegetarian restaurants

6 User models

6.5.1 Train doors

A good approach here is to try and design the system so that it caters for the different ways in which users will try to employ it.

6.5.2 A pressure gauge problem

The aim here is to make the feedback for the two states of 'zero pressure' and 'dangerously high pressure' as different as possible. One way of doing this would be to use a gauge with a linear scale instead of the circular scale (something like a thermometer for example). Another way would be to provide additional feedback, a whistle for example, when the pressure was dangerously high.

6.5.3 The short drawer problem

The best solution here is not to give good feedback for a bad system but to redesign the underlying system. What needs to be done is to build the drawer in such a way that it cannot be pulled all the way out of the table.

7 Feedback and errors

7.7.1 Does it know I am here?

With the traffic lights it is a case of the system making a state change (that of detecting and reacting to the arrival of your car) and you suspecting that it hasn't made the state change.

With the telephone system it is slightly different. The system is still in the same state (holding your call for someone to attend to) but you suspect that it has changed state and completely disconnected you without you realizing it.

The solution is to provide feedback to confirm the real state of affairs to the user.

7.7.2 A modern telephone

The two available choices are audio and visual. When the connection is broken the telephone could be designed to make a loud beeping sound until it was properly 'hung up'. (What is the problem with this approach?) Visually the telephone could have a small warning light built in that only went out when the telephone was 'hung up'.

'Is it good design practice to redesign something so that it then needs extra features in order to function acceptably?' No!

7.7.3 Combined feedback

◆ **Turning a gas ring up under a saucepan on a cooker**
Tactile (the feel of the knob turning). Audio (most gas cookers make a hissing sound that varies with how much the gas is turned up. Also the food being cooked often makes its own noises depending on the strength of the flame). Visual (occasionally I will look underneath the pan to check the strength of flame).

◆ **Doing the same but with an electric cooker**
Tactile (again). Visual (abstract visual feedback, the numbers or whatever marked on the gas knob).

◆ **Turning the volume down on a radio**
Tactile (the feel of the knob turning). Audio (the change in the volume level). Visual (occasionally you will look at the knob).

◆ **Putting the top back on a pen**
Visual (the initial lining up of the pen before it enters the top). Tactile (once the pen is sliding into the top). Audio and tactile (the click as the pen pushes home into the pen top).

◆ **Pressing buttons on a calculator.**
Tactile, visual and with some calculators an audible click. This is the situation for buttons in general.

◆ **Checking if a mechanical watch is still running**
Visual (if it's got a second hand). Audio (if it hasn't).

◆ **A blind person using a white stick as they walk**
Tactile (feeling for obstructions). Audio (the echoes of the taps provide useful spatial information about the environment).

7.7.4 Feedback for microwaves

Microwaves are invisible. Real feedback is impossible and thus we must design abstract feedback. A conventional approach would be to have a little warning light on the front labelled; 'microwaves being generated'. Other, more integrated, approaches would be to make the feedback less 'technical' in nature. For example, installing a purple light *inside* the oven that is only on when the microwaves are being generated. Many users would then think that the purple light *itself* was the microwave generator and that when it switches off so do the microwaves. Although this is not true, it is never-the-less a user model which helps them use the system in a comfortable way. (More about this in Chapter 14.)

Another approach is to have auxiliary visible functions that operate only when the microwaves are being generated, such as an ordinary light to illuminate the oven and a rotating platter to put the food on. Although the user will not see them as directly responsible for the generation of the microwaves, they will still give a feeling of everything switching off safely (including the microwaves) when the door is opened.

7.7.6 Hazard warning lights

Design the hazard warning lights so that the behaviour of just one of the lights cannot be confused with the indicator signal. Ideas along this line are to increase the rate of flashing when the indicators are used as hazard warning lights, or to flash both the indicators and the brake lights together.

7.7.7 A domestic accident

The user is not really interested in whether electricity is being supplied to the ring. What they are really interested in is whether the ring is dangerously hot or not. How could you convey this information?

8 Controls

8.6.1 More action–release switches

Other examples I can think of are:

♦ The button in a lift to hold the doors open

♦ The pedal on a pedal bin that holds the lid open

♦ A Morse Code key

8.6.3 Notating variable controllers

The situation can be complicated by transitions to and from this state. Try notating a hi-fi amplifier with just an on/off switch and a separate volume control.

8.6.4 Continental cookers

When you turn a British gas knob it takes the gas flow from 'off' through 'simmer' and up to end at 'full' (sometimes with the extra feedback for a simmer state). Continental gas control knobs do it differently. They take the flow from 'off' through 'full' and then down to end at 'simmer'. This neatly isolates the simmer state but can be confusing to those used to the British approach.

9 Designing interactive systems

9.6.1 One button

Solving this one involves making the controls very multifunctional. Design it so that different operations can be done by different numbers of presses (click once for the hour, click twice for the minutes) or by holding the button pressed in.

The display can also be multifunctional. Some office buildings have big displays on them showing the time and the temperature. The display switches between them showing each for a second or two. The same could be done here with the hours and minutes, but how would the user know which was which?

9.6.2 Panic button

A few thoughts on this one:

◆ The button could be kept out of harm's way by recessing it in a hole a few centimetres deep.

◆ It must be inconspicuous to use and close to hand.

◆ It must give good tactile feedback that it has been pressed: a definite tangible 'click', but no audio feedback!

9.6.3 Dictaphone controls

The tricky thing is, what do you do about left-handed users? Is it possible to design the dictaphone so that it is in some way symmetrical and can be used by both left- and right-handed users?

9.6.4 More hardware constraints

One possible approach is to build a menu-like interface for the digits. The top row of the display shows the digits 0 to 9 and the user enters the PIN code digit-by-digit by selecting the digits from this list. The single digit to be selected is shown in reverse and the user controls which digit it is by moving this reversed cursor to the left or right using the left and right buttons in the group of four. Pressing the bottom button selects the digit currently under the reversed cursor. Do this four times and you have entered a PIN code.

9.6.5 Lifts

While they are waiting for a lift the user will be interested in which floor the lift is currently on. This gives them an idea of how long they will have to wait. Alternatively as the lift 'knows' all the timing information about its operation (how long it waits at a floor, how long it takes to go between floors) it could even give the user countdown feedback. The user requests a lift and immediately gets a digital display of how many seconds until its estimated time of arrival.

A different approach is to work up the goal tree (Section 11.2 [p 181]) and instead of saying, 'How can we help them while they are waiting for the lift?' to say, 'How can we distract them so they are less aware that they are waiting?' We can alter the environment and include something like a communal pin-board by the lift, or a mirror.

10 Interactive computer systems

10.8.2 Feedback in films

Another relevant scene is the one from *2001: A Space Odyssey* where Dave detonates the explosive bolts on the door of the pod he is in. The detonation of the bolts is a highly protected state requiring several distinct user actions to reach it. (See Exercise 3.4.3 [p 40].)

11 Tasks and goals

11.5.1 Answering machines

The guidelines for Chapter 17 can help you with this one.

11.5.3 Email

If you cannot get very far with this return to it after reading Section 17.4 [p 285].

12 Computer models

12.7.1 Orchestrating lighting

How will the lighting scripts look? (The figure in Exercise 12.7.3 [p 204] can help with this.) Base your tools on the sorts of things that the user will want to do with the lights? Here are some ideas:

- Have more than one light doing the same thing.

- Have lights doing things synchronized to key points in what other lights are doing.

- Have gradual fades up and down between certain levels. (Here the light is at half-strength. Ten seconds later I want it at full-strength. In between I want a gradual fade-up between the two levels.)

12.7.2 More about filtering

One important consideration is what to do where roads meet and merge. If one road is displaying 100 kilometres per hour along its length and it then joins another road where the traffic is restricted, the sudden drop from 100 to 50 kilometres per hour at the intersection will cause chaos.

12.7.4 Demonstration language

Here are some features that could be included:

- Elements fading away.

- Elements shrinking or growing by a specific factor.

- Elements changing colour.

- Rotating elements.

- Certain operations are not instantaneous and so can be given a time duration: the previous four operations, for example.

- The ability to group elements together and refer to them with just one name instead of duplicating instructions with all the component elements.

- Some means of specifying which elements are in front of others in the event of them overlapping.

- Some way of specifying that events are to happen at the same time (in parallel) or one after another (in series).

13 Interaction styles

13.8.2 Direct manipulation and telephones

Decide what are the key entities that are going to be shown on the screen: internal telephones, incoming calls, answering machines and so on. Decide what operations the user needs to be able to perform and then decide how they would achieve them within the computer environment.

If you had telephones with built-in black and white screens you could send a screen image to the screen of another telephone: a bit like a fax but without the paper. Thus you could send text and graphics to other people, or you could set up a shared white-board, a system where both parties draw on the same shared drawing while talking over the telephone.

14 Designing user models

14.7.1 Richness and communication

Handwriting contains several details including how quickly the piece of text was written and, possibly, the sex of the writer. There are also handwriting analysts who claim to be able to extract information about the person's character from the style of the writing.

The human voice can convey many things including the following:

- Social class (in Great Britain)
- Intelligence
- Nationality
- Region they were brought up in
- Whether they are male or female
- Their age
- Their current emotional state
- Their character and attitude to life

And there are many other subtle nuances and signals.

Morse Code may, at first, seem to have an impossibly low bandwidth. However, during the heyday of the telegraph, operators who worked with each other regularly could recognize each other's hand on the key by the style and modulation of their tapping.

14.7.2 Better model choice

The initial message that this arrangement gives to the user is that there is something special about these files and it has something to do with reading. In fact this is not the case. I can read all the files. What is special about these files is that I cannot *write* to them (edit or change them). A more accurate statement of the situation is that the files are not 'read only' but are 'non-writeable' or 'write-protected'. I will leave you to design a suitable icon for this.

14.7.3 Navigation in large buildings

In a building with no windows in the corridors no one has any idea of where north, south, east and west are. Even if they did, the only differences in the corridors that reflect these names are one or two small signs. What about painting the corridors with friezes in keeping with the name? An icy landscape for north, a sunrise for east and so on? People often give directions according to landmarks. This is a good reason for including one or two large details in the friezes that could be used as landmarks: a polar bear or a penguin in the icy landscape and a skyscraper silhouette in the sunrise picture.

The ING Bank building (previously called the NMB Bank building) in Amsterdam uses colour as a navigation aid. Each of its 10 connected blocks is decorated in a different colour. I have also seen car ferries that use different colour schemes for different deck levels.

Although this is an architectural example, there are many parallels with these problems encountered by users navigating through large and complex structures on the computer: for example, deep and large menu hierarchies and getting 'lost in hyperspace' when using hypertext systems.

15 Controls and computers

15.9.2 Foot pedal

Such a foot pedal could be used to control the speed of movement in one dimension through some structure: for example, scrolling through text or moving through a three-dimensional model.

15.9.4 Pop-up menus

Although the state diagrams are a bit ungainly when dealing with large computer systems, this is a good example of their suitability for working out small subparts of an interface.

The solution depends upon catching the first press and then waiting for a fraction of a second for the release. If the release occurs within that time then the user was probably using clicks; otherwise she was probably using press and release.

15.9.7 Loose ends

◆ **Channel switching**
  Confine the interaction to the keyboard. Make the return key take the cursor to the following box and the up and down arrow keys skip to the next/previous box. Better still, cater for both keyboard box selection and mouse box selection.

◆ **Alerting the user**
  Use a sound or a visual signal on screen A.

◆ **Distracting the user**
  Don't put unimportant messages on Screen B. Write them into a file that the user can look at if she really needs to.

15.9.8 The ultimate stylus

The stylus I used had the following degrees of freedom:

◆ X position of nib

◆ Y position of nib

◆ Elevation of body (angle it made with the tablet)

◆ Rotation of body (not about its axis but about the nib's point of contact with the tablet).

◆ Pressure-sensitive nib

Things that could be controlled in a paint system:

◆ Colour mix

◆ Colour density

◆ 'Brush' size

◆ 'Brush' shape

◆ Spread of paint (tilt to the right, paint spreads to the left. A spray-can metaphor)

16 Graphics and animation

16.8.1 Old files

One of the best solutions to this problem I have seen is to colour the icons according to their age. Have them yellowing like old paper or going dull like metal.

When it comes to choosing groups or sequences of harmonious colours to be used together like this, the colour schemes that occur in nature are a good source.

16.8.2 Window grouping

There is already a system around called 'Rooms' that helps with this. However, there are many other approaches to the problem:

◆ Give related windows the same graphic appearance: background colour, frame styles and so on.

◆ Explicitly group windows together so that iconizing one of them causes them all to iconize.

◆ When you have a window set-up you want to keep, make a 'snapshot' of it then have a screen background composed of 30 or so window snapshots. Clicking on the one you want causes the corresponding window set-up to open on the screen.

If a group of windows were shrunk to an icon, what would be the best way to label the icon? (Think back to Section 16.5.1 [p 268].)

17 Design examples

17.6.1 Viewing three-dimensional models

When dealing with the examination of three-dimensional models there are two metaphors that are available to us. The first is to simulate holding the model in front of you. The model is displayed on the screen as though hanging in space and you use the controls to rotate it, tilt it and move it towards and away from you. The second metaphor is a walk-through metaphor. The model appears to be all around you. Your viewpoint remains at two metres above ground level and you use the controls to alter your direction of travel and your direction of view.

When it comes to deciding on the controls, you have to work out how many degrees of freedom each method requires, and then the appropriate mappings between them and the two degrees of freedom of the mouse (or maybe three degrees of freedom if you count the keyboard as well).

17.6.2 Dynamic menu contents

With a system like the octagonal menu, individual options are associated with quite distinct selection movements. It is therefore a good idea to try and preserve the position of the options within the structure throughout any menu reorganization. Re-ordering or re-positioning of the options after one has been deleted would cause the user to have to unlearn all the old movements and learn new movements to select an option.

17.6.3 Supporting voice conversations

I mentioned in the guidelines to Exercise 16.8.1 that natural colour schemes seem to be the most pleasing. It is the same with sound fragments. Electronic beeps are annoying and jarring, but more natural sounds (wood hitting metal) sound less disruptive.

When it comes to fragments of speech, we have a sort of distributed tape recorder. Instead of recording speech just in one isolated linear structure we can record small chunks and attach them to relevant elements in far more complex structures.

Such speech fragments could be used to:

◆ Confirm menu selections: 'Delete'.

◆ Signal the arrival of email, and who sent it: 'Email from Lynda'.

◆ Annotate text and programs in group projects. A piece is shown in blue because Eddy has changed it. I click on it and hear Eddy's voice: 'I changed this because of a bug with displaying circles'.

17.6.5 Intelligent graph

A few other questions are:

- Maximum values of peaks.

- Minimum values of troughs.

- Differences in value between a point on the graph and a certain threshold.

- Projections of points on to the axes and measurement of distances on the axes.

17.6.6 Intelligent answering machines

If the owner were ringing up remotely she might want to do things such as:

- Record a new 'I'm not in' message.

- Listen to the messages left by other people.

- Be able to skip over messages when listening to them.

- Play back messages that have arrived since the last time she played them back.

- Delete some messages and keep others to save on recording space in the machine.

17.6.7 Bookmarks

Operations that the user may want to do with this system are:

- Point to a marker in the list of markers and say, 'Show me the part that this marker refers to'.

- Group associated markers together, a little bit like an index entry.

- Attach text or voice fragments as labels to a marker.

- Bring together just the text that has been marked and flick through it.

17.6.8 Advanced telephones

Group households could have a specially designed telephone where each person living there had a different 'phone number and the telephone gave a different ringing tone for each number. Telephone bills could also be kept separate by each person having a four-digit PIN code which they keyed in before they made a call.

I would like to have a telephone where I could record a sound fragment that the telephone could then use when it rang. If the telephone 'knew' the number of the incoming call I could record different sound fragments each associated with a particular number. Thus for John's number I could have the speech fragment, 'Call from John'.

There are many other interesting possibilities.

17.6.10 Text conversation problems

◆ **Remembering your status indication**
Specify a time limit each time you set the 'Very busy' status on. Have a default time limit that it uses. Have a visual reminder on the screen of the 'Very busy' state that is noticeable but not distracting.

◆ **Security**
The security of any such system is governed by the security of the system in general with respect to login names, passwords and ordinary physical security.

◆ **Overload**
Automated meeting arrangers. I give the list of people to the system and it monitors their availability. When they are all 'Not busy' the system then attempts to contact them all and set up the conversation.

Bibliography

Preface

I mentioned the struggle I had getting the computer to include my PostScript figures in the text. Many other people have had this problem. In fact putting pictures in text with a computer is sometimes such a difficult research problem that there are international workshops organized about it:

Hoover A. Z. (1991). Report on a workshop: getting PostScript into TeX and LaTeX documents. In *Proceedings of the 7th Netherlands TeX Users Group Meeting*, Amsterdam, 1991

1 Introduction

The plane crash I refer to is covered in:

Department of Transport, Air Accident Investigation Branch (1990). *Report on the Accident of the Boeing 737-400 G-OBME*. London: HMSO

Further descriptions of pilot and designer errors can be found in:

Norman D. (1992). *Turn Signals are the Facial Expressions of Automobiles*. Reading, MA: Addison-Wesley

2 Design

Some of the parallels between computer–user interface design and architecture are discussed in one of the many useful papers contained in:

Norman D. A. and Draper S., eds. (1986). *User Centred System Design: New Perspectives on Human–Computer Interaction.* Hillsdale, NJ: Lawrence Erlbaum Associates

There are many books covering the established areas of design for use. Browse your local bookshop and library. Here are some. The last two lay great emphasis upon architecture designed for 'the users'.

Heskett J. (1991). *Industrial Design.* London: Thames and Hudson

Papanek V. (1985). *Design for the Real World: Human Ecology and Social Change.* Second Edition. Chicago: Academy Chicago Publishers

HRH The Prince of Wales (1989). *A Vision of Britain.* London: Doubleday

Vale B. and Vale R. (1991). *Green Architecture: Design for a Sustainable Future.* London: Thames and Hudson

3 Interactive systems

There have been many suggestions for notations for interactive systems. Two examples are to be found in:

Foley J. and van Dam A. (1982). *Fundamentals of Interactive Computer Graphics.* Reading, MA: Addison-Wesley

Wasserman A. I. (1985). Extending state transition diagrams for the specification of human–computer interaction. *IEEE Transactions on Software Engineering,* **11**(8), 699–713

Wasserman's paper can also be found in Baeker and Buxton. A useful collection of papers that coves the whole spectrum of user interface design:

Baeker R. M. and Buxton W. S. eds. (1987). *Readings in Human–Computer Interaction.* California: Morgan Kaufmann.

4 Abstraction and presentation

Of relevance to this chapter and the next are Tufte's useful and beautiful books on presentation:

Tufte E. R. (1990). *Envisioning Information*. Cheshire, CT: Graphics Press

Tufte E. R. (1983). *The Visual Display of Quantitative Information*. Cheshire, CT: Graphics Press

5 More about presentation

The problems of good icon design are well treated in:

Marcus A. (1983). Graphic design for computer graphics. *IEEE Computer Graphics and Applications*, **3**(4), 63–70

This can also be found in Baeker and Buxton (see page 336). There is also a more comprehensive book in the field of information presentation by the same author:

Marcus A. (1992). *Graphic Design for Electronic Documents and User Interfaces*. New York: Addison-Wesley

6 User models

For a general treatment of mental models of all sorts of things the reader is referred to:

Gentner D. and Stevens A.L, eds. (1983). *Mental Models*. Hillsdale, NJ: Lawrence Erlbaum Associates

Norman's introductory paper investigating the different models that play a part can also be found in Baeker and Buxton (see page 336). When it comes to interacting with doors, user models and user interface design in general, another work by Don Norman is a must. First published by Basic Books under the title *The Psychology of Everyday Things* it is now available as:

Norman D. A. (1990). *The Design of Everyday Things*. New York: Doubleday

The fascinating subject of ghost limbs and optical illusions are covered respectively by:

Melzack R. (1992). Phantom limbs. *Scientific American*. **266**(4), 90–96

Luckiesh M. (1965). *Visual Illusions.* New York: Dover Books

The discussion of how our previous experience affects our visual perception draws on material from:

Calder N. (1970). *The Mind of Man.* London: British Broadcasting Corporation

I mentioned that some form of rigorous notation is needed as we start to consider more complex ideas such as mental models of other mental models. Such a notation is introduced in Norman's paper mentioned above, and expanded upon in:

Nielsen J. (1990). A meta-model for interacting with computers. *Interacting with Computers*, **2**(2), 147–160

Finally the disaster with the pressure gauge referred to in the exercises can be found in:

Rolt. L. T. C. (1989). *Isambard Kingdom Brunel.* London: Penguin Books

7 Feedback and errors

For an idea of just how rich the audio world can be have a look at the following book. It is also available in paperback, published by Arrow books:

Hull J. M. (1990). *Touching the Rock: An experience of Blindness.* London: SPCK

A concise and entertaining look at errors (also in Baeker and Buxton, see page 336) is:

Lewis C. and Norman D. A. (1986). Designing for error. In *User Centred System Design: New Perspectives on Human–Computer Interaction* (Norman D. A. and Draper S., eds.) Hillsdale, NJ: Lawrence Erlbaum Associates

8 Controls

I introduced the idea of 'modes' in this chapter. As well as further coverage in this book, the reader should also have a look at this good survey of modes in everything from toasters to telephones:

Johnson J. (1990). Modes in non-computer devices. *International
Journal of Man-Machine Studies*. **32**, 423–438

When dealing with controls, there is one interesting book I have
found that bridges the gap between industrial design and user
interface design:

Barbacetto G. (1987). *Design Interface*. Milan: Olivetti, Arcadia Srl

9 Designing interactive systems

I talked about how difficult it can sometimes be to get to grips with
the separation of the user interface of a system. In the survey of
designers of interactive systems below, some of those taking part
actually made strong statements about the inadvisability or
impossibility of designing the user interface separately from the
rest of the system:

Rosson M. B., Maass S. and Kellogg W. A. (1987). Designing for
    designers: an analysis of design practice in the real world.
    ACM SIGCHI Bulletin 1987, 137–142

10 Interactive computer systems

The increasing use of sound in the user interface is typified by Bill
Gaver's work:

Gaver W. W. (1989). The sonicfinder, an interface that uses audi-
    tory icons. *Human–Computer Interaction*, **4**(1), 67–94

And although I said that using a computer with your eyes closed is
impossible this is not strictly true:

Edwards A. (1989). Soundtrack: an auditory interface for blind
    users. *Human–Computer Interaction*, **4**(1), 45–66

The virtual reality headset is described in:

Fisher S. S., McGreevy M., Humphries J. and Robinett W. (1986).
    Virtual environment display system. In *ACM Workshop on 3D
    Interactive Graphics*, Chapel Hill, North Carolina, 1986

A good example of providing richer feedback for particular modes
is:

Monk. A. (1986). Mode errors: a user-centred analysis and some
    preventative measures using keying-contingent sound. *Inter-
    national Journal of Man–Machine Studies*, **24**(4), 313–327

There are many articles and reports dealing with layered models of the interface. Many of the earlier ones are cast very much in terms of text commands and language. However, they can still be of relevance in the more graphic-oriented world of today's interfaces:

Moran T.P. (1981). The command language grammar – a representation for the user interface of interactive computer systems. *International Journal of Man Machine Studies*, **15**, 3–50

13 Interaction styles

The rich store of user interface ideas to be found in the analysis of human language is discovered and plundered in:

Grudin. J. and Norman. D. A. (1991). *Language Evolution and Human–Computer Interaction*. Report DAIMI PB – 354, Computer Science Department, Aarhus University, Denmark

This work is also to appear in *Proceedings of the Thirteenth Annual Conference of the Cognitive Science Society*, Hillsdale, NJ: Lawrence Erlbaum Associates.

The subject of direct manipulation is introduced and well documented in the following article (an excerpt of which appears in Baeker and Buxton, see page 336):

Shneiderman B. (1983). Direct manipulation: a step beyond programming languages. *IEEE Computer*, August 1983, 57–69

14 Designing user models

I mention 'Rooms' in the text, a metaphor based system that helps with window grouping. The full description is given in:

Henderson, Austin and Card S. K. (1986). Rooms: the use of multiple virtual workspaces to reduce space contention in a window based graphical interface. *ACM Transactions on Graphics* **5**(3), 211–243

The three-dimensional tools 'Cone Tree' and 'Perspective Wall' are described in:

Robertson G.C., Mackinlay J.D. and Card S.K (1991). Cone trees: animated 3D visualizations of hierarchical information. In *Proceedings of CHI'91*. New Orleans. April 1991

Mackinlay J.D., Robertson G.C. and Card S.K (1991). The perspective wall: detail and context smoothly integrated. In *Proceedings of CHI'91*. New Orleans. April 1991

The many facets of virtual reality are given good coverage in:

Rheingold H. (1991). *Virtual Reality*. London: Mandarin Paperbacks

The work on 'computerized reality' at XEROX EuroPARC is described in the two papers:

Wellner. P. (1991). The DigitalDesk calculator: tangible manipulation on a desk top display. *Proceedings of the ACM Symposium on User Interface Software and Technology*, South Carolina, USA, November 11–13, 1991

Newman W. and Wellner P. (1992). A desk supporting computer-based interaction with paper documents. In *Proceedings CHI'92*, Monterey, May 1992

The problems that arise due to the differences between device-oriented models and designer-oriented models are covered in:

Gentner D.R. and Grudin. J. (1990). Why good engineers (sometimes) create bad interfaces. In *Proceedings of CHI'90*, Seattle WA, April 1990, 277–282

On the subject of metaphors, here are two papers concerning the desktop metaphor (probably the most common metaphor in use). The first looks at the boundaries of conformity to a particular metaphor:

Johnson J. (1987). How closely should the electronic desktop simulate the real one? *SIGCHI Bulletin.* **19**(2), 21–25

The second is relevant to the 'rich environments' philosophy and the support of users tasks. It looks at how people organize their office and desk space and contains extracts from some interesting interviews:

Malone T.W. (1983). How do people organize their desks: implications for the design of office automation systems. *ACM Transactions on Office Information Systems.* **1**(1), 99–112

When it comes to all aspects of the underlying relationship between the user and the computer an intriguing book is:

Laurel B. (1991). *Computers as Theatre*. Reading, MA: Addison-Wesley

15 Controls and computers

A good survey of on-screen controls can be found in Marcus's book on graphic design, see page 337. Ideas for new channels for controls can be found in:

Simpson C. A., McCauley M. E., Roland E. F., Ruth J. C. and Williges B. H. (1985). Systems design for speech recognition and generation. *Human Factors* **23**(2), 115–141

Buxton. W. and Myers. B. (1986). A study in two–handed input. In *Proceedings of CHI'86*, New York, NY. April 1986

Harriman C. W. (1985). Alternatives for cursor control: Foot-mouse, pad or view system. *InfoWorld*, **7**(38), 48–50

The DataGlove is described in:

Fisher S. S. (1986). Telepresence master glove controller for dexterous robotic end–effectors. In *Proceedings of SPIE Cambridge Symposium on Optical and Optoelectronic Engineering*, Cambridge, MA, October 26, 1986

As well as sections in Don Normans book (see page 337) there are other books on the market that give an overview of the current input and output technology, such as:

Shneiderman B. (1992). *Designing the User Interface: Strategies for Effective Human–Computer Interaction*. Second edition. Reading, MA: Addison-Wesley

Greenstein J.S. and Arnaut L.Y. (1988). Input devices. In *Handbook of Human–Computer Interaction* (Helander M. ed.), pp. 495–519. Amsterdam:Elsevier

Also, any coverage of computer controls can be lightened up a bit by reading about the DataNose:

Tyson H. R., Hudson S. E. and Yeatts A. K. (1991). A nose gesture interface device: extending virtual realities. In *Proceedings of the ACM Symposium on User Interface Software and Technology*, South Carolina, USA. November 11–13, 1991

16 Graphics and animation

The involvement of graphic designers in the appearance and behaviour of the Motif window manager can be seen if you look at the coverage in Marcus's book (see page 337) or:

Open Software Foundation (1990). *OSF/Motif Window Manager and OSF/Motif Toolkit Preliminary Functional Specification.* Cambridge, MA:OSF

The idea of using a 'miniatures' of a pages of text (or 'stamps' as they are sometimes called) as icons is one of those ideas that lots of people have had at one time or another. Here's a look at the subject:

Nielsen J. (1990). Miniatures versus icons as a visual cache for videotex browsing. *Behaviour and Information Technology.* **9**(6), 441–449

Animation in the world of icons is discussed in:

Baecker R., Small I. and Mander R. (1991). Bringing Icons to Life. In *Proceedings CHI'91*, New Orleans, April–May 1991

Work on fisheye views of structures has been carried out by various research groups including:

Sarkar M. and Brown M.H. (1992). Graphical fisheye views of graphs. In *Proceedings CHI'92*, Monterey, May 1992

The quotation used in the scroll bar figure is an extract from *Common Ground.* Copyright © 1990 by W. Heelis.

17 Design examples

One or two people have independently come up with the idea of directional pop-up menus – myself included. However, none have done more in this direction than Don Hopkins with his Pie Menus:

Hopkins D. (1991). The design and implementation of pie menus. *Doctor Dobb's Journal.* December 1991,16–26

18 Conclusions

The situation regarding patents and copyright in the computing world is ridiculous. You can get information on what is going on and what you can do to help change it from the League for Programming Freedom, by email on: league@prep.ai.mit.edu or:

The League for Programming Freedom, 1 Kendall Square #143, PO Box 9171, Cambridge, MA 02139.

The full reference for Apple's Human Interface Guidelines is:

Apple Computer Inc. (1986). *Human Interface Guidelines: The Apple Desktop Interface.* Reading, MA: Addison-Wesley

A good book that covers many important areas in user interface design, including the good 'closure' of interactions, is:

Thimbleby H. (1990). *User Interface Design.* Wokingham: Addison-Wesley

As the author of the next work says, 'There are thousands of books by people who love computers and a smaller but growing number of books concerned with the hazards to computer workers':

Garson B. (1988). *The Electronic Sweatshop.* London: Penguin Books

Finally, to balance all the academic texts in this bibliography the reader is referred to the two poems, *Man and Machine* and *Work* in the following collection:

de Sola Pinto V. and Warren Roberts F. eds. (1977). *D. H. Lawrence, the complete poems.* London: Penguin Books

Guidelines for exercises

In the guidelines for Exercise 14.7.3 I refer to the ING Bank building. It is an incredible building. The document below is produced by the ING Bank Publicity Section, PO BOX 1800, 1000 BV Amsterdam, The Netherlands. Some of the material is also covered in the Vale's book on green architecture mentioned here on page 336.

Internationale Nederlanden Bank (1992). *Building with a Difference: ING Bank Headquarters.* Amsterdam: INB

The file colouring idea for old files in the guidelines for Exercise 16.8.1 comes from:

Salomon G. (1990). New uses for colour. In *The Art of Human–Computer Interface Design, (Laurel B. ed.)* pp. 269–279. Reading, MS: Addison-Wesley

Interacting and viewing three-dimensional models with two-dimensional tools (Exercise 17.6.1) is a classic problem. Have a look at:

Chen M., Mountford S.J. and Sellen A. (1988). A study in interactive 3D rotation using 2D control devices. *Computer Graphics*, **22**(4), 121–129

Index